Critical Perspectives on Child Sex
and Related Trafficking

Critical Perspectives on Child Sexual Exploitation and Related Trafficking

Edited by

Margaret Melrose
University of Bedfordshire, UK

and

Jenny Pearce
University of Bedfordshire, UK

First published 2013 by
PALGRAVE MACMILLAN

Palgrave Macmillan in the UK is an imprint of Macmillan Publishers Limited,
registered in England, company number 785998, of Houndmills, Basingstoke,
Hampshire RG21 6XS.

Palgrave Macmillan in the US is a division of St Martin's Press LLC,
175 Fifth Avenue, New York, NY 10010.

Palgrave Macmillan is the global academic imprint of the above companies.
and has companies and representatives throughout the world.

Palgrave® and Macmillan® are registered trademarks in the United States,
the United Kingdom, Europe and other countries.

ISBN 978–1–137–29409–8   hardback
ISBN 978–1–137–29408–1   paperback

This book is printed on paper suitable for recycling and made from fully
managed and sustained forest sources. Logging, pulping and manufacturing
processes are expected to conform to the environmental regulations of the
country of origin.

A catalogue record for this book is available from the British Library.

A catalog record for this book is available from the Library of Congress.

Typeset by MPS Limited, Chennai, India.

Contents

List of Table and Figures

Table

Figures

Acknowledgements

Working on developing and completing this book has been exciting and rewarding. We would like to thank Palgrave Macmillan for the support they have provided in making this book happen. Our work as joint editors to compile the final manuscript has made us appreciate the fantastic depth and breadth of the emerging research and literature on child sexual exploitation (CSE). Margaret Melrose has taken an excellent lead on supporting authors throughout the process of creating this book, and on leading most of the editing for the final submission. Jenny Pearce and all authors pay a special thanks to Margaret for taking this work forward. Jenny and Margaret both want to offer a big thank you to all the authors who have worked on chapters included in this book. It has been rewarding to work with such committed and informed colleagues and to have the opportunity to discuss content and to think through the implications of our joint submissions for the longer term development of knowledge and expertise on CSE. We are grateful to Mr. Kris McCann for compiling the bibliography.

As editors working for a research institute that is promoting applied social research, we are mindful that we and other authors rely heavily on the work of colleagues engaged with CSE policy and practice development. We want to thank all those engaged in developing and delivering services to young people affected by CSE. Central to this work is the engagement with young people themselves. We want to acknowledge the work of all young people who have contributed to informing practitioners, policy makers and academics about the impact CSE can have on day-to-day life. We hope that in some way this book will help to make a difference to those lives.

Margaret would especially like to acknowledge that, even though absent, the presence of Leah and Harry Wilkins-McCann give her inspiration to carry on with this work.

Notes on Contributors

Dr Lorena Arocha joined the University of Bedfordshire in 2010. She has conducted research on issues related to contemporary forms of slavery and exploitation, including forced labour, bonded labour or debt bondage, human trafficking and sexual exploitation, in a variety of geographical contexts, including Europe, South Asia and Africa. Her research focuses on examining how 'new' exploitative practices are defined and how this then frames policy responses.

Dr Helen Beckett is a Research Fellow at The International Centre for the Study of Sexually Exploited and Trafficked Young People at the University of Bedfordshire. She has worked as a children's rights researcher for 15 years across the voluntary and statutory sectors and more recently within academia. Her specialism includes sexual exploitation, sexual violence and wider child protection concerns, the implementation of children's rights and the experiences of looked after children and homeless youth.

Dr Isabelle Brodie is a Senior Research Fellow in the Department of Applied Social Studies, University of Bedfordshire. Previously she worked at the National Children's Bureau and Birkbeck College. Isabelle has published extensively on a range of issues regarding vulnerable children and young people, often focusing on their educational experiences. Recent projects have included work for the Scottish Government, NSPCC and the Centre for Excellence in Outcomes for Children and Young People (C4EO).

Carlene Firmin MBE is a professional doctorate student at the University of Bedfordshire. She is currently the Principal Policy Advisor and Head of the Secretariat for the Office of the Children's Commissioner's Inquiry into child sexual exploitation gangs and groups. For five years Carlene researched the impact of criminal gangs on women and girls, at the charity Race on the Agenda, during which time she authored the Female Voice in Violence reports. Carlene also writes a monthly column in *Society Guardian*, and has had papers published in academic books and journals. Carlene was featured in *Glamour Magazine*'s 35 most powerful women under 35 in 2011 and was awarded a London Peace Award in 2008. In 2011 she was awarded an MBE for services to Women and Girls Issues in the New Year's Honours list.

Dr Patricia Hynes is a Principal Lecturer in the Department of Applied Social Studies at the University of Bedfordshire. Her research interests include forced migration in all its forms and human rights. She has conducted research internationally on internally displaced persons, refugees, trafficking and asylum policy.

Margaret Melrose is Professor of Social Policy and Applied Social Research in the Department of Applied Social Studies/Institute of Applied Social Research (IASR) at the University of Bedfordshire and Director of the Centre for Young People, Poverty and Social Disadvantage within IASR. She has been Chair of the IASR Ethics Committee for approximately five years. Over the past 20 years Margaret has worked in a cross-disciplinary context to research a range of topics related to young people and sexual exploitation including vulnerable young people and drug use and young people, poverty and welfare reforms. Her work is nationally and internationally recognised and, in addition to numerous publications, she has been invited to present her work at many national and international conferences. She has previously worked as an advisor to Barnardo's Bristol on 'Working with Sexually Exploited Young People', to the NSPCC on researching service provision for young runaways, to LSBU and Eaves Housing on researching exit routes for trafficked women, and to the Belgian Federal Science Policy Office on research with vulnerable and 'hard to reach' young people.

Jenny Pearce is Professor of Young People and Public Policy at the University of Bedfordshire, UK, where she is Director of the 'International Centre for the Study of Sexually Exploited and Trafficked Young People' and the 'Institute of Applied Social Research'. She is co-founder of the 'National Working Group for Sexually Exploited Children and Young People' (www.nationalworkinggroup.co.uk) and runs a 'Child Sexual Exploitation' research forum in partnership with Barnardo's Children's Charity. She is a member of the Policy Steering Committee of 'Eurochild', Brussels, and is rapporteur with the Council of Europe 'One in Five' Campaign to stop sexual violence against children. She has researched and published on a number of topics related to child protection, child sexual exploitation and child trafficking. She is currently developing the 'Our Voices' Project: a European network of projects challenging sexual violence against children. She is associate editor with the journals *Youth and Policy* and *Child Abuse Review*. Jenny trained as a teacher, and has worked in schools, youth justice and youth and community work. She works in partnership with young people, NGOs and statutory services in Europe to develop opportunities for training, research and curriculum development on child welfare and child protection.

John Pitts is Vauxhall Professor of Socio-legal Studies at the University of Bedfordshire. He has worked as a school teacher; a street and club-based youth worker; a group worker in a Young Offender Institution and a consultant on youth crime and youth justice to the police and youth justice and legal professionals in the UK, mainland Europe, the Russian Federation and China. He is Associate Editor of *Safer Communities* and *Youth and Policy*. He has written extensively about youth justice in England and Wales, most notably in *The New Politics of Youth Crime* (Macmillan, 2001) and in the past six years he has undertaken studies of violent youth gangs in London, Manchester and West Yorkshire, some of the findings of which are recounted in *Reluctant Gangsters* (Routledge, 2008). Since 2007 he has acted as an advisor on violent youth gangs to local authorities and police forces. He was a consultant to the Centre for Social Justice enquiry into violent youth gangs in the UK, published as *Dying to Belong* (2009), and a participant in the Prime Minister's Gang Summit in October 2011. He is deputy chair of the London Gangs Forum and a member of the Children's Commissioner's Inquiry into Child and Adolescent Sexual Exploitation. In July 2011 he was awarded the honorary degree of Doctor of Letters for his outstanding contribution to the development of youth justice in England and Wales.

Nicola Sharp is a Research Fellow within the Child and Woman Abuse Studies Unit (CWASU) at London Metropolitan University. She is also a Professional Doctorate student at the University of Bedfordshire. Over the past 14 years Nicola has held research and policy roles within government and non-governmental settings at both national and international level. As such she has developed expertise in a range of public protection issues affecting vulnerable children and adults. Nicola is a registered consultant for UNICEF. She is also Vice Chair of the English Coalition for Runaway Children, a Member of the Advisory Board for the Centre for the Study of Missing Persons and a Trustee of the NWG Network. Nicola is a first class graduate in Management Sciences (BSc Hons) and a postgraduate in International Policy Analysis (MSc) and Woman and Child Abuse (MA).

Dr Lucie Shuker is a Research Fellow in the Institute of Applied Social Research at the University of Bedfordshire, and a member of the International Centre for the Study of Sexually Exploited and Trafficked Young People. After completing her PhD at the University of Cambridge, she joined the team to undertake a realist evaluation of the DfE-funded Barnardo's 'Safe Accommodation Project', which aimed to address an urgent need for safe accommodation for sexually exploited and trafficked young people, through 1-to-1 support, specialist foster care and training local authority foster carers and those that support them. Lucie is also part of the team working on the gang associated sexual exploitation project, which has been funded by the Office of the Children's Commissioner for England.

Camille Warrington is the Young People's Participation Development Officer at the International Centre for Sexually Exploited and Trafficked Young People, University of Bedfordshire. Her own research focuses on young people's experiences of professional welfare services and facilitating participation of those traditionally excluded from decision making using creative processes. Prior to her current role she coordinated the National Working Group for Sexually Exploited Children and Young People and practised as a qualified youth worker undertaking participatory and rights base work in a variety of voluntary and statutory sector settings including leaving care teams, youth services and provision for young Gypsies and Travellers.

Introduction: Critical Perspectives on Child Sexual Exploitation and Related Trafficking

Margaret Melrose and Jenny Pearce

In 2004 one of the editors of this volume noted that, in the UK, awareness of the issue of child sexual exploitation (CSE) amongst policy makers and practitioners had advanced remarkably since the introduction of Government guidance in 2000 (DoH/HO, 2000) as had practice expertise. At that time this was evidenced by the fact that there were, for the first time, a variety of 'models' in different projects for developing services to provide appropriate responses to meet the needs of young people affected by CSE (Melrose with Barrett, 2004). The critical perspectives presented in this volume on a range of topics further demonstrate the extent to which our knowledge and understanding have developed since that time. We are now able not only to acknowledge the assortment of concerns relating to young people affected by CSE and related trafficking, but also to reflect the critical thinking about these subjects that has developed over time.

Whilst acknowledging that knowledge and understandings have developed since the turn of the twenty-first century it would be remiss of us as editors to suggest that there is any room for complacency. There is not. There is still much more that needs to be known, and done, to respond effectively to the needs of young people affected by CSE and/or related trafficking. In particular, we would point to the need for local safeguarding children boards to acknowledge and recognise fully the existence of CSE and to implement completely the Government guidance of 2009 (DCSF, 2009; see Jago et al., 2011). We would also urge policy-makers to develop a national monitoring and reporting system so that we could reliably know the number of young people involved across the country. We would point to the limited evidence available in relation to the involvement of boys and young men and their specific needs – a limitation that authors in this book repeatedly identify. Furthermore we would suggest there is a need for more research in relation to the life-worlds and concrete circumstances that young people who are at risk, or involved, face on a daily basis – particularly in an age of austerity. Perhaps nine years from now we will be able, more confidently, to address these issues from the basis of sound empirical evidence and the knowledge base from which policy and practice are developed will take another exponential leap forward as it did from the end of the twentieth century to the beginning of the twenty-first.

Below we provide definitions of the terms 'young people', 'child sexual exploitation' and 'trafficking' as they are used throughout this book before moving on to describe the organisation of the book.

Definitions

As they are employed throughout the chapters in this volume, the term 'child' draws on the concept of a 'child' as developed in the UN Convention on the Rights of the Child and refers to any young person up to the age of 18.

The term 'child sexual exploitation' as used throughout the chapters in this book draws on the definition developed by DCSF (2009: 9). That is,

> Sexual exploitation of children and young people under 18 involves exploitative situations, contexts and relationships where young people (or a third person or persons) receive 'something' (e.g. food, accommodation, drugs, alcohol, cigarettes, affection, gifts, money) as a result of them performing, and/or another or others performing on them, sexual activities. … In all cases, those exploiting the child/ young person have power over them by virtue of their age, gender, intellect, physical strength and/or economic or other resources. Violence, coercion and intimidation are common, involvement in exploitative relationships being characterised in the main by the child or young person's limited availability of choice resulting from their social/economic and/or emotional vulnerability.
>
> (DCSF, 2009: 9)

When we refer to the trafficking of children and young people we are drawing on the definition of human trafficking as developed in the Protocol to Prevent, Suppress and Punish Trafficking in Persons, especially women and children, commonly referred to as the Palermo Protocol (2000), which provided the first internationally agreed definition of human trafficking (Article 3). It noted:

a) Trafficking in persons shall meant the recruitment, transportation, transfer, harbouring or receipt of persons, by means of the threat or use of force or other forms of coercion, of abduction, of fraud, of deception, of the abuse of power or of a position of vulnerability or of the giving or receiving of payments or benefits to achieve the consent of a person having control over another person, for the purpose of exploitation.

b) The consent of a victim of trafficking in persons to the intended exploitation set forth in sub paragraph (a) of this article shall be irrelevant where any of the means set forth in sub paragraph (a) have been used.

c) The recruitment, transportation, transfer, harbouring or receipt of a child for the purposes of exploitation shall be considered 'trafficking in persons' even if this does not involve any of the means set forth in sub paragraph (a) of this article.

d) A child shall mean any person under the age of 18.

Whilst we recognise that children and young people are trafficked for a variety of reasons (see Pearce, Hynes and Bovarnick, 2009) the focus in this book is on young people who have been sexually exploited. We are, therefore, drawing on work pertaining to children and young people trafficked for sexual exploitation.

The organisation of the book

In Chapter 1 Margaret Melrose presents four key criticisms of the discourse of CSE. She highlights the ways in which the language through which we understand young people's involvement in sexually exploitative relationships has changed since the introduction of the 2000 guidance (DoH/HO, 2000). This changing language, she contends, has stretched the concept of CSE, rendering its meaning rather fuzzy and making it more difficult to apply in practice. Consequently, sexual practices that may be recognised as 'exploitative', but which do not necessarily suggest that the young person is at risk of *commercial* sexual exploitation, are identified as requiring intervention. Melrose further asserts that the discourse of CSE is produced by, and reproduces, the dominant discourse of childhood in the West and, more specifically, a discourse of *female* childhood in which female sexuality is constructed from within a sexual double standard. Furthermore, the chapter maintains that the discourse of CSE prevents the young people concerned from being understood as anything other than passive victims/objects: thus from within this discursive formation the idea that young people may be acting under their own volition, albeit within severely constrained circumstances, cannot be entertained. The chapter also contends that the discourse of CSE individualises the issue of CSE and fails to account for structural and cultural factors that underpin young people's involvement.

In Chapter 2 John Pitts discusses the issue of sexual exploitation and sexual violence in gangs. He argues that current definitions of CSE are of limited usefulness for understanding sexual victimisation in the gang context. This is because the individualising focus of a coercive dyad proposed by dominant definitions and understandings of CSE does not account for the complexity of relationships between young people in gangs where the distinction between victims and abusers may be blurred. Pitts draws on the work of Matza and proposes a model of 'soft determinism' to understand relations between victims and perpetrators in the gang context. He suggests that in an attempt to shake off a mood of fatalism and to regain some control over events in their lives some young women may drift towards gangs where they may be sexually victimised.

In Chapter 3 Carlene Firmin further develops the argument proposed by Pitts. She maintains that the frameworks of 'CSE', 'domestic violence' and/or 'serious youth violence' do not provide an appropriate basis for responding to peer-on-peer sexual exploitation, violence or abuse. Firmin argues that young people involved in these activities need to be understood as located in gendered and hierarchically organised social fields in which they may be conceptualised as simultaneously victims and perpetrators of abuse. She proposes a new definition that may allow various levels of exploitation and abuse to be recognised and suggests that multiple risk factors need to be taken into account when deciding how to keep young people safe. In order to do this, Firmin argues, there is a need to move beyond the current binary thinking of young people as either 'victims' (of abuse, violence or sexual exploitation) or perpetrators of the same.

In Chapter 4 Jenny Pearce considers issues of consent for young people who are in sexually abusive or sexually exploitative relationships. She argues that 'consent' is a key principle for both practitioners and young people when working together through collaborative partnerships to prevent and address the impact of sexual exploitation. Whilst recognising the impact that both violent and subtle coercion have on the young person's apparent capacity to consent to exploitation, the chapter explores the need to collaborate closely and meaningfully with the young person before and during any intervention. This collaboration means contextualising the exploitation within the changing cultural, social, economic and personal environment the young person inhabits. The chapter therefore argues for a conceptual shift away from a medical model of consent and towards a social model of consent that would enable us to understand the circumstances in which young people may give their consent to abusive sexual relationships.

Drawing on empirical evidence from a study conducted in Northern Ireland (NI), Helen Beckett explores the risk of CSE amongst the looked after population in Chapter 5. She finds that in NI this risk is unequally distributed and that those in residential care are at greater risk than those in other care settings. Beckett suggests that to reduce the risk of CSE for young people in residential care in NI there is a need to develop a holistic, integrated, response that can address a young person's need for protection and support whilst holding perpetrators to account. This approach, Beckett argues, should be developed to replace the short-term, reactive response that currently holds sway and that attempts to contain and control the young people concerned.

In Chapter 6 Isabelle Brodie reviews the evidence and CSE policy development in Scotland. She points to the similarities and differences between Scotland and the rest of the UK regarding understandings of, and responses to, CSE. Brodie finds that there are more similarities than differences and that the overall direction of policy development in Scotland mirrors that in the rest of the UK. However she also points to important differences. Namely, she suggests, the Scottish Guidance is less comprehensive than Westminster guidance

(DCSF, 2009) particularly because it does not suggest the develop-ment of a dual approach that safeguards children and young people whilst simultaneously targeting those who exploit them. Brodie sug-gests there remain a number of issues to resolve in relation to CSE policy in Scotland but notes that to safeguard young people at risk or involved a greater focus on the structures of disadvantage that under-pin involvement may be more important than statutory guidance.

The risk of CSE experienced by young women from South Asian communities who may go missing to escape from forced marriage situations is highlighted by Nicola Sharp in Chapter 7. That young people who go missing are at increased risk of CSE is generally acknowledged in the CSE literature. Sharp maintains, however, that how these risks relate to young women from South Asian communi-ties, who might go missing to escape forced marriage situations, has been under-explored and under-acknowledged in the CSE literature and the literature on forced marriage. By drawing our attention to the risks faced by these young women Sharp highlights a significant gap in the understanding of CSE as it relates to young people from minority ethnic communities. Sharp suggests that the risks faced by these young people should be assessed using multiple indicators. This would mean that those escaping forced marriage situations would be assessed for risk of CSE and should receive a holistic response rather than a 'forced marriage' response.

In Chapter 8, Camille Warrington draws on empirical evidence from a study of young people's participation in decision making about their care when they are engaged in CSE services. She argues that the protective potential of services may be limited or enhanced depend-ing on the degree to which young people are included in decisions about their care. In this chapter, however, Warrington presents evi-dence showing that many young people involved in CSE are routinely excluded from decision making processes. Furthermore, she suggests, even when practitioners are committed to young people's partici-pation, practical issues such as concerns about sharing third party information, conflict between the young person's and practitioner's perspectives, concerns about additional resources requirements, fears about involving young people in a potentially stressful process and the reluctance of service users to attend meetings can prevent young people from being meaningfully included in decision making proc-esses. She proposes that unless professionals consult with and engage young people as partners in developing plans for their care such plans may be subverted by the very young people they aim to protect.

Issues of safety for young people who are looked after and involved or at risk of CSE are addressed by Lucie Shuker in Chapter 9. She asserts that the physical safety of these young people needs to be achieved alongside, rather than at the expense of, relational and psychological security. Shuker suggests that if relational and psychological security are sacrificed in the pursuit of physical safety the young person is likely to experience chronic ontological insecurity, which may itself become a risk factor for CSE. Shuker suggests that physical, relational and psychological security are mutually reinforcing and presents a model to suggest how all three elements of security might be achieved in practice.

In Chapter 10 Lorena Arocha critically reviews how issues of trafficking and CSE re-emerged on the political agenda in the 1980s and came to be defined as global social problems. She suggests that because the UN defined trafficking as a security issue, threatening the sovereignty of nation states, these issues gained global prominence. Arocha analyses developments at the European level as a case study example to illustrate her argument. Arocha argues that there are many contradictions in trafficking and CSE policy making at the European level and points to a tendency to conflate trafficking and CSE. This she suggests can have negative impacts on those who are trafficked for purposes other than CSE. Arocha also highlights a tendency in contemporary social policy to individualisation, which results in the de-politicisation of trafficking and CSE and means that the complex global social processes that create the conditions for trafficking and CSE are not addressed.

In Chapter 11 Patricia Hynes discusses the way that statutory services have led approaches to understanding and addressing child protection in general and CSE and related trafficking in particular. She draws on lessons that can be learnt from approaches that acknowledge the strengths of the voluntary sector, raising examples of how minority ethnic and migrant community organisations can hold important knowledge about trafficking and CSE. She notes that children trafficked for CSE will invariably be victims of other related forms of exploitation and discusses how NGOs may have particular approaches that enable better engagement and identification of the problems involved.

Collectively and individually the contributions to this volume provide us with a range of interesting and stimulating perspectives for considering a variety of topics relevant to young people involved or at risk of CSE and related trafficking. As the editors we are pleased to have facilitated such a valuable contribution to this field of endeavour and trust that our readers, whether policy makers, practitioners, other academics, researchers or students will consider our efforts worthwhile.

1
Young People and Sexual Exploitation: A Critical Discourse Analysis

Margaret Melrose

Introduction

Although the title of this chapter contains the phrase 'sexual exploitation' this is not a term I will employ uncritically in the following discussion. The chapter will present a critical analysis of the discourse of 'child sexual exploitation' (CSE) and I will therefore refer to 'young people's involvement in commercial sex markets' and/or 'participation in commercial sexual transactions' in place of this term.

In this chapter I make four key criticisms of the CSE discourse that currently dominates academic debate and determines policy and practice development in the UK. Firstly, I argue that there has been an expansion of the discourse since the turn of the twenty-first century. This has rendered the meaning of the term rather 'vague' and 'ambiguous' (Asquith and Turner, 2008; Melrose, 2012a, b). I suggest that the expansion of this discourse lends the concept a certain elasticity which means that a variety of situations and behaviours can be interpreted as 'child sexual exploitation' (Melrose, 2012a).

Secondly, I argue that the discourse is predicated on, and reproduces, two more fundamental discourses. These are firstly a discourse of 'childhood' that dominates Western thought about 'children' and 'childhood' and secondly a discourse of '*female* childhood' – because, despite its pretentions to gender neutrality, the imagined child of CSE discourse is invariably female and as such young men are largely rendered invisible by it (Dennis, 2008; Melrose, 2010). The idea of childhood on which the CSE discourse is predicated imagines children

9

as dependent, innocent, pure, unable to exercise choice and unable to enter contracts, whilst the discourse of female childhood constructs female sexuality from within a sexual double standard that sees women 'primarily as objects of male desire' (Powell, 2010: 174). I therefore argue that the CSE discourse is produced by, and reproduces, particular understandings of 'children' and 'childhood' and particular understandings of adolescent female sexuality.

Thirdly, I argue that CSE discourse positions the young people concerned as *always* and *inevitably* passive victims/objects and thereby tells only particular and partial truths about them. I suggest that these partial truths primarily serve the interests of fundraising and campaigning arms of organisations that work with these young people rather than the interests of the young people themselves.

Fourthly, I contend that the individualising character of CSE discourse reduces young people's involvement to a problem of the (individual) morality/immorality of those who would pay for their sexual services and/or an individual problem of the behaviour of the young people. This directs attention away from the social, economic and cultural arrangements and processes that render young people vulnerable to involvement in commercial sex markets. It thereby obscures wider concerns with young people's poverty and socio-economic disadvantage: the very factors that, in conjunction with other dynamics and experiences, underpin involvement in those markets (Melrose, 2010; Pearce, 2009; Phoenix, 2001; 2002). In other words, I argue that the 'sexually exploited child' of the CSE discourse is abstracted from the concrete conditions of her life and (re)presented as the pitiful personification of a corrupted or defiled ideal of Western childhood.

I conclude the discussion by considering debates about the 'mainstreaming' of sex in contemporary culture and locating young people involved in commercial sex markets in what has been described as an 'unprecedented sexualised, sex-crazed and sex-everywhere culture' (Powell, 2010: 1).

In undertaking this critical analysis it is not my intention to suggest that young people's involvement in commercial sex markets is acceptable or necessarily advantageous to them, or that involvement in those markets should be condoned. I am not suggesting that involvement in commercial sex markets is never exploitative or that we should not be concerned with trying to protect young people from involvement in those markets. What I am arguing is that the way in which the dominant CSE discourse constructs such involvement (and consequently determines, in policy and practice, how the protection of young people involved is approached) does not meet young people's social and economic needs and therefore does not protect them adequately.

Expanding discourse

CSE discourse fundamentally conditions how young people's involvement in commercial sexual transactions is accounted for and thereby determines responses in policy and practice. In other words, discourses have material effects and these effects make themselves felt by delimiting what can or cannot be said (or thought – and therefore done) about any particular issue or topic (Eagleton, 1991).

Discourses are 'strongly implicated in the exercise of power' (Willig, 2001: 107 cited in Allen, 2003: 216) and 'dominant discourses derive considerable power from their entrenchment within discursive fields such as the legal system, religion and the family' (Allen, 2003: 216). Over the past 12 years a particular discourse of CSE has achieved dominance, conditioning understandings and determining responses to young people who are involved in commercial sex markets (Melrose, 2010; 2012a, b).

There has been an historical shift in the language through which young people's involvement in these markets has been apprehended and understood: from 'abuse through prostitution' during the mid to late 1990s to '*commercial* sexual exploitation' in the early years of the twenty-first century and most recently an expansion of the concept to 'sexual exploitation' (e.g. DCSF, 2009). This new and expanded language means that the concept of CSE no longer *necessarily* signals young people's abuse through prostitution or in *commercial* markets (Melrose, 2012a, b). Arguably this new language stretches the concept to the point of meaninglessness and in practice this means that distinguishing CSE from other forms of adolescent sexual activity has become increasingly difficult (Melrose, 2012a).

The CSE discourse was promoted from the late twentieth and early twenty-first century by campaigning organisations (such as children's charities) so as to establish a distinction between the involvement of young people and the involvement of adults in commercial sex markets (Melrose, 2010; 2012a; O'Connell-Davidson, 2005). This distinction enabled campaigning organisations to claim that young people's involvement in commercial sex markets was a form of sexual abuse and thus to argue that children and young people who were involved should be afforded a child protection response rather than criminalisation and punishment (Barnardos, 1998; Melrose, Barrett and Brodie, 1999). The success of these campaigns resulted in the introduction of new government guidance (DoH/HO, 2000) in relation to the treatment of young people involved and, since its introduction, the 'discursive separation of child and adult prostitution' (O'Connell-Davidson, 2005: 44) has become ever more firmly entrenched (Melrose, 2012a).

The discursive separation of adult and young people's involvement in commercial sex markets means that the weight of historical and contemporary, national and international, evidence regarding adult involvement in sex work is largely overlooked when the involvement of young people is considered. Research on adult engagement in sex work demonstrates that, for both young and old, males and females, the decision to enter commercial sex markets is frequently taken in the context of social deprivation, unemployment and poverty (Andrieu-Sanz and Vasquez, 1989; Barrett, 1994, 1997; Crosby and Barrett, 1999; Cusick, 2003; Edwards, 1992; Gibson, 1995; Green, 1992; Hardman, 1997; Matthews, 2008; Melrose, 2010; Melrose, Barrett and Brodie, 1999; O'Connell-Davidson, 1995, 1998, 2005; O'Neill, 1994; 1997; O'Neill, Goode and Hopkins, 1995; Phoenix, 2001; Pitts, 1997).

Their lack of economic autonomy and their dependence on adults of course means that young people who become involved in sex work are vulnerable in ways that adults are not (O'Connell-Davidson, 1998). However, this is no reason to suppose that evidence to explain the involvement of adults might not equally apply to young people. It can be no coincidence that, for example, in the United Kingdom the majority of those involved in commercial sex markets are single parent mothers and young people for whom state welfare benefits are 'completely inadequate or wholly absent' (O'Connell-Davidson, 1998: 14; q.v. Melrose, 2010; 2012c).

Alongside poverty, many adults and young people who become involved have experienced a range of debilitating processes. Many of those involved have histories of family discord and, for some, 'child sexual and physical abuse provides a fundamental stage and set of experiences which make the decision to enter prostitution more probable' (Matthews, 2008: 66). In short, in relation to both adults and young people, the reasons for becoming involved are complex; 'there is no simple or single answer to the question of how people become involved' (O'Connell-Davidson, 2005: 46) or why they become involved. Moreover, the dynamics involved may be contradictory (Matthews, 2008).

Predicates of the discourse of child sexual exploitation

The sociology of childhood has enabled us to recognise that our contemporary understandings of 'children' and 'childhood' derive from a discourse of childhood that emerged in Europe in the mid-eighteenth century (Aries, 1962). This discourse, promoted primarily by developmental psychology 'in a pact with medicine, education and government agencies' (James, Jenks and Prout, 1998: 17), has since become deeply ingrained in Western thinking about 'children' and 'childhood'. This discourse constructs childhood as 'an inadequate precursor to the real state of human being, namely being "grown up"' (James, Jenks and Prout, 1998: 18).

The 'child' is discursively constructed as the opposite of an 'adult' and is thus assumed to embody all of those qualities and characteristics that an adult does not. Children are imagined as passive and incapable of independent action; innocent as opposed to worldly-wise; dependent as opposed to independent or autonomous; pure as opposed to tainted; irrational as opposed to rational (Brace, 2003 cited in O'Connell-Davidson, 2005). Furthermore, children are assumed to be asexual and childhood is imagined as a period of sexual innocence (Bragg and Buckingham, 2010; Haydon and Scraton, 2002; Pilcher, 1996). As Kincaid writes:

> The child is that species which is free of sexual feeling or response; the adult is that species which has crossed over into sexuality.
> Kincaid (1992: 7 cited in O'Connell-Davidson, 2005: 93)

According to the UNCRC definition of a 'child' a child or young person does not become 'adult' and thereby 'cross over into sexuality' until they are 18, which renders adolescent engagement in sexual activity before that age somewhat problematic. As Pilcher (1996: 78) writes, 'Western ideologies around sexuality and childhood mean that the pairing of "children" with "sex" is morally inappropriate' and 'evidence of childhood sexuality undermines ideas about what childhood should "properly" be.'

In addition to imagining childhood as a period of sexual innocence childhood is envisaged through a gendered mode of discourse that constructs male and female childhoods quite differently. As a consequence, when adolescent sexuality is considered it is not thought of in the same way for boys and girls. Male and female sexuality is imagined within the 'double standard' of (hetero) sexuality that constructs male sexuality as active and pursuant and female sexuality as passive and accommodating (Allen, 2003; Cohen, 2011; Haydon and Scraton, 2002; Hird and Jackson, 2001; Powell, 2010). This mode of discourse considers girls' sexual desire as an 'aberration' (Cohen, 2011: 13): their sexual expression is permissible only in 'preparation for reproduction and motherhood' (Cohen, 2011: 13; q.v. Powell, 2010; Haydon and Scraton, 2002) and they are sanctioned for expressing their sexuality outside of a 'love relationship' (Cohen, 2011; Haydon and Scraton, 2002; Powell, 2010: 42). Conversely, girls are 'constantly reminded to emphasise their femininity, to respond to and excite the male gaze' but are 'negatively labelled should they be confident, assertive or sexually active' (Cohen, 2011; Haydon and Scraton, 2002: 167; Powell, 2010).

In the dominant discourse of CSE a 'child' and a 'young person' are conflated, which is arguably 'infantalising' (Bragg, 2012: 408) and misleading given that developmental approaches to the study of childhood demonstrate significant changes occurring in young people between the ages of 11 and 18. It is also misleading in the sense that the majority of young people who become involved in commercial sex markets tend to be between 15 and 17 years old (Jago et al., 2011). Thus the majority are not pre-pubertal children as the terminology of CSE might imply.

Creating victims and objects

The CSE discourse cannot and does not account for the sexual agency of young people who become involved because this discourse suggests that *all* young people are coerced, manipulated or forced into selling or exchanging sexual services by predatory or abusive adults (usually men, who are often masquerading as boyfriends) (Melrose, 2010).

The grammatical construction of CSE discourse establishes in language that the young people concerned are *always*, and *inevitably*, passive objects or 'things'. This is because the verb 'to exploit' is transitive verb, requiring a direct object (the thing that is exploited) and an implied subject – 'the exploiter'. By constructing the young person as an 'object' that is exploited the discourse of CSE manages, in one phrase, to negate the idea that the young people concerned might be exercising their own agency. This discursive construction thereby establishes that these young people are not acting autonomously and not acting under their own volition, and they cannot therefore be understood as social actors in their own right (Melrose, 2012b). If the CSE discourse establishes that the young people concerned are not acting autonomously or exercising volition then by implication their involvement in commercial sexual transactions must be understood as forced or coerced on the one hand or as irrational action on the other.

There is limited evidence to support the idea that young people who become involved in commercial sexual transactions are always and inevitably passive objects that are groomed, forced or coerced into commercial sexual activity or that they are acting irrationally (Harris, private communication, 2011). On the contrary, there is evidence to suggest that some of these young people may be making constrained, but rational, choices within the context of highly diminished circumstances and opportunities (Melrose, Barrett and Brodie, 1999; q.v. Scott and Skidmore, 2006; Montgomery, 1998; O'Connell-Davidson, 2005). In these conditions young people may be exposed to social networks that serve only to reinforce marginalised and disadvantaged social identities and statuses (i.e. they only have access to negative social capital) (Wacquant, 1998) where only their bodily capital has any value (Bernstein, 1999). In these settings sexuality represents a form of symbolic capital (Powell, 2010: 48) and for some young people it may 'make sense' (Phoenix, 2001) to exploit their symbolic capital in commercial sex markets.

A 'youthful' body has a very high premium in Western culture (not just in the sex industry but in the culture generally), which is why 'older' women are exhorted by advertising campaigns and cosmetics manufacturers to 'dispel the signs of ageing' and to invest in all sorts of anti-ageing products and treatments. Young people involved in sex markets are similarly aware that there is a premium on youth in the sex industry and know that the younger they are, or look, the more they can earn (Melrose, Barrett and Brodie, 1999). Discussing boys involved in the sex industry, for example, Gibson (1995: 163) noted,

> There is a lot of pressure on the boys to look as young as possible. The younger they are, the more physically and emotionally underdeveloped they appear, the more they are in demand. They have a 'sell-by date' of up to the age of nineteen.

Youthfulness is therefore a very important commodity in the sex industry. Just as adults are able to opt for sex industry 'careers' as a viable alternative to no or low income, so young women and young men are able to exploit their symbolic capital and their 'youthfulness' by selling or swapping sexual services for financial gain. In conditions of socio-economic marginalisation this might represent the 'best' way to survive when confronted with limited opportunities for income generation (Melrose, 2010; 2012c).

Individualising child sexual exploitation

The young person who becomes involved in commercial sex markets voluntarily, as a result of exercising their own agency, is an anomaly that CSE discourse cannot accommodate. The idea that young people might make an autonomous decision to sell or swap sex threatens the system of binary opposition that generates understandings of what children and young people are (O'Connell-Davidson, 2005). It also undermines the binary opposition between adults (who are able to enter contracts to sell sex if they wish) and children (who, by virtue of the fact that they are children, are unable to enter such contracts). Furthermore, it destabilises the binary opposition that distinguishes the exploited from the exploiters and the victims from the villains. From within the dominant CSE discourse, therefore, young people who *wilfully* or *voluntarily* engage in such actions cannot be considered either as 'children' as they are conventionally understood or as 'victims' of 'exploiters'. These young people therefore need to be bracketed off from the category of 'child' – and yet they are not (chronologically) 'adult' (i.e. they are not 18). They also need to be bracketed off from the category of 'victim' since if they are acting autonomously they clearly cannot be considered 'victims' of abusive or predatory adults.

These troubling contradictions cannot be accommodated by the dominant CSE discourse because, as I have argued, the terminology of this discourse means that the young people concerned can only be understood as passive objects/victims. From within this discourse if these young people cannot be understood as 'victims' or as 'innocent children' then they must be understood in some way as being 'children' or 'victims' who have something 'wrong' with them *as children* or *as victims*.

Regarding these young people as having something 'wrong' with them results from a tendency within CSE discourse to individualise the problem of involvement in commercial sexual transactions (Melrose, 2010). This mode of discourse encourages a narrow focus on the individual actions of the predatory adults involved in paying young people for sexual services or otherwise encouraging them to exchange sexual favours. It also encourages a focus on the individual actions and behaviour of the young people themselves. This discourse would thereby suggest that there is something that needs 'fixing' with young people who independently engage in commercial sexual activity because this discourse suggests that the young person is deluded, irrational, suffering from low self-esteem, false consciousness and/or other related (psychological) problems (Melrose, 2012b). It does not therefore enable a consideration of what it is about contemporary social, economic and cultural arrangements and processes that might drive young people towards commercial sex markets. Neither does it identify 'the specific social processes that create the conditions of exploitation' (Cabezas, 1998: 85) nor facilitate an understanding of what might wrong with a society in which sex work appears as the 'best option' for those who are 'vulnerable and/or financially impoverished' (Fusco, 1998).

Instead the CSE discourse suggests that the behaviour (and even the patterns of thought) of young people who are involved needs to be changed, as does that of those who would exploit them. By focusing attention on the individual behaviour and morality of those who would pay for their sexual services and/or by focusing concern on the alleged psychological and/or behavioural problems experienced by the young people, this discourse fails to account for the political, economic and cultural conditions that shape young people's involvement in commercial sex markets.

If the currently dominant discourse through which the young people concerned are imagined and apprehended does not enable them to be considered as active human subjects and does not enable the social, economic and cultural conditions that underpin their involvement to be accounted for then a question arises about whose or what interests are served by this discourse.

Fundraisers in organisations that promote the dominant CSE discourse, like their predecessors in the nineteenth-century social purity movement, need to promote an image of young people who are involved that will appeal to the values of white 'middle class Christians' (Doezema, 1998: 36) from whom those organisations garner much (financial) support. As Doezema (1998: 44) has pointed out, 'sickening stories of child abuse galvanise public opinion and get donations'. Thus, in order to rouse public opinion and ensure financial support, experienced practitioners and policy makers are required by fundraisers, campaign managers and press officers to present their detailed understandings of these complex issues in simplistic terms and media sound bites so that the young people concerned are *necessarily* presented as 'innocent victims' (Melrose, 2012b).

The image of children selling their bodies, as Montgomery (1998: 140) has argued, is a 'powerful metaphor' that provokes 'indignation and outrage'. The passive victim/object image of CSE discourse is thus a powerful marketing and fundraising tool that serves the interests of campaign managers and fundraisers very well. But this is not to say that it equally serves the interests of the young people concerned.

By casting young people involved as passive objects unable to exercise agency and act autonomously CSE discourse does not serve the interests of the young people concerned. It does not serve their interests by insisting that selling or swapping sex can be reduced to a problem of the immorality of individual adults who pay or otherwise encourage them to participate in commercial sexual exchanges. Neither does it serve their interests to individualise such participation or to reduce it to matters of 'low self-esteem' or related psychological problems. And nor does it serve their interests to obscure the social, political and economic inequalities that underpin involvement or the cultural conditions that makes involvement possible.

Sex in the mainstream

In contemporary Western culture sexuality is an important currency and sex is a commodity that sells – not just for those who trade it in commercial sex markets. The value of this commodity is well understood by (amongst others) mainstream entertainment, advertising and information technology industries. It is largely due to the activities of these industries that the metaphor of 'seduction' is a key motif in marketing campaigns for various goods ranging from food to cars and the fulfilment of sexual fantasies is promised through the consumption of a range of products.

These developments have been described variously as the 'sexualisation' of culture (Attwood, 2006; 2010; Bailey, 2011; Gill, 2007; 2010; Levy, 2005; Papadopoulos, 2010; Walter, 2010), the 'pornification' of culture (Attwood, 2010; Gill, 2003; McRobbie, 2004) and the 'mainstreaming' of sex (Attwood, 2010; McRobbie, 2004). This process involves

> the blurring of boundaries between the pornographic and the mainstream; new forms of sexual encounter (phone/cyber sex) and a growth in commercial sex services and new spaces for sexual entertainment (e.g. escort agencies, lap dancing clubs and sex tours, internet sites).
>
> Bragg (2012: 409)

It is claimed that the mainstreaming of sex is also *sexualising* (Bailey, 2011; Papadopoulos, 2010) but, because of Western ideologies of sexuality and childhood, scant attention has been paid to what children and young people might 'bring to the process of sexualisation' (Walkerdine, 1997: 169–70 cited in Bragg and Buckingham, 2010: 130). Rather, 'blame' for young people's access to sexual knowledge, sexualised behaviours and the 'sexualisation of culture' more generally is usually 'laid at the door of external forces, most commonly the media and consumer culture' (Bragg and Buckingham, 2010: 129). Adult sexuality and sexually explicit material available through various media and information technologies is thus accused of intruding on 'the sanitized space of natural childhood' (Walkerdine, 1997: 169 cited in Bragg and Buckingham, 2010: 130). This returns us abruptly to the dominant Western discourse of childhood, which informs the discourse of CSE, and which assumes that children are either asexual or sexually innocent (Bragg and Buckingham, 2010; Haydon and Scraton, 2002; O'Connell-Davidson, 2005; Pilcher, 1996). They are thus assumed to be incapable of bringing anything to the process of sexualisation. As Powell (2010: 16) has argued,

> In defending the concept that children and young people need protection from sexual exploitation, Western society has become invested in the idea that we cannot simultaneously allow them any sexual agency at all.

At the same time, however, sex and sexuality have become so central to late-modern Western culture – and youth culture in particular – that sex has become part of the territory on which what it means to be a child or teenager is constantly being 'defined, reasserted and worked over' (Bragg and Buckingham, 2010: 135). To feel that she is desirable, primarily to men, remains a powerful determinant of a young woman's sense of self worth and identity (Allen, 2003; Hird and Jackson, 2001; Levy, 2005; Powell, 2010; Walter, 2010). It is, for many young girls, the means by which 'they feel they are worth something in the world' (Cohen, 2011: 8). In this cultural context many young women who are not necessarily vulnerable to involvement in commercial sex markets regard sex and their sexuality as a commodity. Sexuality is treated as an instrumental 'tool' and sexual favours are traded as a means of 'gaining acclaim socially' (Levy, 2005: 146).

Young women growing up in this cultural context understand from a very early age that they are valued primarily for their sexual attractiveness and come to regard their bodies as commodities to be improved, customised, enhanced and exploited through diet, an endless barrage of beauty regimes and/or surgery. For some this body enhancement is to advance their general attractiveness whilst for others it is in the more specific pursuit of successful careers as 'glamour models' and 'lap-dancers' – that is, their bodies are regarded as things to exploit to improve their chances of success in 'mainstream' sex industry careers (Coy, 2009a cited in Papadopoulos, 2010; Melrose, 2012a).

The growth in demand for cosmetic surgery would suggest that many young women view their bodies as instrumental tools through which they can achieve other goals. In 2003, for example, 11,300 breast augmentation operations were performed on young people aged 18 or younger in the USA (Zuckerman and Abraham, 2008). In the UK a 2006 survey suggested that a quarter of girls were considering plastic surgery by the time they were 16 (Walter, 2010: 68) and the number of labial reduction operations has risen steeply in the UK in recent years (Walter, 2010: 108). Through such procedures young women are exercising agency to fulfil dominant values of heterosexual attractiveness and thereby augmenting the value of their symbolic capital (i.e. their sexuality) to improve their chances of 'success' in the mainstream sex industry and/or their attractiveness to men.

Young women from less affluent backgrounds, whose potential to enhance their symbolic capital through expensive procedures might be more limited than their more affluent sisters', are no less influenced by the idea of a lucrative career in the mainstream sex industry and/or making themselves attractive to the male gaze. These young women, however, may not have the means to achieve success in that industry: they may not be able to afford bodily enhancements and/or they may not have connections to the necessary contacts and social networks. These young women are therefore more likely to find themselves at the illegitimate rather than the legitimate end of the sex industry continuum where they are confined to the lower echelons of a highly differentiated and hierarchically organised sex industry (Bernstein, 1999).

Conclusions

This chapter has provided a critique of the CSE discourse by highlighting four key limitations. Firstly, it has asserted that the expansion of the discourse has rendered the concept of CSE rather vague and meaningless. In practice, therefore, it is harder to identify what 'sexual exploitation' is, and when it is identified we might no longer necessarily be considering young people who are abused through prostitution or through participation in commercial sexual exchanges (Melrose, 2012a).

Secondly, the chapter has stressed that the CSE discourse is produced by, and in turn reproduces, dominant conceptions of 'childhood' and dominant ideologies in relation to adolescent female sexuality which deny female sexual agency. The conflation of 'adolescents' with 'children' in this discourse tends to infantalise the young people being considered.

Thirdly, the discussion has contended that the CSE discourse tells only partial truths about the young people who become involved and cannot accommodate or account for those young people who become involved independently of coercion or manipulation by predatory adults (Melrose, 2010). The discourse is incapable of acknowledging the agency of these young people since the language positions them always and inevitably as passive objects/victims. The discussion has suggested that whilst this may serve the fundraising interests of agencies working with young people who are involved it does not necessarily serve the interests of the young people concerned.

Fourthly, the chapter has argued that the CSE discourse tends to reduce young people's involvement to an individual problem of the (im)morality of adults who exploit them and/or individual behavioural and/or psychological problems located in the young person. By doing so, this discourse abstracts the young people from the concrete conditions of their lives and obscures the social, economic, political and cultural conditions that underpin involvement in commercial sex markets and makes participation in them make sense.

By considering the mainstreaming of sex in contemporary popular and youth culture the chapter has pointed to the ways in which young people, particularly young women, may make active choices to pursue legitimate careers in the contemporary sex industry. It has however indicated that not all young people will be able to succeed in legitimate sex industry 'careers' and, as a result of socio-economic disadvantage, some may find themselves left with only illegitimate options available to them. These cultural conditions, combined with the social, economic and political circumstances of young people's lives, need to be taken into account if we are properly to understand and appropriately respond to young people's involvement in commercial sex markets. To do this we need to move beyond the discourse of CSE and recognise that some young people will make 'poor' choices whilst respecting the choices they make.

2
Drifting into Trouble: Sexual Exploitation and Gang Affiliation

John Pitts

Gangs? What gangs?

This chapter considers sexual violence and child sexual exploitation (CSE) in youth gangs. However, at present, many UK social scientists remain sceptical about the very existence of youth gangs. The sceptics do have a point of course. There are discernible historical continuities between youth subcultures past and present and the sometimes misplaced social anxieties they engender (Pearson, 1983). Moreover, the term 'gang' tends to be used indiscriminately in popular discourse, the media and the criminal justice system and, all too often, its use is stigmatising and racist (cf. Alexander, 2008). And there are, of course, many different kinds of adolescent groups in the UK, engaged in relatively innocuous adolescent misbehaviour that are wrongly identified as 'gangs' (Aldridge, Medina and Ralphs, 2008).

Nonetheless evidence that violent youth gangs exist and that their existence poses a serious threat to the safety and wellbeing, and in some cases the lives, of the children, young people and adults who live in gang-affected neighbourhoods is now substantial (Andell and Pitts, 2010; Balasunderam, 2009; Bullock and Tilley, 2003; Centre for Social Justice, 2009; Matthews and Pitts, 2007; Palmer, 2009; Palmer and Pitts, 2006; Pitts, 2008; Youth Justice Board, 2007).

A 'gang' is understood as:

A relatively durable, predominantly street-based group of young people who (1) see themselves (and are seen by others) as a discernible group, (2) engage in a range of criminal activities and violence,

(3) identify with or lay claim over territory, (4) have some form of identifying structural feature, and (5) are in conflict with other, similar, gangs.

(Centre for Social Justice, 2009: 1)

However, a not unreasonable concern with the corrosive effects of erroneous description, pernicious labelling and discriminatory policing amongst some academics has meant that the impact of gang violence upon its almost invariably socially disadvantaged victims is often minimised and at worst denied (cf. the critique of such unbalanced *Left Idealism* in Lea and Young, 1984; Matthews and Young, 1992; Young and Matthews, 1992).

But, as Elliott Currie (1986: 18) has observed:

This minimisation of the impact of crime and an unwillingness to make the link between poverty and crime finds its corollary in an idealisation of the criminal as a kind of proto-revolutionary (which perpetuates) an image of progressives as being both fuzzy-minded and, much worse, unconcerned about the realities of life.

This 'fuzzy-mindedness' is particularly evident when UK social scientists confront the question of sexual victimisation in gangs, because it requires them to reconcile their commitment to challenging the demonisation of socially disadvantaged young men with the reality of the sexual victimisation of socially disadvantaged young women (Hallsworth, 2011; Hallsworth and Young, 2008).

The mature response would be to recognise that social and economic polarisation, acute social disadvantage and institutionalised racism inevitably have profound social, cultural and behavioural effects, one of which might be to drive some young men into a caricatured, hyper-masculinity which, as the data on gang-related fatalities and sexual offences attests, can have catastrophic consequences for other, similarly disadvantaged, young people (Pitts, 2008). To the neutral observer this might appear to be a sociological truism, but it has proved an ideological contradiction that even some academics of professorial rank have been unable or unwilling to reconcile, and this accounts for the paucity of research and scholarship in this important area of criminology.

Sexual exploitation

Current definitions of CSE are not very helpful in discussions of sexual victimisation in youth gangs. This is because they juxtapose an essentially passive victim with a predatory perpetrator. Thus they present a world in which an exploiter deliberately exploits; an abuser deliberately abuses or a seducer deliberately seduces. This model of a coercive dyad in which perpetrators wilfully transgress normative and legal prohibitions continues to inform both the political debate about, and interventions with, 'sexually exploited' children and young people, and whilst it describes the child sexual abuse encountered by the police and children's services well enough, its individualising focus fails to capture the complexities of the actual and perceived sexual exploitation of adolescents, particularly if those adolescents are involved with gangs.

The victimisation of young women in gangs?

The Metropolitan Police define 'gang rape' (subsequently re-badged as 'Group Sexual Assault' – GSA) as 'a sex attack by three or more people'. A study by Scotland Yard's Operation 'Sapphire', which investigates sex crimes, revealed that in 2008/9, the Metropolitan Police recorded 93 'gang rapes' compared with 36 in 2003/4. Moreover, the number of attacks involving four or more attackers appears to have grown over the period, whilst the average age of victims fell. In 1998/99 48 per cent of victims were under 19, whereas by 2008 this proportion had risen to 64 per cent. Thirty-six per cent of these young women were aged 15 or younger. In 2008/9 42 per cent of suspects were aged under 19, compared with 38 per cent in 2003/4, whilst 8 per cent of them were identified as white, 32 per cent as black and 24 per cent as 'different ethnicities'. The ethnicity of the remaining 36 per cent is unknown. The proportion of white victims fell from 69 per cent in 1998/99 to 50 per cent in 2008. During the same period, the proportion of black victims rose from 17 per cent to 34 per cent. In London, the boroughs with the highest rates of gang rape were Lambeth, Croydon, Newham, Southwark, Westminster and Hackney.

In gang affected neighbourhoods young women are also at heightened risk of other forms of violent crime. In my study of youth gangs in Waltham Forest (Pitts, 2008) I found that in the two years from 1 January 2005 to 31 December 2006, there were 493 incidents of *gun-enabled crime* in the borough. The term *gun-enabled crime* covers everything from threats with a replica firearm to wounding and murder. Table 2.1 shows that gun crime tends to be perpetrated by young people under the age of 20 and that African-Caribbean children and young people are heavily over-represented as perpetrators and that perpetrators are, overwhelmingly, male.

Whilst the victims of gun-enabled crime are still disproportionately African-Caribbean there are also far larger numbers of White Caucasian children and young people being victimised. Even more striking, perhaps, is the fact that whilst only 5 per cent of gun crime suspects in Waltham Forest were young women, they constituted around 30 per cent of gun crime victims. Unsurprisingly, perhaps,

Table 2.1   Gun-enabled crime in Waltham Forest in 2007

Ages of Perpetrators	Percentage
1–10	11%
11–20	53%
21–30	30%
Ethnicity of Perpetrators	**Percentage**
White Caucasian	18%
Black African-Caribbean	59%
Asian	10%
Gender of Perpetrators	**Percentage**
Male	92%
Female	5%
Ages of Victims	**Percentage**
1–10	19%
11–20	27%
21–30	27%
Ethnicity of Victims	**Percentage**
White Caucasian	39%
Black African Caribbean	31%
Asian	13%
Gender of Victims	**Percentage**
Male	69%
Female	30%

Source: Metropolitan Police CRIS Data (2007).

gun-enabled crime in Waltham Forest was concentrated in or near the major gang neighbourhoods and overlapped with street crime and drug-dealing hotspots.

Sexual exploitation in gangs

That sexual relationships within gangs are exploitative should not surprise us since the violent youth gang, as distinct from the adolescent peer group, is essentially exploitative; both in its dealings with the outside world and in the quality of relationships within the gang. As a young respondent in South East London observed:

> It's not just people robbing any old women on the street, they are robbing their so-called friends or the so-called breddrins, the same people rob each other because they think we're in the same situation.
>
> (Pitts, 2008: 42)

He said that whilst there is plenty of money around, 'friendships are possible' but when the money runs out, 'friends' are quite likely to turn on one another. Adult respondents interviewed by Palmer (2009: 16) on a North West London housing estate noted:

> Half of the shootings that have happened over the last 10 years – do you know that the parents of the kids that have been shooting each other was boyfriend and girlfriend or close friends?

Jason, a young respondent from the same estate, said:

> I've been set up a few times but I'm not watching no faces because that's life. You don't know the brers ... face covered, it might be your own friends.

In this predatory, exploitative, 'dog-eat-dog', world, the respect ascribed to a young man is determined in large part by his ability to 'do' what he believes to be the right kind of 'masculinity'. Jock Young writes:

> Young men facing such a denial of recognition turn ... to the creation of cultures of machismo, [specifically] to the mobilisation of

one of their only resources, physical strength, to the formation of gangs and to the defence of their own 'turf'. Being denied the respect of others they create a subculture that revolves around masculine powers and 'respect'.

(Young, 1999: 63)

Relationships between male gang members are characterised by competition rather than connection (Bourdieu, 1993) and an instrumentality wherein others come to be perceived as either a means to an end or a potential threat (Palmer and Pitts, 2006; Harding, 2012). In such situations, Elias (2000) argues, we see the erosion of 'reality congruence' and its concomitant, a diminution in 'mutual identification' and tolerance.

Mullins (2007), drawing on the work of Walter B. Miller (1958), suggests that the consequent desire on the part of men to maintain personal autonomy means that to connect emotionally with a woman would threaten that autonomy, thus leading to what Statham (1984) describes as *psychic celibacy*; a repression of emotion that keeps women mentally and emotionally *at arm's length*. As Rodger (2008: 8) observes: 'Where marginality, social exclusion or sectarianism emerges, the sense of empathy for the other and the mutual restraint on behaviour are absent'. Arguably, this situation has been exacerbated by recent cultural changes within violent youth gangs.

Los-Angelisation

In some gang-affected towns and cities in England, the last decade has witnessed a fragmentation of older-established gangs and the proliferation of younger, more anarchic ones. These new groupings appear to be less concerned with the acquisition of wealth and more concerned with building a reputation for extreme violence. This transition has paralleled, and possibly been driven by, a process in which local gang traditions have been supplanted by a bricolage of elements absorbed from a globalised gang culture; mediated via film, the Internet, music and PlayStation games (Hebdige, 1979; Levi-Strauss, 1966; Valkenburg and Peter, 2007; Weitzer and Kubrin, 2009). As such, this new, synthetic, 'gangsta' culture tends, necessarily, towards caricature and exaggeration (Hagedorn, 2008).

This is worrying because demonstrations of hypermasculinity (Young, 1999) through group sexual assault (MPS, 2012) and gang-related sexual violence (Firmin, 2010, 2011) are central elements of this new synthetic/authentic, hyper-real, way of discharging the 'gangsta' role. This is compounded, some argue, by the tidal wave of readily accessible pornography available on the Web (Flood, 2009) and the capacity of individuals to generate home grown versions of this via 'sexting' (Ringrose et al., 2011). This 'sexualisation' or 'pornification' (Attwood, 2010) of culture in general, and 'gangsta' culture in particular, perpetuates the association between masculinity and predatory sexual prowess which, as Coy (2009a) observes, justifies sexual violence and exploitation.

The girls in the gang

Most of the studies of girls and young women who become involved with violent youth gangs have been conducted in North America. The much smaller body of UK research has focussed largely on the question of whether 'gang-involved' young women are passive subjects or active agents. This line of enquiry appears to proceed from the assumption that if we demonstrate that a young woman has been victimised we are denying her capacity for agency, and this has led to studies which, whilst 'ideologically correct', understate the very real risks of gang involvement for both boys and girls (Batchelor, 2009; Young, 2009). Recent North American research acknowledges that the relative powerlessness of many gang-involved young women means that although they do exercise agency, they do so in a situation of, sometimes severe, constraint (Miller, 1998, 2001, 2009).

These studies suggest that many young women who become involved with violent youth gangs have been subject to parental neglect and suffered psychological, physical and sexual abuse at home, school or elsewhere (Miller, 2001). Joining the gang tends to be a process of 'seduction' rather than 'coercion', sometimes following in the footsteps of an older sister, or more often, an older brother, who is already a gang member; or starting a relationship with a gang-involved boy or young man. For many of these young women the gang appears to offer a way out of, and protection from, a difficult family situation; 'real' friendship; a sense of being appreciated and popular; excitement and money. Franklin (1988) and Burton (1990) produced similar findings in their studies of gang-involved African-American young women, as did Cepeda and Valdez (2003) in their study of Mexican-American girls. Indeed, Cepeda and Valdez contend that gang involvement

> may be the 'rational choice' in the face of the limited options and opportunities available to them.
>
> (Cepeda and Valdez, 2003: 15)

However, as the authors note, most girls eventually came to realise that there was a heavy price to pay for gang involvement and that although they are associated with gangs, they could never become 'full members'. Instead, they were, in the main, classified as 'girlfriends' with specific roles and tasks such as 'looking good', 'being available' for 'leisure time' when the gang was not busy and being 'put aside' when they were.

Where young women do take part in gang activities, like holding or transporting money, drugs or weapons, it is because they are less likely than boys to be caught. The girls in Totten (2000) and Cepeda and Valdez's research (2003) felt that they had to keep proving that they were worthy of gang involvement because, if they lost status, they were vulnerable to assault and sexual exploitation by gang members, sometimes with the active support of their own 'boyfriend'.

Cousineau (2002) found that some girls stayed in the gang because it was the only alternative 'home' they had and that it was better than the one they had left. Not only did they think that they had nowhere else to go but, because they had cut their ties with non-gang-involved peers, but they also had nobody to turn to. Thornberry and colleagues (1995: 12) suggest that this may be because one of the social costs of the sexual practices of gang-involved young women is that they are stigmatised and marginalised by 'other types of young females, male gang members, and the community'.

Beyond this, for Cousineau's young women, leaving the gang usually meant finishing a relationship with a 'boyfriend', attempting to construct or re-build a social network, re-entering education, training or employment, and dealing with the health problems resulting from poor nutrition, drug abuse and unprotected sex. When girls did leave the gang it tended to be the result of an event or a series of events that altered the girls' perception of the gang as a safe place to be. This could be an arrest followed by incarceration, being badly beaten up, seeing this happen to a friend, or being forced into behaviours, such as prostitution, which they found unacceptable.

Sexual exploitation?

All too often, the gang-related sexual behaviours with which we are concerned appear to be neither wholly constrained in the sense of the coercive dyad proffered by the CSE system, nor freely chosen. And this reality requires us to consider the socio-cultural context and the existential conditions in which such choices and non-choices are made.

It is clear from both the North American and more recent UK research that young women who become involved with gangs are likely to be used by male gang members not only for sex but to discharge a range of high-risk tasks which the males are anxious to avoid. They may, moreover, live with the threat of violent retribution if they fail to comply with their demands. However, as Firmin (2009: 34) observes, these relationships are complex:

> Women who are involved in gangs can occupy a number of roles, including: perpetrators ... victims ... partners ... (and) can be targeted by gangs. Women associated with rival gangs can also be targeted with violence (including rape); and associates: partners, sisters and mothers might be involved with hiding drugs and weapons, washing blood-covered clothing, etc. Even where they have no formal involvement, partners can serve to 'glamorise' gang members, and to put pressure on them to provide the material wealth associated with criminal behaviour.

The idea that 'sexual exploitation' of young women in youth gangs is, for them, *normal* in the sense that they regard it as mundane, commonplace and, hence, unproblematic, is questionable because it ignores the pathos of their lives and the context in which these abuses occur. It also fails to explain the mechanisms whereby the young women make the transition from conventional, or mainstream, sexual attitudes and practices to behaviour that is regarded by all but the most die-hard post-modernists, who welcome anything that bends a norm as a valuable contribution to life's rich tapestry, as socially deviant or, indeed, bizarre.

It is difficult to believe that the young women who are subjects of, or who submit themselves to, such practices, like giving oral sex to a group of boys on demand, are unaware of the differential status and esteem ascribed to the hierarchically ranked modes of sexual practice within their own social milieu. In almost all cases, one imagines, they are only too aware of how their sexual behaviour is regarded by their peers, who describe them variously as 'slags', 'skets' or 'links'. So whilst it may be true that they regard the abuse as 'normative', in the sociological sense, for girls occupying their lowly status, this does not mean that they are unaware that these sexual practices are at odds with prevailing mainstream social norms as well as the, admittedly contradictory, norms and values pertaining in their own social milieu. So, why do they do it; what are the rewards, and how do they overcome the social prohibitions which make it possible?

The social field of the violent youth gang

Some social scientists, drawing upon the work of Pierre Bourdieu, have suggested that within the social field of the gang, sexual practices which might otherwise be regarded as taboo become a 'normalised' role requirement. Although Bourdieu never wrote about youth gangs, his work on social field theory has become a key point of reference in the academic debate about them (cf. Hagedorn, 2008; Harding, 2012; Pitts, 2008; Wacquant, 2008).

Bourdieu eschews individualising explanations, arguing that because human behaviour is primarily a product of the social fields in which human beings are embedded, these social fields must be analysed independently of the characteristics of their inhabitants. Social fields, he argues, are shaped by the broad 'determining structures' of class, family and ethnicity, but their specific form is determined by the struggle 'between 'agents' antagonistically oriented to the same prizes or values' (Bourdieu, 1993: 22). This struggle creates status hierarchies, 'pecking orders', in which each position in the hierarchy induces a set of motivations that are subjectively experienced as *what should be done*. Thus, what Bourdieu calls the 'social fate' of individuals is sealed in large part by the role demands, which they experience as a *chain of objective requirements* placed upon them.

> You learn it just by hanging around. ... You know what you are supposed to do and not supposed to do really. Just like what you are allowed to do at school. They don't even need to explain it.
>
> (Harding, 2012: 40)

Recent studies (Firmin, 2010; 2011) suggest that the roles played by girls and young women in gangs are similarly hierarchically ranked and that these roles carry with them a *chain of objective requirements*. Firmin identifies at least three distinct roles played by girls and young women in violent youth gangs: *Girlfriends* (aka *Wifeys*), *Gang Girls* (aka *Links*, *Slags* or *Skets*) and girls who are *Loosely Affiliated*.

The Girlfriends of high status male gang members occupy a similarly elevated position. They might carry or hide weapons, drugs or money for their boyfriends, but in return they receive expensive gifts and protection from rival gangs and other girls. However, Girlfriends can sometimes slide down the pecking order to become Gang Girls. Firmin (2011) writes about Miranda, who, at the age of 14, was permanently excluded from school and under the supervision of a Youth Offending Team (YOT). At this point she met her boyfriend (aged 19), who was a high status gang member. Although Miranda did well at the YOT outside she was recruiting other girls into the gang, selling drugs, transporting firearms and committing serious acts of violence. At 16 she started a relationship with a 27-year-old drug dealer. When this relationship broke down, however, she lost face and began engaging in group sex with several lower status gang members at once. Gang Girls are usually fairly young; aged from 12 upwards, and are shared by gang-involved young men. Should one of these girls become pregnant by a high status gang member, a situation which can be perceived as a bid to establish a more solid relationship with him, they may be attacked by other Gang Girls endeavouring to 'bring them back down to earth', or indeed to induce a miscarriage.

Loosely Affiliated Girls may have friendships or sexual relationships with high status members of several different gangs. Whereas the status of Girlfriends and Gang Girls flows from their dependence upon male gang members, the status of Loosely Affiliated girls is a product of their independence from any particular gang or gang member. Their power flows from being custodians of secrets concerning the whereabouts of money, drugs and guns, planned 'moves' against rivals and the ebb and flow of the 'respect' accorded to, and hence the vulnerability of, high status 'playas' (Harding, 2012). But how do these young women know what the role requirements of the social field of the gang are? They know, says Bourdieu, because they are the unwitting bearers of *habitus*:

> those aspects of culture that are anchored in the body or daily practices of individuals (or) groups … It includes the totality of learned habits, bodily skills, styles, tastes, and other non-discursive knowledges that might be said to 'go without saying' for a specific group
> (Mauss, 1934: 63)

which they simultaneously inherit, ingest, adapt and reproduce. Habitus, says Bourdieu, is the mechanism whereby objective social structures become embodied within a set of personal cognitive and somatic characteristics. But, inasmuch as these young women are, as it were, 'brought into being' by the habitus of their social field through their participation in it, they also reproduce that social field. Although Bourdieu describes this process as *agency* it bears little resemblance to the notion of freely chosen action by an autonomous actor that underpins the agency versus structure debate that trundles on in conventional sociology.

Whilst Bourdieu provides an important perspective from which to understand how social relationships and status hierarchies operate within the social field of the gang, he presents us with a closed system. Put another way, if the habitus of the social field effectively constitutes the actors within it, how can they ever do anything differently, or indeed, anything different? But of course they do. As Harding (2012) observes, only 5 per cent to 10 per cent of young people affiliated to gangs in their early teenage years are still involved by their early 20s. This finding echoes those of the Edinburgh Study of Youth Transitions (2005), which found that in a sample of over 4,000 school students, 'self-nominated' gang affiliates constituted 20 per cent of the cohort at age 13, but this had fallen to 5 per cent by the age of 17. And, in line with what we know about the criminal careers of young women in general, the involvement of girls in gangs is of even briefer duration. Whereas in Edinburgh at age 13, the numbers of boys and girls claiming to be gang-affiliated were similar, by 17 three times as many boys as girls claimed affiliation. Moreover, when girls do leave the gang they are more likely to pursue conventional routes to academic and vocational success; suggesting that their involvement is both briefer and less embedded.

Drifting into trouble

In contrast to the notion of *habitus* Matza (1969) posits a process of *habituation*. Thus, in place of what we might call Bourdieu's *hard determinism*, Matza's theoretical stance is one of *soft determinism*: explaining deviant social action as a product of *drift*; of choices made, not made and half made, or agency exerted, in a situation of existential and social constraint. For Matza, *drift* is triggered by the need to shrug off a *mood of fatalism*; the sense that one is powerless and acted upon, and a desire to restore a *mood of humanism*; to regain some control over events. This explanation is congruent with much of the North American research in this area. Whilst Bourdieu would see the actions of gang-involved young women as a function of the immanent role requirements of their social field, some North American studies of girls from abusive or negligent families in gang affected neighbourhoods suggest that affiliation, the sexual demands it might entail and the violence they risk notwithstanding, may nonetheless hold the promise of a greater level of control over their lives (Burton, 1990; Cepeda and Valdez, 2003; Cousineau 2002; Franklin, 1988; Miller, 2001). Indeed, Cepeda and Valdez (2003) suggest that in participating in proscribed sexual activity and other deviant activities they are resisting the passivity and submissiveness associated with traditional female gender roles.

In Melanie Klein's terms, this 'transgression' may in fact be a bid for health; a movement away from the abusive environment in which they are trapped and an attempt to take control of their lives. McMullen (1987), writing about young men and women selling their bodies for sex in London's Soho notes that although the need for money may shape their involvement in prostitution in important ways, it is the 'buzz' of the momentary power that these ostensibly 'powerless' young people are able to exert over potentially dangerous 'punters' that holds them there.

How do they do it? Matza (1964) suggests that 'delinquents', because they are continually exposed to mainstream norms and values, can only engage in such socially deviant behaviour by employing *techniques of neutralisation* with which to negate the conventional moral bind, persuading themselves that conventional norms cannot apply to them in a particular social situation. These neutralisations, Matza argues, are elaborated in a situation of *company* in which a process of *sounding* – conversations with similarly situated peers to establish the propriety of particular actions in particular circumstances – takes place. In the case of McMullen's young people, they were able to persuade themselves that they were not 'prostitutes' but 'working boys' and 'working girls' who were 'only doing it for the money'. In the process, the sense of the authorship of, or responsibility for, the ensuing deviant action becomes blurred, thereby loosening further the conventional moral bind and facilitating the *drift* into 'social deviance'.

Neutralisations may take the form of a *denial of responsibility*, with subjects arguing that they were victims of special circumstances over which they have no control (in the case of rape this is obviously true of course); the *condemnation of the condemners* wherein their accusers are depicted as hypocrites who are no better than they are, or an *appeal to higher loyalties*, wherein loyalty to friends or associates is seen to trump conventional norms.

This said, as Sykes and Matza (1957: 9) have pointed out, there is, and always has been, a 'subterranean tradition' of delinquency amongst young people, characterised by

an emphasis on daring and adventure; the rejection of the prosaic discipline of work; the taste for luxury and conspicuous consumption; and the respect paid to manhood and violent 'exploit'.

This helps to explain why some young people opt, albeit sometimes briefly or episodically, into an alternative 'social field', 'lifeworld' or 'normative ghetto', in which different, and possibly proscribed, forms of behaviour are experienced as permissible or, indeed, a 'role requirement' of involvement (Bourdieu, 1993). Hence, Charlotte Appleyard's cry of dismay at:

teenagers as young as 16 passed out on the street, with their friends unable to help because they were too drunk to care. No one bats an eyelid – the culture is that each and every night, you stay up until dawn and drink until you are insensible. ... There is absolutely no restraint – one rep tried to pull off my friend's bikini-style top while the crowd around us laughed hysterically. Everything is seen as a joke, which means that complete strangers feel entitled to grope you. Many girls are simply too drunk to fend them off. By the early morning, the beach is littered with heaving bodies – and sex is as casual as a handshake.

(Appleyard, 2011)

This is not, of course, a description of the violent youth gang on vacation, but the post-A-level antics enjoyed by thousands of middle class English adolescents every summer and it challenges the model of CSE suggested by both social field theory and the 'coercive dyad'; directing us instead to a consideration of the social and cultural contexts within which, and the existential circumstances under which, such hedonistic trysts may occur. Moreover it suggests that social norms and sexual mores may be as much a function of a place or a social field, as an expression of the predilections or inhibitions of individuals.

However, the fact that many young people may comfortably occupy a plurality of moral spheres is not to suggest that those at the bottom end of the social structure are similarly free to indulge their desires before returning to a rewarding world of middle class propriety. Of course the desire to shake off the conventional bind is probably as strong for them as it is for their middle class counterparts, but as Wacquant (2008) has observed, these 'urban outcasts' are not free to opt in or out of the social field of the gang at will, because a defining feature of the neighbourhoods in which gangs are most prevalent is that residents have nowhere else to go (Pitts, 2008).

3

Something Old or Something New: Do Pre-Existing Conceptualisations of Abuse Enable a Sufficient Response to Abuse in Young People's Relationships and Peer-Groups?

Carlene Firmin

Introduction

Evidence in the UK has identified that children and young people experience violence and sexual exploitation in their intimate relationships (Barter, 2009; Pearce, 2009) or in their peer groups and street gangs (Beckett et al., 2012; Firmin, 2010, 2011; OCC, 2012a). In response, policy makers and practitioners have applied pre-existing conceptualisations of 'domestic abuse', 'CSE' and 'serious youth violence' to address this 'peer-on-peer' abuse, with each involving different definitions, policy frameworks and operational responses.

This chapter assesses the applicability of pre-existing conceptualisations, and questions whether any sufficiently account for the age and gender specific characteristics of peer-on-peer abuse. With reference to Connell's theory of 'hegemonic masculinity' and drawing upon Bourdieu's concepts of 'social fields' and 'habitus', this chapter proposes a new conceptual framework for understanding 'peer-on-peer' abuse, embracing the significance for our understanding of CSE when perpetrators are under 18 and may have experienced victimisation in previous contexts.

By considering children and young people's experiences within gendered, age-specific social fields, this chapter questions the identification of the exploited and the exploiter in pre-existing conceptualisations.

By identifying exploitative environments within which abusive relationships are formed, this approach should assist a more accurate identification of multiple layers of exploitation within children and young people's relationships, and consequently improve responses to peer-on-peer exploitation.

The abuse

Extensive evidence of peer-on-peer abuse exists, much of it involving sexually exploitative situations. NSPCC states that 'two thirds of contact sexual abuse experienced by children aged 0–17' was committed by someone aged under 18 (Radford et al., 2011); Barnardos (2011a) CSE services stated that a quarter of service users were abused by peers and Jago and colleagues (2011) have highlighted young people's experiences of sexual exploitation perpetrated by peers. In their Inquiry into Sexual Exploitation in Gangs and Groups (OCC, 2012a) the OCC reported that 29 per cent of identified perpetrators were aged under 19.

Young women are pressured and coerced into sexual relationships (Hoggart and Phillips, 2009; Maxwell and Aggleton, 2010; Noonan and Charles, 2009; Coy and Kelly, 2011) and, according to Burman and Cartmel (2006), 3 per cent of young women have been forced to have sex with their partners. Barter's (2009) work found that one in three girls experienced sexual violence from a partner.

Depending on the context within which sexual violence takes places three definitions are currently employed to describe peer-on-peer abuse. These are:

- 'Domestic Violence' (when accompanied by explicit violence)

  Any incident of threatening behaviour, violence or abuse (psychological, physical, sexual, financial or emotional) between adults who are or have been intimate partners or family members, regardless of gender or sexuality.

  (HO, 2011a: 6)

- 'Serious Youth Violence' (when motivated by, or occurring within, a street gang context)

  Any offence of most serious violence or weapon enabled crime, where the victim is aged 1–19' i.e. murder, manslaughter, rape, wounding with intent and causing grievous bodily harm. 'Youth violence' is defined in the same way, but also includes assault with injury offences.

(London Safeguarding Children Board, 2009: 6)

- 'Child Sexual Exploitation' (please see introductory chapter for definition).

These definitions were not designed with peer-on peer abuse in mind. In particular the definition of CSE notes an age gap between victim and perpetrator as underpinning the power imbalance that facilitates exploitation. The definition of domestic abuse also assumes an adult perpetrator. As a result theorists and professionals seek to capture the phenomenon by applying conceptualisations of

- adult-on-adult abuse (domestic violence);
- adult-on-child abuse (child sexual exploitation); OR
- non-relational and gender-neutral child-on-child violence (serious youth violence).

Current responses

The difficulty of conceptualising sexual violence between peers makes it difficult to identify and address. It is therefore imperative that the phenomenon is better understood. The following composite case study illustrates the significance of peer-on-peer abuse for practice.

A street gang is made up of young men aged 12–16. Members of the gang have a range of backgrounds. Some members live in households where there is domestic violence, at least one has been known to social services as a victim of child sexual abuse. Members of this gang are influenced by elders in the local area who form an older gang aged 18–25. Boys in the younger gang offend on behalf of the older gang. Over time the younger boys have become increasingly violent and harmful to others in the local area.

Boys within the younger gang have a number of female peers – some are considered girlfriends and others are friends. Over an extensive period of time the boys sexually assault these girls in people's homes, at parties, in parks and other local outdoor spaces. Meanwhile the girls gradually began offending alongside the boys who were assaulting them. If the girls do not have sex with boys they are physically attacked, so sex is exchanged for safety. The majority of the boys and all of the girls are aged 14–16.

The above case study could be defined as 'CSE', 'domestic abuse' or 'serious youth violence'. Professionals currently apply the three definitions inconsistently and definitional choices result in different policy frameworks and operational responses being employed each of which I consider insufficient.

If the case is defined as CSE, safeguarding guidance (DCSF, 2009) would be employed and specialist CSE services could be offered by organisations such as Barnardo's, the NSPCC, The Children's Society and/or smaller local projects. Many of these services are joined to projects that work with children who go missing and are age-specific, targeting children under the age of 18. The majority of children accessing services are girls and young women, and the perception of CSE is that it generally impacts girls: however, emerging evidence and practice in this field are challenging this view and, whilst in the minority, a number of services also work with boys. Nevertheless, applying a CSE definition might create an operational response that appears to be gender-neutral but which in practice may be gender-specific.

Furthermore, CSE is policed differently across the country and policing is targeted, in the main, at adult perpetrators: some local forces have dedicated CSE teams; others have sexual violence teams, public protection teams or child abuse investigation teams who hold responsibility for this work. Specific exploitation offences can be used for charging these offences, such as those which reference 'grooming' or 'trafficking'. However, forces also employ harbourers' warnings and abduction notices to disrupt instances of abuse.

For the girls in the case study who are considered 'girlfriends', but who are exposed to physical and sexual violence, their experience may be described as 'domestic abuse'. This would prompt a response from the Home Office led Integrated Policy to Tackle Violence against Women and Girls (HO, 2011b) and local multi-agency-risk-assessment-conferencing (MARAC) would provide the multi-agency setting for risk management. Services offered include refuges offered by Women's Aid, Refuge and smaller local projects, in addition to Rape Crisis provision and sexual assault referral centres. Services are mainly targeted at adult women although emerging evidence suggests that a number rape crisis services have been extended to work with children aged 14-upwards. Following the change to the definition of domestic abuse to include 16–17 year olds there is the potential that refuge and MARAC arrangements may also be extended to some children aged 16-upwards. Domestic abuse services tend to be gender-specific, designed to work with women. Specific and dedicated policing responses are in place for domestic abuse and organisations such as Respect and DVIP work with adult perpetrators. However, there has been little programme development within youth justice settings to work with perpetrators under 18.

As the sexual violence described in the case study occurred within a street gang all the exploitation could be defined as 'serious youth violence'. Whilst serious youth violence is the responsibility of the Home Office, at a local level strategic responsibility currently sits between community safety partnerships and police forces, and many areas host multi-agency gang groups. Successive governments have published strategies to tackle gangs and serious youth violence (HO, 2008; 2010; HM Government, 2011). The most recently published strategy included recommendations targeted at girls and young women and referred to sexual violence within gangs for the first time. In 2012 the Government funded 13 new services, which are still being developed at the time of writing, to support young people (mainly girls) who have experienced sexual violence in gang-affected neighbourhoods. Programmes to tackle serious youth violence, however, have tended to focus on boys and young men who use violence against other boys and young men. These continue to be offence focused, generally seeking to tackle knife possession, anger-management and gang association/exit, rather than relationship-based violence.

The fact that these three definitions, when employed, result in three distinct policy, strategic, and operational responses is unsurprising given that

- CSE and serious youth violence target child victims, whereas domestic abuse services tend to focus on adult victims
- Domestic abuse responses are gender-specific whilst CSE policies and services, although appearing to be gender-neutral are (often)

implicitly focused on young women, whilst services to tackle serious youth violence have been implicitly targeted at boys
- Domestic abuse and CSE responses generally assume perpetrators to be adults, whereas serious youth violence services tend to work on the basis that everyone involved is a young person

As a result current definitions and the operational responses that flow from them do not enable professionals to account for the age and gender specific aspects of peer-on-peer abuse, or to conceptualise 'exploitation' accurately. Given that all of those involved in peer-on-peer abuse are children, one may seek to draw upon safeguarding policy/practice more generally to afford a more consistent response than the three definitions already considered.

Child protection activity is 'undertaken to protect specific children who are suffering, or are likely to suffer, significant harm' and safeguarding and promoting the welfare of children is defined as 'protecting children from maltreatment, preventing impairment of children's health or development ensuring children are growing up in circumstances consistent with the provision of safe and effective care' (DfE, 2012). However, there have been increasing concerns voiced about the system's ability to safeguard adolescents (Education Select Committee, 2012). At present the system

- Is generally focused on protecting younger children where the victim's agency is rarely identified;
- Recognises the impact of the home and the family as social fields within which abuse takes place rather than a peer group, school or neighbourhood;
- Responds better to cases of abuse faced by older young people outside of the home when the abuse is committed by adults and there is a clearly identified child 'victim' rather than potential child 'perpetrators';
- Struggles to protect children who display agency either as victims or as perpetrators; and
- Seeks to manage and control the behaviour of older children in order to protect them from their own 'risky behaviours' rather than contribute to challenging the harmful social fields that older children may be navigating.

A question of culpability

The inconsistencies outlined could be explored in relation to young people's culpability. Children in England and Wales can be held criminally responsible for 'violence' or 'abuse' from the age of ten. However, they are unable legally to consent to sexual activity or marriage, be considered as victims of domestic abuse or commit acts of domestic abuse, until they are 16. Nevertheless, a 14-year-old boy who physically assaults his 14-year-old girlfriend could, theoretically, be convicted of committing an act of sexual violence against her whilst being unable to consent to sexual activity or be in an abusive relationship with her. Research undertaken on adolescent development (Coleman, 2012) notes that there is no definitive time period of 'adolescence', and the cut-off point of 18 years to signal the end of 'childhood' in policy is somewhat artificial.

Whilst the age at which a young person can lawfully consent to sexual activity is 16 years in the UK, other issues can restrict or remove a child's ability to consent to sexual activity beyond that age. For example, the definition of CSE is not based on the age of consent but on a child's 'limited availability of choice' and an exploiter's 'power over them' (DCSF, 2009). 'Limited choice' allows for agency but does not imply free consent (Melrose, Barrett and Brodie, 1999). As Pearce (this volume) suggests, it is important to consider the circumstances in which young people consent to abusive or exploitative relationships.

Although critical consideration of victimisation and consent is underway (Pearce, this volume; Powell, 2008), consent from the perspective of those who commit harm, beyond the age of criminal responsibility, requires further exploration. Young people can commit acts of sexual violence to which they are not legally able to consent. Furthermore, cultural, societal, familial and peer-group influences may shape understandings of consent, and create behavioural pressures. It is possible, for example, that boys could commit acts of sexual violence and harm in order to survive as a 'male' in gang contexts, and/or that girls consent, in a constrained way, to sexual activity in order to survive in similar contexts. A continuum of consent would enable us to consider whether the legal and definitional restrictions on consent are applicable to peer-on-peer abuse, ensuring that the place of power, control and choice are accurately identified when we are seeking to prevent and intervene in abusive situations.

Building on current thinking about survival and consent (Pearce, this volume), when children navigate gang-affected spaces they may use violence to survive; a technique which they do not perceive is required in every environment they navigate. Hallsworth and Young refer to the 'survivalist mentality' (2011: 68) of young people who engage in serious youth violence. This attitude was echoed by boys and young men previously interviewed by the author. Interviewees referred to the neighbourhood risks and the pressures to conform to dominant masculinities to explain the mentality they adopted:

> People want to be seen as like the alpha male, like the rude boy, the bad boy. They'll be scared of him, they want to be the biggest, the best.
>
> (Firmin, 2011: 49)

In violent social fields it is possible that young people can simulta-neously perpetrate violence *and* be victims of it or when we consider CSE it could emerge young people are being exploited to exploit. The limitation of the vast majority of theorising about serious youth violence is that it conceptualises 'survival violence' within a violent social field but not necessarily with a 'hyper-masculine' or 'exploita-tive' social field. The author's research into the impact of serious youth and gang violence on women and girls identifies 'the gang' as a 'hyper-masculine' environment (Firmin, 2013). However, in other research this hyper-masculinity is implied rather than stated, acknowledging that boys commit the majority of serious youth vio-lence but failing to reference gender norms, stereotypes or masculini-ties and femininities.

The challenge: Conceptualising violence within gender and age sensitive social fields

Currently used definitions, policies and practices are rooted in preva-lent models of abuse derived from specific cultural or ideological positions. Feminist academics, for example, identify sexual violence as 'gendered': rooted in gendered inequality and power relations, and disproportionately affecting women (Horvath and Kelly, 2009; Kelly, 1988). Gendered violence can be further explored through the con-cept of 'hegemonic masculinity' (Connell and Messerschmidt, 2005).

Hegemonic masculinity can be constructed individually, within a group and/or at a regional and global level (Hatfield, 2010). It 'legitimates hierarchical gender relations between men and women, between masculinity and femininity, and among men' (Messerschmidt, 2012: 58). For the purposes of this work the concept is considered in relation to (a) gender-based violence and (b) the notion that hegemonic masculinity gives rise to subordinate masculinities (based on class and/or ethnicity) and that may develop alongside 'emphasised' femininities (Connell and Messerschmidt, 2005).

Research demonstrates that the gendered character of young people's lives affects the codes that determine or influence their behaviour (Noonan and Charles, 2009), and can sometimes lead to forms of violence against women being regarded as permissible (Coy and Kelly, 2011; EWAV, 2010). Research by Barter (2011) demonstrates that boys in the UK are more likely to commit acts of 'peer violence' and 'partner violence'. These findings concur with international literature, and particularly US research into 'dating violence'. To this extent Barter concludes that 'partner violence' is 'a thoroughly gendered affair' (2011: 103).

Powell's (2008) work identifies the gendered nature of sexual violence in young people's relationships with reference to broader gender inequalities, and relational inequalities between masculinities and femininities. Applying Powell's work to gang-affected neighbourhoods, or young people's peer groups, requires a consideration of the extent to which social fields interact with one another and impact on the behaviour of individual young people.

As Figure 3.1 illustrates, children, and relationships between them, exist within multiple social fields. Within each social field are particular social rules that children attempt to play in order to navigate them safely. When conceptualising peer-on-peer exploitation it is useful to consider whether the rules of each social field are harmful, and if so whether these rules and/or other agents (such as older gang members), groom children to exploit one another. Pre-existing definitions of CSE and domestic abuse are predicated on a fundamental power imbalance between victim and perpetrator conceptualising this by considering individual relationships in a vacuum, removed from the context within which they occur. However, if abusive relationships between young people take place in exploitative social fields it seems unhelpful and unrealistic to define them, or attempt to intervene with

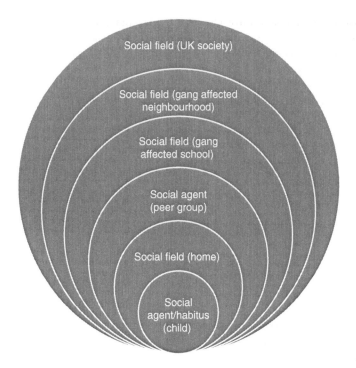

Figure 3.1   A model for understanding peer-on-peer abuse and exploitation

them, without considering the power imbalances that exist between young people and the social fields they are navigating. Whilst within their own relationships or peer groups young people may be powerful, those young people also sit within broader hierarchies of inequality and power which may render them relatively 'powerless'.

The hegemonic masculinity that defines the social fields that young people navigate, and within which they form and develop their identities, are evidenced through a range of literatures. International and UK-based research on the sexualisation of childhood (e.g. Aapola, Gonick and Harris, 2005; Coy 2009a; Family Lives, 2012; Papadopoulos, 2010) in general, and the specific impact of music (Weitzer and Kubrin, 2009), Internet imagery (Peter and Valkenburg, 2007), 'sexting' (Ringrose et al., 2011) and pornography (Flood, 2009) identifies the inequality in societal gender relations: 'the sexualisation of culture is identified as a context that reinforces gender inequality by designating women as sexually available and objectified, perpetuates associations of masculinity and predatory sexual prowess, and justifies sexual violence' (Coy, 2009a: 2).

At the local level, research has identified attitudinal, discursive and structural hegemonic masculinity within peer groups (Barter, 2009; Franklin, 2004), schools (Butler, 1999; Ringrose and Renold, 2011), care homes (Barter, 2006) and neighbourhoods (Anderson, 1999; Wood, Barter and Berridge, 2011). The links between hegemonic masculinity and the disproportionate involvement of boys in violent crime (Newburn and Stanko, 1994) has been well documented. This, coupled with the consensus within the literature on the relationship between gender inequality, the sexualisation of childhood and gendered violence (Papadopoulos, 2010; Coy, 2009a) is demonstrative of the harmful social fields within which young people are forming identities and relationships. The power hierarchies within and between these social fields, and young people's experiences as social agents within them, are critically important to the conceptualisation of peer-on-peer abuse. The negative and limiting impact that such social fields have on girls' 'space for action' (Jeffner, 2000: 1) must be considered alongside the restrictions that they place on boys to express and embody alternative masculinities (Talbot and Quayle, 2010). Within this it is important to consider the operation of a gendered hierarchy at multiple levels: gendered power relations are not two-tiered. Cross-equalities perspectives would allow for age and gender to become compounded and create power hierarchies between men and boys. If some children are being groomed to be abused within certain micro and macro social fields, are some children being groomed to abuse? Within this one must leave space for individual agency and responsibility; however, the interaction between children and other influential individuals, which can determine or constrain behaviour, cannot be discounted.

Unlike broader debates about 'partner violence', 'domestic violence' and 'child sexual exploitation', research into serious youth violence embeds young people's use of violence within a peer group or neighbourhood context (Firmin, 2008; 2010; Hallsworth and Young, 2011; Pitts, 2008; Thrasher, 1927). Rather than considering whether individual or familial vulnerabilities solely contribute to young people's experience of violence, the Chicago School identified that the neighbourhood within which gangs were located remained the same even when the individuals living within those neighbourhoods changed. The notion of a gang-affected neighbourhood can also be considered within the lens of Bourdieu's social fields. Drawing upon labelling theorists' location of social norms within places, for example neighbourhoods, the prevalent norms within social fields require attention. When the gang-affected neighbourhood or school is the social field within which peer-on-peer abuse takes place, to what extent do individual agents within that social field play the rules of the game by assuming hyper-masculine identities?

Extensive research has explored the gendered identities of adults; how adults 'do' gender and the roles of men and women in constructing masculinities and femininities (Butler, 1999; Connell and Messerschmidt, 2005; McNay, 2000; Talbot and Quayle, 2010). It has also considered the ways in which state and social institutions require gender conformity and the relations of domination and subordination between the sexes that develop as a consequence. Consideration of the ways in which children's identities are gendered or whether children may be active in constructing these identities is less well developed. Gendered hierarchies persist within environments navigated by children (Mac an Ghaill, 1994; Thorne, 1993); however, there is limited understanding of how boys understand and construct their gender identities. If peer-on-peer abuse and 'exploitation' is gendered, to what extent are young people responsible for constructing these gendered dynamics and to what extent do gendered social norms and hierarchies within families, neighbourhoods and societies contribute to the construction of gender identities that are harmful to the young people concerned?

Whilst boys commit the majority of peer-on-peer abuse (Barter, 2009), it is less clear whether these acts mirror those of adult male perpetrators. In their critique of 'bullying' theory Ringrose and Renold state that 'to be constituted as victims is to position boys as "feminine"' (2011: 187). This challenge equally applies to 'peer-on-peer abuse' where victimhood is associated with femininity. Working with a clear victim/perpetrator divide results in the assumption that when boys are committing the harm, they cannot simultaneously be victims. And yet, when we seek to view this abuse within social fields, and as a part of multiple relational hierarchies, there is the potential for boys to be understood as *both* exploited and exploiters. Until we are able appropriately to conceptualise this abuse within its appropriate context it is too great an assumption to extend the term 'domestic violence' or 'child sexual exploitation' to peer-on-peer abuse.

Conclusion: Thinking differently about the problem

To define peer-on-peer abuse in general, and peer-on-peer sexual exploitation specifically, one must account for:

- The gendered hierarchies within young people's relationships;
- The impact of age and adolescent development on young people's culpability, particularly in relation to their identity and ability to consent; and
- The relationship between young people's agency, power, and the social fields within which they navigate.

Applying the traditional definition of CSE requires a victim on the one hand and a perpetrator on the other. However, children can simultaneously exploit and be exploited when their relationships, peer groups, gendered identities and relational hierarchies are conceptualised within broader social fields. Applying the proposed framework could enable an accurate identification of victims, perpetrators, agency, responsibility, power imbalance and exploitation, which is required to define and respond to the phenomenon. Whilst all sectors can agree that children are experiencing the phenomenon in question, there is far less agreement on the dynamics of the abuse. This inconsistency places children at potential risk of further harm, rendering professionals unable to agree on the nature of what is happening and what is required to keep children safe.

As a working definition it is recommended that the following is tested:

> Physical, sexual, emotional and financial abuse, and coercive control, exercised within young people's relationships, characterised by inequalities of power, and influenced by gendered hierarchies, within and external to their relationships.

This definition enables professionals to conceptualise young people's relationships within multiple environments, and assess the extent to which the impact of the social environment(s) as well as the children involved need to be addressed. By considering the potential impact of the social fields navigated by, and influencing, children, this chapter proposes a new conceptualisation and working definition to be tested with future research. This process will identify both the power held by young people and the multiple levels of exploitation at play. In order to understand the behaviour of young people we need accurately to conceptualise the rules of the game they are playing. Testing whether and how interventions challenge the rules, as well as the players of the game, will assist in the improved protection of children from peer-on-peer abuse.

4
A Social Model of 'Abused Consent'

Jenny Pearce

Introduction

[T]hey question you a lot and say 'did you try to run away?' and they think you didn't try to get away. They think you wanted it. They doubt you.

People's stereotype is, 'girls like that, that's what they do'.

A lot of their attitude is 'you're just a little slapper – a slapper who likes sleeping with older men – they think it's just kids coming onto older men.

(Quotes from young people in the 'What Works for Us' WWFU Group, Annual Report, 2011)

These young people are challenging the assumption that they are consenting to CSE. In this chapter I argue that too often young people's 'consent' to CSE is taken for granted or assumed, and by default, the young person feels blamed for the abuse they experience. I argue that this is intricately linked to our current understanding of young people's 'consent' to sexual activity which is based on a medical model that assesses their intellectual capacity to understand and use contraceptives. This is inadequate as a framework for understanding the pressures on those who might be sexually exploited. A 'social model' of consent would enable consent to be contextualised, shedding light on how 'consent' may be distorted through abusive and exploitative relationships and/or contexts. This would eventually challenge what I call 'condoned consent': the process by which some practitioners may fail to identify and challenge sexual exploitation. Without a social model helping us to contextualise 'consent', too many young people are left feeling that they are responsible for the abuse they experience.

My argument draws from work on disability that has distinguished between a 'medical model' of disability: placing attention on the disabled person's individual capacity to access able bodied society; and a 'social model' of disability: placing attention on how society isolates people with disabilities through disabling environments and prejudiced attitudes. Although criticisms have been lodged against placing medical and social models of disability in opposition to each other (arguing that this is oversimplified), many campaigners have asked for a stronger focus on the social and environmental factors that present barriers to access to mainstream society (Oliver, 1996). This is not at the expense of promoting the need for continued medical advancements, but is advocated to ensure that an inclusive approach challenges prejudice and promotes inclusion.

Transferring this to my thoughts about consent, I argue that a social model of consent would address the social and environmental features that impact on young people's ability to consent and help practitioners to assess the different ways that a young person's capacity to consent can be abused, exploited and manipulated. I consider four ways that a social model of consent helps us to understand how consent can be abused: 'coerced consent' where the child is subtly and/or violently manipulated into consenting to sexual activity; 'normalised consent' where societal attitudes about violence and sexual relationships suggest that exploitation and violence may be inherent and, therefore, be expected as 'normal'; 'survival consent', where poverty can be a 'push factor' for young people consenting to sex in exchange for money or other gifts; and 'condoned consent' where practitioners fail to recognise sexual exploitation, thereby condoning it. These four forms of abused consent can operate separately and in conjunction with each other. Exploring their meaning within a pursuit to embrace consent as a social issue gives us a better understanding of how consent can be abused in sexually exploitative contexts and relationships.

Child sexual exploitation

I am employing the definition of CSE as given in the introduction of the book (DCSF, 2009). Recent research carried out by Firmin (2010, 2011, and this volume) suggests that this comprehensive definition needs further recognition of peer-on-peer sexual exploitation: situations where young people either entice each other into exploitative situations or actively abuse each other. Peer-on-peer abuse has been noted in just over a quarter of cases where research into CSE has occurred (Beckett, 2011; OCC, 2012a; Jago et al., 2011). When I refer to young people in this chapter, I do not overlook the fact that increasingly large numbers of prepubescent children are being exploited (Barnardo's, 2011b). My focus, however, is on those who, over 13 years of age are not protected through legislation that classifies all sexual activity with those under 13 as statutory rape (Sexual Offences Act (SOA) 2003). I also refer to those between 16 and 18 years of age who are still classified as children entitled to protection from abuse according to the UNCRC (1989). It is important to note here that the concept of 'childhood' referred to in UK policy and practice is strongly influenced by notions of 'innocence' as understood by the Western World. The relationship between 'childhood' and 'innocence' promotes the need for the adult community to protect the 'vulnerable child', a promotion that is specific to particular economic and social forms that separate children from the adult community. Whilst acknowledging that notions of 'childhood', and therefore of 'protection' of the child vary across the world, this chapter refers to CSE as understood within the UK.

Why our current understanding of consent is inadequate

Prior to the SOA 2003, there had been considerable concern that the meaning of 'consent' was confused, governed by case law and deemed to be unsatisfactory. The Home Office publication 'Setting the Boundaries' (HO, 2000) introduced a statutory definition of consent, outlined in sections 74 to 76 of the SOA 2003.

Section 74 of the SOA notes that 'For the purposes of this part of the act, a person consents if he agrees by choice, and has the freedom and capacity to make that choice'; Section 75 clarifies that

> it is accepted that the complainant did not consent if certain circumstances apply. These include the use, or fear of use, of violence against

the complainant or other person; the complainant being unlawfully detained; being under the influence of substances (causing the complainant to be stupefied or overpowered); asleep or unconscious or unable to communicate because of physical disability.

Case Law later extended 'disability' to include mental disability. Section 76 notes that

if a defendant intentionally deceived the complainant or impersonated a person known to the complainant, it is also assumed that the complainant did not consent to the sexual activity.

Despite this advanced clarity, concern is expressed that variations in interpretation and in the application of the SOA continue (Scott, 2010). Prosecutions for CSE, rape and other sexual offences remain low, failing to reflect the levels of abuse experienced (Kelly, Lovett and Regan, 2005). Questions have been asked about why it is difficult for sexually exploited children and young people to understand what consent to sexual activity means and why it is difficult for them to be identified and supported by practitioners who might think that the child is 'choosing' their relationships (Jago and Pearce, 2008). My argument is that some (not all, but some), of the answers rest with our confused interpretation of what 'consent' to sexual activity actually means and how it can be manipulated and abused.

Whilst legislation noted above provides some clarity, the complex social problems that influence individual situations are complex and are not yet fully understood. Practitioners face contradictory messages in upholding legislation which outlaws sexual activity for those under 16 whilst simultaneously working to prevent the spread of sexually transmitted infections (STIs) and unwanted pregnancies. They are faced with the dual requirement of advancing child protection procedures whilst also minimising harm through STIs and teenage pregnancy (FPA, 2009). Research shows that despite low levels of young people's self reporting of sexual activity, there is increasing worry about the health issues facing young people. As noted by Coleman,

Since research on this topic started in the 1970s the numbers becoming sexually active in adolescence have increased substantially. Whilst sexual activity varies according to region, social background, and ethnic group, we can say that some-where between 30% and 40% of young people in the UK have had sexual intercourse by the time they reach the age of 16. ... The most recent evidence from the NHS Contraceptive Services Report3 shows that 29% of young women attending sexual health services who are under the age of 16 are using the pill ... More worryingly, it appears that in the region of 20% of adolescents use no contraception at first intercourse. This may be because sex is unplanned, or because of alcohol or drug use at the time. The younger the age of those having sex, the higher the numbers using no contraception.

(Coleman, 2012: 134–35, 145)

The most commonly used guidelines assisting an understanding of consent are those developed through the need to determine whether a child under the age of 16 should be given contraceptive advice or services. These are the Fraser Guidelines, developed as a result of the Gillick case (1982). Mrs Gillick took her local health authority and the Department of Health and Social Security to court to stop doctors from giving contraceptive advice or treatment to under-16-year-olds without parental consent. The case went to the House of Lords in 1985, who ruled in favour of the original judgment delivered by Mr Justice Woolf that

whether or not a child is capable of giving the necessary consent will depend on the child's maturity and understanding and the nature of the consent required. The child must be capable of mak-ing a reasonable assessment of the advantages and disadvantages of the treatment proposed, so the consent, if given, can be prop-erly and fairly described as true consent.

(Woolf, 1985)

The Fraser Guidelines noted that an assessment should be based on whether

- the young person will understand the professional's advice
- the young person cannot be persuaded to inform their parents
- the young person is likely to begin, or to continue having, sexual intercourse with or without contraceptive treatment

- unless the young person receives contraceptive treatment, their physical or mental health, or both, are likely to suffer
- the young person's best interests require them to receive contraceptive advice or treatment with or without parental consent

(www.gpnotebook.co.uk)

Whilst the medical profession has taken a lead in considering how to define and understand consent (Wheeler, 2006), the reality for many practitioners is that the commitment to a 'harm minimisation' approach may well conflict with a child protection approach that pursues inquiry about potential abuse. Recent initiatives have encouraged awareness of the complex issues facing those who are trying to decide if the young person is capable of consenting to receiving sexual health services or is being abused into consenting. 'The FPA (2011) have provided an overview on the law regarding consent' the Crown Prosecution Service guidelines advise health practitioners about how 'competency' might be undermined, asking for an assessment of whether a child is being coerced into unwanted sexual activity, and, if so, how and when confidentiality should be breeched so that child protection agencies can offer support (CPS, 2012); and innovative guidelines from the General Medical Council note the importance of protecting children from abuse and neglect, encouraging appropriate information sharing if a health practitioner does have concern for a child's welfare

> sharing information appropriately is essential to providing safe, effective care, both for the individual and for the wider community. It is also at the heart of effective child protection. It is vital that all doctors have the confidence to act on their concerns about the possible abuse.
>
> (GMC, 2012: 22)

The Royal College of General Practitioners Adolescent Health Group produced toolkits on 'Confidentiality and Young People' (RCGP, 2011) to help practitioners make decisions about if and when confidentiality should be breeched, noting that the young person may be coerced and not freely consenting to sex, suggesting warning signs such as a power imbalance between the patient and their sexual partner(s), for example if there is an age gap of more than five years. The guidance notes that the younger the age,

> the more cautious GPs should be about assuming they are competent to consent to sex, and a query could be raised as to why they are so sexualised.
>
> (RCGP, 2011: 22)

Although this guidance above has been developed specifically by and for health care professionals, the Government has also outlined specific guidance to all practitioners working with children, focusing on how to implement multiagency work in identifying, sharing information about and supporting sexually exploited children and young people (DCSF, 2009). However, subsequent research showed that under a quarter of Safeguarding Children Boards were implementing the guidance (Jago et al., 2011) and despite all the work noted above, there remain real concerns that health care professionals assessing the young person's capacity to consent do not identify the early warning signs of CSE and do not share important information with other services early enough to ensure preventative interventions (OCC, 2012a). Further than this, assessment of Gillick competencies against Frazer guidelines do not enable a critical appraisal of the social pressures and structures that might impact on the relationship between consent and abuse.

Below I explore the ways that a 'social' rather than a 'medical' model of consent can help us to understand the ways consent can be abused, and by default, then help us to better identify and work with sexually exploited young people.

The social model: A typology for understanding abused consent

To take this further I identify four categories of how consent can be abused: coerced consent, normalised consent, survival consent and condoned consent. They may occur independently of each other or may be interdependent. I have separated them out solely to try to illustrate the range of complex issues that need to be engaged with in order to develop a 'social' model of consent.

Coerced consent

Much of the research into CSE has explored the process whereby an adult 'grooms' a child. The grooming model aimed to help practitioners, parents, carers and young people understand the stages through which an abuser would identify victim(s), flatter them with promises of love, make them feel special and cared for, offer gifts, separate them from their school, friends and family and eventually begin to abuse them (Scott and Skidmore, 2006). Grooming may take place on or off line, often involving a combination of technology and personal face-to-face contact (CEOP, 2011). Usually, although not always, the grooming is accompanied by the abuser encouraging the young person to become dependent upon alcohol and/or drugs, so that dependence on their abuser for love and 'supplies' is unified. Once dependent, the abuser invariably forces and/or coerces the young person into sexual activity with other abusers.

In these cases, the young person may appear to be consenting to sexual activity, however misguided or displaced their conviction of choice might be. Indeed, they may protect their abuser, saying that they are in love and exercising 'choice' over their own actions. Although many young people do reach a point where they want to leave, but can't, the coercive nature of this form of abuse can mean that the 'love' can be so deep that they reject interventions that aim to support them, return to abuser(s) and indeed, may visit abuser(s) in prison following the abuser's prosecution for CSE. That is, even after a court convicts an abuser for exploitation, the young person may still remain attached, wanting contact with their abuser.

These stages of grooming are well researched and the SOA 2003 (section 15) legislates specifically against grooming as a means of coercion for CSE. Whilst the stages and mechanics of grooming are understood, there is a long way to go to fully appreciate the impact of the grooming on the young person's capacity or willingness to consent to exploitation and to deliver core training to all child care staff so that they understand how to work with the presenting behaviour. Therapeutic work with sexually exploited children has drawn on attachment theory to help understand the way that consent is abused through abusive and disorganised attachments (see Corby, Shemmings and Wilkins, 2012; Howe, 2011 for more information on disorganised and abusive attachments and child protection).

Practitioners have suggested that an effective way of breaking the attachment to the abuser is through developing alternative 'good ' attachments, so that the young person begins to experience dependency on a non-abusive, rather than an abusive, adult (SECOS, 2012). Through such intervention, the young person can begin to compare the experience, understand what a 'good' relationship feels like, start to engage in debate about why and how their capacity to consent has been manipulated and begin to distance themselves from the abuser(s). For this to be affected, a substantial period of time is needed for the practitioner to engage and maintain contact with the young person, to build trust and confidence and eventually facilitate an understanding of the difference between the 'good' attachment and the abusive experience. The practitioner needs to feel secure in their post, needs supervisions to manage the conflicts and disappointments of working with a young person who comes back and forth with different messages and who might continue to return to abusive attachments. This is not an immediate quick fix but a long term intervention. There is a genuine worry that short term funding and targeted 'outcomes'-led interventions that focus on six month cycles of provisions will undermine efforts to secure long term 'good' attachments with children who are exploited through coerced consent.

It is clear that research into the impact of grooming can advance our understanding of 'coerced consent', addressing the social pressures that influence a child's capacity to consent to sexual activity. More work is needed to help understand this better as it is enacted for boys and young men who might experience CSE, and as grooming develops further through the use of mobile phones, social networking sites and other media. This could be advanced through further evaluations of existing work that draws on attachment theory to help provide tools for the young people to challenge and move away from abuse.

Normalised consent

My second category in the typology of the social model of abused consent is developed through considering the way that sexual violence is argued to be 'normalised' in young people's intimate relationships. There has been an increasing awareness from work of the Ending Violence against Women and Girls strategy (HO, 2011b) that sexual violence against girls in intimate relationships is underreported and poorly understood. In addition The Home Office 'teenage relationship abuse campaign' (HO, 2011c) recognises worries about teenagers becoming both victims and perpetrators of abusive relationships. More recently, concern about the sexualisation of youth and the pornographication of culture (see 22 January Radio Four 'Woman's Hour'), has called for a 'revolution' in sex education in schools to address the 'hyper-sexualized British culture which facilitates sexual bullying and "sexting" (where people send sexually explicit text messages)'. The backdrop to this concern touches on Government concerns about the sexualisation of youth (Papadopolous, 2010).

Despite concerns about the ways that children are sexualised and how sexual violence and pornography may be 'normalised' in popular culture, little has been done to research the impact this has on young people's understanding of consent in intimate relationships (Powell, 2010), and in particular sexually exploitative relationships. Research findings from the United States on Adolescent Intimate Personal Violence (AIPV) have focused on the psychological and medical response for teenagers experiencing domestic violence in their relationships. After establishing that AIPV was a problem for many young people in America, including those in same sex relationships, assessments were made about why particular adolescents were violent in intimate relationships. For example, some research showed that violence was more common after a couple had children, with 78 per cent of adolescents experiencing AIPV during the three months after giving birth who had not experienced IPV before delivery (see Keeling and Mason, 2008). Other studies focused on the impact of loss and bereavement on boys' capacity to develop healthy relationships, as research showed that 14 per cent of violent teen fathers had lost their own father when children (Tan and Quinlivan, 2006). However insightful, this research has focused on medical and individual psychological issues facing children in violent relationships rather than the pressures on young men or women to consent to violent and/or exploitative sexual activities. That is, it has not addressed the ways that violence impacts on the young person's capacity to consent to abusive relationships.

Some innovative research in the UK has tried to capture an understanding of the extent of violence experienced by teenagers in intimate relationships and to explore whether this then becomes 'normalised' (Schutt, 2006). In her work on 'teen dating violence' (emotional, physical and sexual) Barter (2009; 2011) argues that gendered power relations and the impact of social disadvantage need to be accounted for so that the context in which such violence occurs, and the meaning it holds for young people, can be explored. Drawing from interviews with 82 young people, 44 boys and 38 girls, from a range of agencies and organisations working with disadvantaged young people across the south-west of England, Barter's research (2011) showed that many young people appeared to accept violence as a normal, although unwanted, aspect of being in a relationship. More than half of the young women in the study said they had experienced a sexually violent relationship before they were 18. In addition, work undertaken by Firmin (2010; 2011) shows a worrying acceptance of violence as an integral part of sexual activity between young people, particularly exaggerated for those living in gang-affected neighbourhoods where the status of boys and young men is directly related to their demonstration of 'hyper-masculinity' and where girls and young women are routinely abused as a result. This resonates with work of the 1990s which noted that 'because masculinity is a behavioural response to the particular conditions and situations in which men participate ... men do masculinity according to the social situation in which they find themselves' (Messerschmidt, 1993: 83–4) and more recently by Kelly, who notes that such violence means that specific masculinities and femininities are (re) created through its ongoing use (Kelly and Gill, 2012). This endorses some of the arguments made by those working on the Violence against Women and Girls Strategy (HO, 2011a) where an understanding of the impact of gendered power relationships on both boys and girls is called for in both gay and heterosexual relationships. That is, we need a better understanding of the social pressures on young people who might assume that there is no option other than to be violent or receive violence within their sexual activity.

Current research at the University of Bedfordshire is exploring this through research funded by the Office of the Children's Commissioner for England as part of their Inquiry into Child Sexual Exploitation in Gangs and Groups. Interviews are being held with up to 180 young people who live in gang-affected neighbourhoods. Although the young people's interviews are not yet complete, the interim report gave a tentative preliminary analysis of the themes emerging from the first 68 interviews, conducted across four different research sites (Beckett et al., 2012).

Half of these interviews were conducted with young women, half with young men. Preliminary findings suggest that sexual violence was 'normalised' for many research participants, to the point where rape was not recognised as such and where sexual violence was an accepted tool for initiation, intimidation and retaliation between and within rival groups. Over and above this acceptance of sexual violence as a weapon of conflict, the research showed that young women's' 'reputation' and consequent respect was graded depending upon her sexual activity. Not all young women were viewed as having equal (or in some cases any) rights to assent to or decline sexual activity. In particular, young women who are sexually active with more than one partner are viewed by some as having lost their right to withhold consent.

This repeats what we know from the early feminist debate about heterosexual relationships, which argues that young women are classified and graded according to their sexual activity. If a young man is promiscuous in heterosexual relationships, he is advancing his masculinity; if a girl is promiscuous she is a 'slag', but if not, she is a 'drag'. The 'slag/drag' dichotomy labelled 'bad girls' (sexually active) as 'anyone's' and 'good girls' (not sexually active or monogamous) as 'boring'. As soon as the 'slag' label is given, the young woman loses all right to say no to sex (Lees, 1993; McRobbie, 1991). Whilst further exploration is needed about how to counter the pressures on some young men to demonstrate their achievement of 'hegemonic heterosexual masculinity' through sexual violence, so too is a better understanding of the impact of pressures such as the slag/drag dichotomy on young women's capacity to consent to exploitation.

Whether our concern is more general, focusing on the sexualisation of youth culture and the pornografication of society overall, or more specific, focusing on the impact of social, economic and familial disadvantage on particular groups of young people, it is evident that we need to develop a better understanding of the impact that these social pressures have on young men's and young women's understanding of what it is to consent to sexual activity. An incorporation of such awareness into sex and relationship education in schools and in basic training for youth, social work and legal practitioners may begin to counter the more individual approach to considering consent through the medical model described above.

Survival consent

My third category within the social model of abused consent typology is what I call 'survival consent'. This recognises the impact that poverty may have on young women and men's decisions to swap, sell or exchange sex for some form of reward, gift or money. It draws on adult sex worker literature that talks of 'survival sex': the use of sex in exchange for money, accommodation or other gifts to alleviate the pressures of poverty (Phoenix, 2002). In terms of understanding women's role in the sex industry, and in selling sex in particular, the feminist movement is divided between radical feminists who argue that prostitution is an inherent part, and violent expression of, patriarchal society, defining 'victims' in need of rescuing; and pragmatic feminists who argue that the sale of sex is not illegal, that work in the sex industry can offer financial reward and independence that may not be available elsewhere, and that some women and men may actively choose to consent to sex in exchange for payment.

These debates about adult sex workers have been applied to young people by those who question the shift to a 'child protection' discourse that places all those under 18 as victims of CSE needing child protection through safeguarding approaches, from a 'criminal justice discourse' that places those over 18 as active agents making their own decisions, needing control through the criminal justice system (Melrose, 2010). Such authors argue that protection from exploitation should be afforded regardless of age. The onus therefore should be on understanding the means through which commercial sexual exploitation is linked to exploitation per se (through poverty, deprivation and a dominant ideology of reward through financial gain) rather than on the Western focus, which constructs children as vulnerable and in need of particular protection.

Whilst the history of CSE is situated in language that positions children as 'involved in prostitution' (DoH/HO, 2000), the more recent discourse of CSE (DCSF, 2009; DfE, 2011a) inevitably positions the young person as a victim, 'supposedly' unable to play an active role in whether they consent to sexual activity in exchange for payment or not (Melrose, this volume). I say 'supposedly' because despite guidance positioning the young person as a victim, and encouraging awareness of the impact that exploitation and abuse has on their ability to consent, many practitioners do still assume that a young person is consenting to their own exploitation, an assumption that I explore further under my fourth category of the social model of abused consent typology: condoned consent.

Being mindful of the debates explored above, we see that Survival Consent recognises that many young people may be taking what they see as informed decisions about exchanging sex for payment. To help practitioners understand the dynamics at play, Scott and Skidmore (2006) described young people in these circumstances exercising 'constrained choice': that is, faced with few other alternatives, and little awareness of choices available to them, young people may think that they play an active role in 'deciding' to consent to sex that is exploitative and abusive. That poverty and deprivation can be 'push factors' into further exploitation is evident from the recent inquiry into CSE in groups and gangs which noted that in 58 written submissions and all site visits

> material inducements to victims were identified. These included money, drugs, alcohol, food, accommodation, phones or phone top up credits, gifts, debts and links to adults involved in prostitution. Such financial coercion was particularly apparent in cases where children were homeless and on the streets, had run away or were drug/alcohol dependent.
>
> (OCC, 2012a: 41)

Research into CSE has repeatedly shown a high correlation between children living in poverty, experiencing local authority care and going missing, and vulnerability to CSE (Chase and Statham, 2005; Pearce, 2009; CEOP, 2011; OCC, 2012a). Undoubtedly, in some circumstances, young people may not be 'groomed, or coerced' into swapping sex for reward. They may feel that they are taking the best action for themselves by exchanging sex for accommodation, funding or gifts to alleviate their adverse circumstances. Indeed, some may consider that their very survival depends upon them consenting to exploitative or abusive sex. Young people should neither be penalised for this, nor assumed to be making informed choices about their well-being. A social model of consent will ask practitioners to be mindful of the financial and other social pressures facing young people, recognising the pressures on the young person when they exercise agency to relieve the poverty and deprivation experienced. Most agencies that are established to support young people in CSE are not designed to address these wider social issues. However, it is important that practitioners are mindful of the pressures experienced by young people living within a dominant culture that values new clothing, possessions and economic gain. Recognising the impact of poverty on young people's actions will help to understand why some may appear to consent to sexually exploitative situations in return for some financial or other reward.

Condoned consent

> This child has a very vivid imagination. I'm not even going to record a lot of our conversation because it's clearly not true.

> I know that she's been in front of a jury and told a story about being raped over there. I know she wasn't believed ... I mean we are asking the court to believe a 15 year old girl against four or five adults.
>
> > (Pearce, Hynes and Bovarnick, 2013: 77–94)

My final category within the typology of a social model of abused consent is 'condoned consent'. Condoned consent is where professionals, either through lack of awareness or through purposeful action, fail to recognise CSE as abuse, and blame the child or young person for consenting to the predicament 'they have got themselves into'. In some situations, as was the case with the first quote above, this may be through sheer disbelief that such terrible abuse can happen. In others, as with the second quotation above, it might be from recognition that children will not be believed. To take the case further would be to lead the young woman into situations where she would face disbelief, an experience that could be further damaging to her. In other cases practitioners may be thinking that it would be better to accept the situation as resources are not available to cope with the aftermath of 'lifting the stone' (Jago et al., 2011). In situations involving same sex exploitation, the practitioner may believe that the young person is 'experimenting' with sexual activity and consider that to intervene would be to undermine the child's right to explore their sexual orientation. In others, practitioners may themselves be confused about how to judge whether a child or young person is consenting. Indeed, the OCC inquiry (2012a: 47) noted that the inquiry panel were presented with 'confused and inconsistent understanding on the part of both professionals and young people of the concept of consent to sexual activity' and that rather than being seen as victims of abuse

> [c]hildren and young people who were sexually exploited were frequently described by professionals in many localities as being

'promiscuous, 'liking the glamour', engaging in 'risky behaviour' and being generally badly behaved.

(OCC, 2012a: 47)

I separate condoned consent into two forms: Firstly, it may be *unconscious*. This would be where practitioners are poorly trained or supported to recognise CSE or to understand the impact that it has on the child's capacity to consent to sexual activity. This is not unlikely, as the compulsory core training in social work, education, police, youth work and youth justice fails to identify and address CSE as a child protection issue. Reviews in child protection services such as Munro (2011) and Laming (2009) singularly fail to mention CSE, to explore the nature of abuse involved or to look at ways that practitioners can address the complex issues involved. With this backdrop, it is understandable that some practitioners may not understand what CSE is, or its impact on children's capacity to consent to abusive sex. This can be remedied through a review and change to core curriculum, the provision of post qualifying training and a recognition of the importance of support and supervision to staff working in child protection.

The second and more dangerous form of condoned consent is what I call professional negligence: consciously turning a blind eye to recognised exploitation of children. This may occur when professionals are aware that consent is being condoned but do not intervene because they lack the resources to support an intervention, or the time or commitment to address the issues involved. CSE is excused through attitudes of acceptance: that 'they will do it anyway' and 'they want to live like this'; of resignation: 'there is so little we can do anyway' and 'they are 16 so they can consent and it is the medic's concern to decide competence'; of denial 'it's not really happening as badly as this chaotic teenager is describing'; or finally through ageism: 'they are nearly 18 anyway so will transfer to adult services before we can impact on their lives'. Whilst this latter rationale has been used to excuse lack of intervention with many troubled teenagers approaching 18, (Rees et al., 2011) the former are documented through research to be particularly applicable to practitioners failing to address the problem of CSE (Barnardo's, 2011a; OCC, 2012a; Pearce, 2009). Anne Marie Currie opens her campaign report 'Cut Them Free' (Barnardo's, 2011b) by saying that 'No child can consent to their own abuse'.

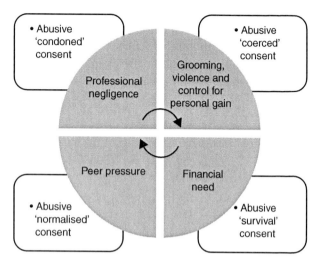

Figure 4.1 A social model of abused consent

Until this is embedded within every practitioner's approach to working with sexually exploited children and young people, professional negligence through condoned consent will continue.

Conclusion

This chapter has proposed four categories of abused consent within a typology of a social model for understanding abused consent. The diagram below shows how these categories can be interwoven, supporting and endorsing each other as justifications to overlook CSE.

I have argued that whilst the medical model for understanding consent is helpful, and more recent guidelines for health care practitioners do rightly encourage awareness of how exploitation and abuse may impact on a young person's capacity to consent, there is still a dearth of materials available to help all practitioners understand the impact of social and economic pressures on young people 'consenting' to exploitative sexual activity. A social model contextualising abused consent can help us to start this process.

5

Looked After Young People and CSE: A View from Northern Ireland

Helen Beckett

Introduction

This chapter considers the issue of child sexual exploitation (CSE) with specific reference to looked after adolescents. Drawing on the findings of a large scale study undertaken in Northern Ireland (NI) the chapter explores the prevalence and nature of CSE amongst adolescents in care. The chapter argues that whilst there are significant levels of CSE within the adolescent looked after population, the heterogeneous nature of both young people's individual biographies and their care experiences means that not all looked after young people experience similar levels of risk. Identifying disproportionate levels of risk within the residential care population, the second half of the chapter explores potential contributory factors to this and some important principles for responding to risk within this population. Highlighting the importance of a holistic approach to understanding risk and resilience, the chapter emphasises the need to move beyond a short-term, reactive response to concerns (that frequently centres on controlling or containing the behaviours of the young person) to a more holistic, integrated response (that addresses the protective, support and rehabilitative needs of the individual child and holds the perpetrator to account). Although the chapter draws predominantly on data from NI, consideration is also given to learning from other jurisdictions and the applicability of the NI findings for elsewhere in the United Kingdom (UK).

Sexual exploitation and the looked after population

Over the last decade CSE has received increasing attention across the UK and a series of reports have highlighted the existence of this form of child abuse, noting the variety of forms it can take and the multiple challenges inherent in responding to it (Scott and Skidmore, 2006; Clutton and Coles, 2007; Jago and Pearce, 2008; OCC, 2012b). Whilst acknowledging that no child is immune from this form of abuse, studies have repeatedly identified particular life experiences that are associated with increased vulnerability. These include:

• Being in care;
• Prior (sexual) abuse or neglect;
• Family dysfunction (domestic violence, family breakdown, parental drug or alcohol misuse);
• Going missing or running away from home or a care placement;
• Substance misuse;
• Disengagement from education;
• Social isolation and/or low self esteem;
• Association with negative peer groups/peers who have been sexually exploited; and
• Homelessness.

> (Beckett, 2011; CEOP, 2011; Clutton and Coles, 2007; Harris and Robinson, 2007; OCC, 2012a; Pearce, 2009)

Whilst acknowledging the increased risk associated with these vulnerability factors, it is important to recognise that their presence is not necessarily predictive of an experience of CSE. It is the interplay of these and other factors – together with exposure to someone who would take advantage of these vulnerabilities, and inadequate protective structures to mediate against that risk – that culminate in a young person being abused through CSE. This interconnectedness has not always been recognised when considering the vulnerability of looked after children to CSE, with their vulnerability often presented as singularly related to their care experience. The data presented in this chapter demonstrates that to attribute risk of CSE to the care experience is an oversimplification of the issue; as indeed is the alternative discourse of locating the cause of young peoples' vulnerability in their individual biographies. Their vulnerability stems from a complex interplay of many factors including: elements of the care experience, ongoing repercussions of pre-care experiences, effectiveness of support structures, the extent and nature of exposure to risk, and personal strategies for negotiating this.

A further important factor that warrants greater consideration is the heterogeneity of the looked after population and the unequal distribution of risk across it. Noting the cited reasons for the increased risk of CSE within the care population – multiple placement moves, frequent changes in social worker, lack of positive attachments and negative peer associations (Beckett, 2011; Coy, 2008, 2009b; DHSSPSNI, 2006) – it is apparent that not all looked after young people will have experienced these to the same degree, or experienced similar levels of associated vulnerability. In a climate of ever decreasing resources, it is important to move beyond considering the looked after population as a homogeneous whole, in order to map patterns of particular risk and respond accordingly – the findings presented below offer useful learning in this regard.

The Northern Ireland context

Recent statistics reveal a total of 2,644 looked after children in Northern Ireland at March 2012. This equates to a rate of 61 per 10,000; similar to that of England (59 per 10,000) and lower than that of Scotland and Wales (92 and 156 per 10,000 respectively) (BAAF, 2012). Just over half of these children were male whilst 48 per cent were female. Just under half (46 per cent) were aged 12 or older, the age cohort under consideration in this chapter (DHSSPSNI, 2012). As in England, the majority (74 per cent) of looked after young people in Northern Ireland are in foster care placements. A further 11 per cent are in at home placements, with 9 per cent in residential care and the remaining 6 per cent in other placement types (DHSSPSNI, 2012). As is also the case in other parts of the UK, young people aged 12 and over are more likely to be in residential placements than their younger counterparts, with 17 per cent of 12–17 year olds in residential care (DHSSPSNI, 2011). At 30 June 2012, there were 360 residential places in NI across 52 residential homes, averaging six to seven places per home. Unlike England, the majority of residential care placements are provided by the Health and Social Care (HSC) Trust, with private providers accounting for only 18 per cent of residential placements in NI (DHSSPSNI, 2012).

As in the rest of the UK, looked after adolescents in NI are recognised to be at particular risk of experiencing CSE. A series of reports and policy documents have repeatedly identified this risk, and the accompanying risks for other young people, throughout the last decade (Beckett, 2011; DHSSPSNI, 2006, 2008; DoJ, 2011; Dudley, 2006; HSC Board, 2010; Martynowicz, Toucas and Caughey, 2009; Montgomery-Devlin, 2008; NICCY, 2009; Raws, 2001; RQIA, 2011; Sinclair and Geraghty, 2008). However, in spite of this recognition, NI has not yet introduced dedicated guidance on CSE. In the absence of such guidance, the principles and procedures that underpin current responses to CSE are drawn from a number of different documents introduced almost ten years ago when knowledge about the issue was much more limited than is currently the case (ACPC, 2005; DHSSPSNI, 2003; HSSB et al., 2004). Whilst these safeguarding documents outline a number of important principles for addressing CSE they do so within a narrower definition of CSE than that currently governing responses in England and Wales. As such, the current categorisation of CSE fails to incorporate the full range of sexually exploitative experiences identified in research or the range of relevant offences recognised in sexual offences legislation. In the absence of a more comprehensive articulation of the issue, professionals can experience confusion with regard to the boundaries of CSE and the identification of appropriate responses to it. This is particularly the case where victim and perpetrator are of a similar age, an emerging issue in both NI and the rest of the UK (Barter et al., 2009; Beckett, 2011; Beckett et al., 2012; Firmin, 2010; Jago et al., 2011).

Other factors that have impacted upon the effectiveness of statutory responses to CSE within NI include the historical dominance of 'the troubles' and the subsidiary status accorded social issues within this; experiences of/attitudes to statutory authorities and the 'internal policing' of certain communities; and the taboo nature of sex and sexuality within a traditionally religious society. The focus in recent years on institutional abuse, whilst clearly valid and necessary, has also inadvertently drawn attention away from other forms of abuse such as CSE, as has the subsidiary status traditionally afforded to concerns about adolescents within the UK child protection system (Beckett, 2011; Calder, 2001; Harper and Scott, 2006; Melrose, 2004; Pearce, 2010).

The study

The primary data presented in this chapter is drawn from an in-depth two year study of CSE in NI, undertaken in 2009–11. The study was conducted on behalf of Barnardo's NI and funded by the Department of Health, Social Services and Public Safety NI (DHSSPSNI). The definition of CSE used in the research was based on that used in statutory safeguarding guidance in England and Wales (DCSF, 2009; Welsh Assembly, 2010). The study adopted a multi-method approach, with strong ethical underpinnings (see Beckett, 2011 for a full discussion).

The research sample

A total of 1,102 CSE risk assessments were completed by social work practitioners across the five HSC Trusts and the quantitative data presented here is drawn from these. The majority (71 per cent) related to looked after young people aged 12–17 years inclusive, representing two-thirds of the entire looked after population of this age within NI. The remainder related to young people who were supported by social services but not looked after at the point of assessment (included as a point of reference for comparative levels of risk).

One quarter (25 per cent) of the looked after sample for whom risk assessments were undertaken were aged 12–13 years; 36 per cent were 14–15 and 39 per cent were 16–17 years old. There was an equal gender split and very little variation in terms of ethnicity (95 per cent described as white), but this is to be expected given the ethnic composition of the NI population. The majority (62 per cent) were in non-familial foster-care or kinship placements, with a further 20 per cent in residential care, 11 per cent in 'at home' placements and the remainder in secure care (2 per cent) or 'other' placement types (5 per cent). Virtually all (98 per cent) had been known to social services for at least a year, with half known to social services for ten or more years at the point of inclusion in the study.

Patterns of CSE within the looked after population

Social workers identified CSE to be an issue of concern for one in seven (14 per cent) of the looked after population. The three main types of CSE identified within this were:

Abuse through prostitution: Under Part 3 of the Sexual Offences (NI) Order 2008 it is an offence to abuse a child through prostitution, either through paying for the sexual services of a child or inciting, arranging or controlling this (articles 37–40). 'Payments' are not necessarily monetary: they can include the provision of goods or services (including drugs and alcohol) at a reduced cost or to discharge a debt.

The 'party house' scenario: This was the most common type of CSE identified within the study. These scenarios shared many similarities with the abuse of a child through prostitution but in these cases the exchange was generally less apparent upfront, with payment or trade off demanded, or forcefully taken, respectively after a period of grooming and/or partying at houses with 'free' alcohol and/or drugs.

Sexually exploitative relationships: These 'relationships' generally involved young people under the legal age of consent in, what they perceived to be, consensual sexual relationships with boyfriends or girlfriends who were generally much older. Most of these cases related to heterosexual relationships, however, a number of single-sex relationships were also identified. Although tangible goods were part of the currency of exchange in some of these situations, in most others, the returns for the young person were more intangible, relating to attention, affection and/or a sense of belonging.

Internet exploitation, child abuse images and trafficking for the purposes of CSE were also identified but much less frequently than those cited above. Considerable overlap was observed between different forms of CSE, in terms of those perpetrating the abuse, their modus operandi, and the young people being targeted. Many cases were identified in which young people experienced several different forms of CSE, either concurrently or in succession, with one form of abuse sometimes leading into another.

As in other studies, the rate of CSE identified for young males (5 per cent) was significantly lower than that for young females (23 per cent). However this does not necessarily equate with lower rates of experience. Professional participants acknowledged that males are less likely to report experiences of CSE due to societal expectations of masculinity and/or fear of being labelled as homosexual. Some also identified an unintended bias in their identification of concerns between the genders and a greater discomfort in talking to young men about these issues, all of which may reduce the likelihood of males reporting incidents or seeking support.

The vast majority (92 per cent) of looked after young people for whom CSE represented a concern were under the legal age of consent when concerns were first identified. The majority were between 12 and 15 years old, with initial identification occurring most commonly at 14 years. This mirrors findings from elsewhere in the UK, which show 14–15 years as the most common age at which CSE is first identified (Barnardo's, 2011a; CEOP, 2011). It should be noted, however, that age of first identification does not necessarily equate with age at onset of the exploitation, with cases as young as 10 identified by professionals within the research.

In over half (55 per cent) of cases CSE had endured at least a year; in 19 per cent it had lasted for three years or more, with a number of cases reported to have continued for eight or ten years. The prolonged nature of the exploitation, sometimes continuing long after statutory agencies became aware of concerns, raises serious questions about the effectiveness of existing responses. A further worry was the finding that in half of cases, concerns about CSE emerged after entry into care – in half of the remaining cases, concerns from the pre-care period continued after entry to care. This raises questions about whether elements of the care experience may increase the risk of CSE for some young people, or whether the relationship between the two is purely incidental.

Given the frequency with which the care population are identified as disproportionately experiencing CSE it is particularly interesting to note that the rate of concern identified for the overall looked after population (14 per cent) within the NI study is only marginally higher than that for other young people who were known to social services but not in care (13 per cent). Where significant differences do emerge is when these findings are broken down by placement type, with young people in residential care disproportionately represented in cases of concern.

The sexual exploitation of young people in residential care

More than half of CSE cases identified within the looked after population came from residential care, despite this population representing only 20 per cent of the overall sample. This equates to a rate of 41 per cent within the residential cohort, compared to 11 per cent in at home placements and less than 5 per cent for non-familial or kinship foster care. Females in residential care emerged as at particular risk with sexual exploitation identified as an issue of concern for almost two-thirds (64 per cent) of this group.

There is no singular explanation for the observable over-representation of young people in residential care amongst CSE statistics. As explored below, their vulnerability stems from a complex interplay of factors: some relate to the ongoing impact of their pre-care life experiences or individual biographies whilst others are associated with the care experience (specifically the residential care experience) itself.

Individual biographies and the ongoing impact of pre-care experiences

It is widely recognised that many looked after adolescents have experienced traumatic life experiences prior to entry into care that continue to impact upon their daily lives years after the event. The study identified a number of pre-care experiences that appeared to increase vulnerability to CSE in the present including: prior sexual abuse or other abusive experiences; absence of positive role models and nurturing relationships; family dysfunction; and a lack of boundaries within the home. A clear link was observable between these earlier experiences and present vulnerability factors such as low self-esteem, an unmet need for love and significance, inability to self regulate, low levels of resilience, inadequate support structures, patterns of absconding and drug or alcohol misuse.

Many young people with previous experiences of abuse and/or neglect lived in heightened states of anxiety, absconding, misusing drugs and/or alcohol (and sometimes sex) to meet their need for stimulation and/or block out debilitating negative emotions. A particular issue for those who had previously been sexually abused was their premature sexualisation and low self-esteem/self worth. Some such individuals appeared to experience CSE in a comparatively positive light, noting that 'at least they were getting something for it this time'. Some had become so desensitised to abuse that they did not view what was happening to them as unusual or wrong. A stark theme emerging in relation to this was the 'normalisation' of rape amongst young females with repeated experiences of abuse: as one young person explained: 'me being raped, is like you having a cup of tea'.

For many young people who entered the care system in adolescence, absence of boundaries and parental discipline, and the patterns of risk that ensued, were also key contributory factors to ongoing risk of CSE when in care. Case file reviews revealed examples of adolescents brought into care after months or years of inadequate parental control; misusing alcohol and/or drugs, associating with unsavoury older individuals in the community and suspected CSE within this. In a number of cases, such patterns of behaviour had been established as young as 9 or 10 years of age. Addressing such entrenched patterns of behaviour presents a significant challenge for professionals working with them upon their entry into care.

Impact of the care experience

This discussion notes from the outset that for many young people, particularly those who end up in stable placements akin to a family environment, the care experience provides a safe setting in which to receive appropriate support to deal with the impact of their pre-care experiences and rebuild their lives. For others, however, the care experience can serve to compound existing difficulties and vulnerabilities, rather than alleviate them. This is particularly true of those entering the care system in adolescence when patterns of risk within the community are already established and appropriate placements in the community are harder to source and sustain. It is also particularly true of those who failed to receive appropriate support to deal with both their entry into care and the reasons for this, and those who are exposed to further instability and insecurity within the system in terms of where they live and/or who is responsible for their care.

Young people in residential care are frequently those who have experienced less positive care pathways in terms of their access to these rehabilitative factors, rendering them vulnerable to alternative sources of perceived emotional and physical security. Whilst some young people are able to realise these foundational needs within a protective and supportive residential care setting, for others the residential care experience serves to further compound their difficulties and increase their vulnerability to CSE. Four significant risk factors, specific to the experience of residential care, were highlighted within the study. These were:

• The population of young people directed towards residential care and the consequent population mix within this;

- Behavioural norms amongst some residential populations;
- Specific targeting of residential units by perpetrators; and
- Systemic restrictions on staff's ability to safeguard from this.

Population mix

Young people placed in residential settings are often those who display more complex needs and/or challenging behavioural issues, the various manifestations of which impact upon the dynamics of group living both in terms of peer interaction and staff capacity to invest in supportive therapeutic relationships with residents. A particular concern in relation to the population mix in residential care is the culture of sexual bullying, intimidation and assaults and the co-placement of those displaying sexually harmful behaviour with those particularly vulnerable to exploitation. A further related issue is that frequently young people who have experienced/are experiencing CSE are placed in residential care in response to these concerns, thus introducing risks for other residents (Clutton and Coles, 2007; Munro, 2004). A number of examples were identified within the study of sexually exploited young females introducing other young people in the unit to their abusers, either unwittingly or at the instigation/coercion of the abuser(s).

Behavioural norms

High proportions of the residential population in the NI study were observed to be misusing drugs, solvents and/or alcohol, disengaging from education, engaging in underage sexual activity and/or associating with 'risky' adults; all known risk indicators for CSE (see Beckett, 2011). The prevalence of each of these factors was significantly higher amongst the residential population than their peers in other placement types. Thus concerns were expressed about the impact of exposure to such behaviours or risks within such a confined environment and the impact of peer pressure within this. Residential staff reported patterns of young people coming into their units and quickly adopting the behaviours of other residents, including those that led them into sexually exploitative situations. This was true even where no such concerns existed prior to entry into the unit. Younger residents, aged 12–14 years, were noted to be particularly vulnerable to this.

Going missing, a significant risk factor for CSE, was identified as a particular issue in terms of behavioural norms within the residential care population, with 60 per cent having been missing overnight or longer on one or more occasions in the last year (compared to 20 per cent or less in other placements). The research identified this as a pattern of behaviour rather than a one-off incident, with young women more likely to abscond than young men and the risk of absconding increasing with age. It is widely recognised that young people go missing for a range of reasons, including both push (getting away from something) and pull factors (drawn to something). In the case of residential care this can include being unsettled or feeling unsafe in their placement (bullying, sexual intimidation and so on) and peer influences and behavioural norms of going missing within the unit.

Targeting of residential units

The study found clear evidence of young people in residential units, being specifically targeted by perpetrators. Two main reasons were identified for this: the fact that the young people were known to be vulnerable because of their past experiences and the fact that abusers perceived them to be less protected than their peers in the community (see below).

Inadequate systemic responses

Many professionals working with young people entrenched in sexually exploitative situations were very vocal about their inability to manage risk adequately within the residential setting. This is rarely a reflection of lack of effort on their part; rather it reflects the perceived inadequacy of the structures within which they work and the limited tools at their disposal to defend against the manipulative techniques employed by abusers. Two of the key issues repeatedly identified as conspiring to prevent effective protection in residential units were staff's inability to monitor mobile phone use or stop young people leaving a placement, even when they knew that they were going to an abuser. Whilst restraint based options do exist to facilitate the latter, staff did not feel sufficiently equipped and/or supported to avail of these in exercising the corporate parenting duty of the HSC Trust.

Responding to the sexual exploitation of young people in residential care

CSE is never an easy issue to address. Frequently recognised challenges include variable levels of awareness, the 'hidden' nature of the problem, low levels of reporting and, frequently, the co-existence of other presenting problems that cloud identification of abuse. Extricating young people from sexually exploitative situations is also complicated by the fact that, for them, the negatives are generally linked to some positives, whether this is access to drugs or alcohol, or a sense of belonging and affection. Young people's differential understandings of risk, and the infrequency with which they view themselves as victims in need of help, further militate against protecting them from CSE.

In the absence of an adequate ability to manage risk within the residential scenario, a frequently utilised response to concerns about CSE in NI is to place young people in secure accommodation. Although there are some potential benefits associated with a period in secure accommodation there is also a series of negatives. These include the message young people receive when they are locked up as opposed to their abuser, lack of evidence of meaningful change that lasts beyond the period of containment, and increased exposure to risk through links established whilst securely accommodated.

An effective response to young people affected by CSE in residential care, and indeed for adolescents in care more generally, must move beyond this type of short-term reactive response to a more holistic, integrated response that acknowledges the multi-faceted nature of risk and addresses the protective, support and rehabilitative needs of the individual child. If, for example, a young person is returning to their abuser because of substance misuse, this is unlikely to change if the substance dependency is not simultaneously addressed. Similarly, if they are drawn to their abuser because of a need for attachment or affection, alternative meaningful relationships will be the key to sustaining ongoing disengagement from the abuser.

Professionals need to be further supported to understand the complex nature of CSE and the many psychosocial factors impacting upon a young person affected by it. Whilst many professionals revealed insightful understanding of these issues, others appeared to struggle with the ostensible contradictions inherent in many CSE cases: particularly young people's perceived 'choice' to return to their abusers, despite professional attempts to 'rescue' them. Responses to a sexually exploited young person will vary considerably depending on whether those working with him/her perceive him/her to be a victim or a willing participant in their experiences. The complex reasons that young people may seemingly 'allow' themselves to be exploited, many of which may be beyond the control of the young person, therefore need to be better understood. Professionals also need to be supported to identify vulnerability in the midst of challenging behaviour and seeming disregard for professional support.

A further vital element to protecting young people at risk of CSE is a safe supportive environment. Asked what was key to this within the residential setting, young people who participated in the research identified two core components: (a) a sense of 'home', safety and belonging and (b) positive relationships with staff. Where young people felt that staff genuinely cared about, and for, them, they were more likely to confide in them, listen to them and be persuaded by them. Some of the therapeutic approaches currently being implemented in residential units in NI were contributing to the realisation such provision by enhancing staff capacity to work with residents in a more effective (and less reactive) manner.

It is critical that all these elements are underpinned by a proactive multi-agency approach. The study identified numerous examples of promising practice in this regard in relation to managing risk within residential care, including 'unofficial' police visits to residential units and regular meetings between local police and unit staff, but ongoing professional tensions were also observable in many areas. These related primarily to a lack of clarity about the relative responsibilities of police and social care professionals in responding to concerns about CSE within the residential care population and confusion as to the practicalities of information sharing. Given that both these issues were identified as key contributory factors to the failure of statutory bodies to protect from CSE in recent serious case reviews, it is vital that resolution to these challenges be identified.

Conclusions

Although this chapter has identified numerous individual vulnerabilities and system inadequacies it is vital to reiterate that none of these is the actual *cause* of CSE. CSE exists because individuals are willing to abuse young people in this manner: individual vulnerabilities and system failures just make it easier for them to do so. Ultimate culpability firmly rests with the abusers and, as such, proactive pursuit and prosecution of these individuals must form a central element of any response to CSE, in addition to the victim-focused work outlined within this chapter.

Recognising this, the overriding message that emerges from the NI study is that, despite the efforts of many dedicated professionals, there are current failures in the duty to safeguard looked after children and young people from CSE. Beyond the shortcomings in the fields of prevention and prosecution, there are serious shortcomings in responses to those who are being abused through CSE and those at immediate risk of the same. A clear indicator of this is the prolonged periods of time over which many cases of CSE had continued: often months or even years after statutory services became aware of the risk. In a number of cases, this failure to protect not only failed that young person, but other young people also, who were subsequently introduced to the abusive network through this individual. This risk was particularly present for young people in residential care.

There is a clear need for a more proactive risk-minimisation strategy that is premised on a more nuanced understanding of the heterogeneous nature of the looked after population and their care experiences. Such an approach should acknowledge the varying biographies and experiences of different looked after adolescents and pay cognisance to the co-existence of inter-related contributory factors operating at the individual, community and societal levels. Identified patterns of vulnerability can be used to inform and direct targeted preventative work with those young people likely to experience heightened risk of CSE during their care experience. Specific consideration should be given to population mix within residential care, with the identified risks associated with a residential care experience an explicit consideration in decisions about placement patterns and care plans. Central to all of these developments should be the voices of those who have experienced CSE and can help us identify meaningful and effective ways to engage young people in efforts to safeguard them from CSE.

6

Young People, Trafficking and Sexual Exploitation: A View from Scotland

Isabelle Brodie

Introduction

This chapter reviews evidence regarding child sexual exploitation (CSE) in Scotland. As devolution has progressed across the UK, there has been growing interest in the different routes taken in respect to social policy and welfare reform (see, for example, Arnott and Ozga, 2008 and Phillips, 2003 regarding education; Scott and Wright, 2012 regarding policy development; Smith and colleague 2009 regarding health). More recently, there has been a recognition that new alignments are appearing which may or may not present challenges to the coherence of UK policy and practice, or represent 'real innovation' in the way that services are delivered (Scott and Wright, 2012: 441). In turn there have been calls for more empirically and theoretically grounded work which examines the extent and nature of difference in the four nations of the UK (Paterson and Iannelli, 2007). Such calls can be linked to broader interest in evidence-based policy, and raise questions about how evidence is shared and interpreted across the UK. This chapter seeks to contribute to such sharing of evidence in respect to the issue of CSE and policy development on this issue in Scotland.

Melrose (2012a, this volume) has described the evolution of CSE discourse from one of 'children abused through prostitution' to that of 'child sexual exploitation', and suggests that this change in discourse and the expansion of the concept it implies has not always been helpful. As knowledge concerning CSE has developed, the concept can seem like the many headed hydra also described as 'elastic' (Asquith and Turner, 2008; Melrose, 2012a) – carrying the weight of too many social anxieties, from the 'premature' sexualisation of childhood (Papadopoulos, 2010) to sexual violence against women on a much broader scale. This elasticity also carries with it certain challenges for policy, in that it can be viewed as being linked to, or having implications for, many different areas – for example, health, housing, welfare benefits and family support. More specifically, there are questions about the balance that is achieved in policy regarding the safeguarding of children and young people, in terms of different age groups and specific vulnerabilities.

Whilst media and political interest in CSE means that there is a certain amount of enthusiasm for legislative and policy change, there are differences across the UK in terms of how such development is taking place. This chapter considers the process of such policy development in Scotland, which, at the time of writing is developing rapidly. The content of the chapter is based mainly on a scoping review of CSE undertaken for the Scottish Government in 2012 (Brodie and Pearce, 2012) and which is helping influence the direction of policy on CSE in Scotland. The scoping review involved a literature review, a review of available statistics, and a consultation with 'expert' practitioners during a one day seminar. It is important to emphasise that this was a small-scale piece of work, albeit one that should set the scene for further research, policy and practice development.

The chapter begins by considering the background to policy development regarding CSE in Scotland. It will then examine the nature of the research evidence from Scottish-based studies, and how this relates to evidence from throughout the UK regarding the scale and nature of CSE. The chapter will also consider the views of practitioners working within this context, and the perceived challenges and opportunities that exist within their practice contexts in respect to supporting young people at risk or experiencing CSE. The chapter concludes that the evidence leans towards similarity rather than difference across the UK, and to this extent there are important lessons to be learned in Scotland from the experience of policy development in England and Wales.

Policy background and context

The early history of CSE in Scotland closely mirrors that in the rest of the UK. Research in the late 1990s highlighted concerns about children and young people involved in prostitution (Buckley and

Brodie, 2000; Melrose, Barrett and Brodie, 1999). The emergence of these concerns can be traced to campaigns by major children's charities, who commissioned and used academic research to further their arguments that young people's (under-18s') involvement in prostitution should be decriminalised (see, for example, Barnardo's, 1998; Melrose, Barrett and Brodie, 1999).

It is significant that this criminalisation is also apparent in Scotland, where the approach to work with 'troublesome' young people and young offenders has been distinct by virtue of the Scottish Children's Hearing System, introduced in the early 1970s as a result of the Kilbrandon Report. The Hearing System emphasises the need to address youth offending within a child welfare, rather than criminal justice, framework and undertakes this using a multi-agency panel. However, grounds for referral to the Hearing System have traditionally included that of 'moral danger'. Though this category is due, at the time of writing, to be removed, it is a reminder of 'difference' in the way in which Scottish policy – even that generally considered benign – regarding children and young people has been constructed, and the 'gendering' of this.

As a result of these campaigns guidance on young people involved in prostitution was issued in England in 2000; parallel guidance was issued slightly later in Scotland (Scottish Executive, 2003). This defined CSE in much the same terms as the Westminster guidance of both 2000 and 2009, and the Welsh guidance of 2010:

> Any involvement of a child or young person below 18 in sexual activity for which remuneration of cash or in kind is given to the young person or a third person or persons. The perpetrator will have power over the child by virtue of one or more of the following – age, emotional maturity, gender, physical strength, intellect and economic and other resources e.g. access to drugs.

The guidance retains the language of 'children and young people involved in prostitution' and is less comprehensive in scope than the Westminster guidance issued in 2009. An obvious gap in the Scottish guidance is the idea of the 'dual approach', which emphasises the need to disrupt the activities of abusers as critical to the protection of young people. This has important implications for the development of local child protection policy, in terms of training and supporting professionals in the gathering evidence and sharing intelligence information, and for the partnership between police and other professional groups.

The idea of CSE is recognised, however, in other policy documents concerning young people and sexual abuse. The National Child Protection Guidance (2010) includes CSE as a type of child abuse. Similarly, statutory guidance on *Safeguarding Children Who May Have Been Trafficked* (Scottish Executive, 2009) identifies CSE as one of the reasons for, and outcomes of, trafficking. This guidance emphasises that professionals need to be alert to the signs that a child may be trafficked, and the need to develop local protocols on the issue.

The concept of 'grooming' is also recognised in Scottish legislation via the *Protection of Children and Prevention of Sexual Offences (Scotland) Act 2005*. This includes 'meeting a child following certain preliminary contact' (s1); that is, where a person arranges to meet a child who is under 18, having communicated with them on at least one previous occasion (in person, via the Internet or via other technologies), with the intention of performing sexual activity on the child. However, there is a significant lack of evidence regarding the extent to which this legislation has been applied to cases of CSE in Scotland (e.g. Association of Chief Police Officers' (ACPO) submission to the Petitions Committee, 2011). This has raised questions about how well CSE is being recognised, and whether appropriate action is being taken against abusers.

More recently, it has been argued that policy and practice concerning CSE have not kept pace with the rest of the UK. This position has been most strongly advocated by the children's charity Barnardo's, which, since the late 1990s, has been at the forefront of developing work to support children and young people affected by sexual exploitation across the UK (Barnardo's, 2011a). This has resulted in a petition to the Scottish Government that was examined by the Petitions Committee in July 2011. The Barnardo's petition asked the Scottish Government to:

- commission new research on the nature and scope of CSE in Scotland;
- report back on all action points set out in the 2003 Scottish Government guidance on Vulnerable Children and Young People Sexual Exploitation Through Prostitution; and

- review and develop dedicated Scottish Government guidelines on CSE, updating the 2003 guidance and incorporating the relevant parts of the 2010 National Child Protection Guidelines (http://scottish.parliament.uk/GettingInvolved/Petitions/PE01393).

Local authorities and other relevant organisations were invited in late 2011 to submit their views to the Petitions Committee, firstly in response to the question of whether more research into CSE should be commissioned; and secondly, whether the Scottish Government should update the 2003 guidance (see www.scotland.gov.uk/petitions for access to these submissions). Seven submissions were received from NHS area health boards, ACPO, Glasgow City Council and an independent agency working with young people in relation to Internet exploitation. The responses are interesting as they provide some insight into the current views of practitioners. Obviously, the sample is small and it may well be the case that only the most pro-active and engaged with the issue have responded (Barnardo's, in a letter to the Committee, expresses disappointment at the level of response). However, they can be considered alongside the views of practitioners attending the expert seminar which took place as part of our review. Whilst most agreed that more could be done, there was also a strong view that the issue was on the agenda and that there were some striking examples of good practice in Scotland, on the part of both statutory and voluntary agencies. Respondents to the Petitions Committee also emphasise that there is local activity taking place, through CEOP ambassadors in schools to raise awareness, local practice guidelines and so on.

Similarly, the submissions to the Petitions Committee recognise that the landscape has changed in respect to CSE, partly as a result of social and technological change, partly as a result of growing awareness of the issue. To this extent, there is an acknowledgement that guidance needs to be revisited and more research needs to take place. However, views are more mixed on the degree of regulation which should be introduced – from unequivocal agreement that more detailed statutory guidance is required (Lothian and Grampian area health boards) to the view that new research and information should be used by local Child Protection Committees to develop their own guidance. ACPO states that despite sustained partnership engagement, the implementation of local protocols has not been achieved – but seems less sure about how this should be addressed.

In the mean time, a series of prosecutions for CSE have taken place in England, attracting a high level of media attention. So far, there have been no such cases reported in Scotland. However, questions in the Scottish Parliament have drawn attention to the issue and requested information on the action to be taken by the Government. Following consideration of the evidence submitted, the Petitions Committee has also launched a public inquiry into CSE, due to report in May 2013. In January 2013, the Scottish Children's Minister announced a new strategy to address CSE. This will aim:

- to pilot improved identification of potential victims;
- to improve the way in which CSE is identified by the police;
- to encourage victims to come forward through a new National Confidential Forum; and
- to set up an expert group to capture the lessons of CSE cases elsewhere in the UK and make recommendations to the Scottish Government (http://www.scotland.gov.uk/News/Releases/2013/01/exploitation-action30012013).

Clearly, then, policy development in Scotland is proceeding rapidly. However, this raises interesting questions in respect to the research, policy and practice nexus. More specifically, to what extent does the existence of *specific* guidance and a practice framework predict the development of good practice? Alternatively, what are the policy and research conditions for the development of good practice in respect to young people who are sexually exploited?

The knowledge base

As noted above, the amount of research focusing specifically on CSE in Scotland is very limited indeed. No empirical research has taken place that examines the nature and prevalence of CSE throughout Scotland. Also, no research has examined how CSE is perceived by different professionals working with children and young people, or the role played by, and experience of, specialist CSE services. It is also worth noting that the studies that have been undertaken have had a narrow geographical focus, taking place in urban, central Scotland.

There are, however, two strands of research evidence that provide important information. Firstly, there is evidence from research studies in Scotland, some of which focus on CSE, but also research that examines the experiences of a wider group of children and young people who are disadvantaged in different ways, which suggests that these experiences may make them more vulnerable to CSE. Secondly, there is evidence from UK studies which have also included Scotland.

Following the 2003 guidance, some small-scale research studies took place, mainly focusing on the experiences of children and young people in the care system (Dillane, Hill and Munro, 2005; Munro, 2004), and those living in secure accommodation (Creegan, Scott and Smith, 2005). However, future research should also take account of other types of placement in Scotland, including those looked after at home (proportionately higher than in England). This 'at home' group is known to have poorer outcomes educationally (McClung and Gayle, 2011) and is especially vulnerable on a range of indicators. Whilst such differences are not definitive, they suggest some interesting lines of enquiry in respect to how the issue of CSE is being addressed by services – for example, that awareness raising in the care system does not focus solely on residential placements.

The socio-economic disadvantage that often constitutes the bedrock of CSE has been well-documented (Beckett, 2011; Brodie et al., 2011; Creegan, Scott and Smith, 2005; Dillane, Hill and Munro, 2005; Jago et al., 2011; Melrose, Barrett and Brodie, 1999; Scott and Skidmore, 2006). There is extensive evidence attesting to the high levels of child poverty in Scotland, as in the rest of the UK (Joseph Rowntree Foundation, 2011). Other factors include absence or exclusion from education, family disruption and abuse, and going missing from home or care. Obviously, such disadvantage is no less present in Scotland, but it is important to scrutinise some of the evidence within the present discussion. The absence of information on some of these indicators may, for example, highlight information gaps which may be significant when considering the need for new guidance for professionals working with young people.

Going missing from home and care is widely recognised as placing young people at increased risk of CSE. Wade (2002) surveyed 3,000 children and young people in Scottish schools. The study, which also drew on data from agencies working with runaways, estimated that 9,000 children run away or are forced to leave home each year in Scotland, where going missing is defined as 'overnight absence' (see also National Policing Improvement Agency, 2012). Other data highlights that, in terms of missing incidents and persons reported to police, Scotland reflects UK patterns, with concentration of such incidents amongst young people aged 12 to 17, and within this group a higher proportion of young women than young men (NPIA, 2011). There is evidence of higher rates of youth homelessness in Scotland than in other parts of the UK (Quilgars, Johnsen and Pleace, 2008). Stonewall Scotland (2009) has highlighted the vulnerability of young lesbian, gay, bisexual and transsexual (LGBT) people having sex with strangers in exchange for accommodation. Interventions to support young people who go missing have included follow-up from police (University of Stirling and Ipsos MORI Scotland, 2010) and evaluation of refuge provision (Malloch, 2006) – interestingly, the latter research highlighted that young people who were sexually exploited were identified by staff as especially challenging to work with, and the refuge provision was not perceived as appropriate. Similar findings were identified in earlier research into the use of secure accommodation (Creegan, Scott and Smith, 2005), which questioned the value of placing young women who had been sexually exploited in this type of provision, and the expertise of staff in dealing with these issues.

Studies examining the experience of violence amongst young people, including relationship-based violence, have included Scotland (Barter et al., 2009; Burman and Cartmel, 2005). The 'normalised' nature of sexual and other violence amongst gang-associated young people is also identified in Scottish research. Bannister and colleagues (2010) interviewed service providers and gang-involved young people in five case study sites throughout Scotland and included consideration of gender roles in gangs. It was found that girls and young women rarely participated in gangs on equal terms, but tended to participate on the basis of a relationship with a gang member. Girls were 'portrayed as the frequent catalyst of conflict' (para 3.18, p. 30) between gangs, either through spreading rumours or entering into relationships with boys from rival gangs, sleeping with multiple partners across territorial divisions as well as actually fighting with young men (para 2.36). Young men talked about gang-involved young women in 'derogatory and disparaging ways' (para 3.17) and a sexual double standard was in operation. Young women recognised this, and reported that young men were verbally abusive and controlling towards young women in the gang. Young women were acknowledged to be vulnerable to sexual assault, including rape, by more powerful gang members. These findings are significant in the light of findings emerging from research into the relationship between CSE and gang membership (Beckett et al., 2012) and the current inquiry into this issue in England by the Office for the Children's Commissioner (OCC, 2012a).

Scotland included: The evidence from UK studies

Concern continues to be expressed about the reliability of statistics regarding the prevalence of CSE in Scotland as in the rest of the UK (see, for example, All Party Parliamentary Group, 2012). These concerns can be related to a number of factors: an overall lack of awareness resulting in variable levels of reporting; different definitions of CSE; difficulties in extracting relevant information from existing databases; and a tendency to rely on information from organisations working with sexually exploited young people, rather than cross-sections of the population. There is also a skewing of data towards girls, and a concomitant lack of information about boys who are sexually exploited (Lillywhite and Skidmore, 2006; Asquith and Turner, 2008; Melrose, 2010).

CEOP's (2011) 'thematic assessment' produced a UK-wide audit of current knowledge regarding the scale of CSE using data from police forces, Local Safeguarding Children's Boards (LSCBs), children's services and service providers. However, no separate analysis was carried out on the Scottish information and there are no plans to undertake this (CEOP, 2012, personal communication). Scott and Skidmore's (2006) sample of 557 young people in contact with Barnardo's services throughout the UK did not seek to explore differences according to UK country of origin – but this study reinforces the key point, that the life experiences and conditions which may place children and young people at risk of CSE are likely to be similar in Scotland, and at present there is no data which suggests a difference in the scale of the problem.

Similar issues have been identified in regard to data on trafficking, including trafficking for CSE. Data on trafficking is also relevant to thinking about the scale of CSE in Scotland. This can include trafficking from abroad as well as the movement of children and young people around the UK. Research carried out for the Scottish Commissioner for Children and Young People (2011) analysed statistics from the UK Border Agency Office for Scotland and Northern Ireland regarding

National Referral Mechanism referrals of children received between April 2009 and August 2010. A total of 14 referrals had been received, and of these five demonstrated reasonable grounds for suspecting they had been trafficked. The characteristics of these 14 were examined: three were male and 11 female. In ten of the cases the exploitation was sexual; in four cases it was forced labour; there was one case of domestic servitude (in one case both sexual exploitation and domestic servitude were alleged). The majority of these involved children aged 14–18, though two children were under five.

The same research study also obtained further data from CEOP regarding trafficking between March 2007 and February 2010. Of the 17 cases recorded, four were identified as trafficking for CSE. The authors note, therefore, the need to recognise that the trafficking of young people takes place for many different types of exploitation, and should not be assumed to involve sexual exploitation. Marie and Skidmore (2007) surveyed Barnardo's specialist services for sexually exploited young people, plus a smaller number of services working with children who go missing from home or care. This survey investigated services' direct and indirect knowledge regarding internal trafficking, specifically the number of internally trafficked young people they had supported, who had trafficked them, and where to and from. Seventy-six young people were identified by 16 services as having been internally trafficked. The majority of these were young women. Young people were moved from places in Scotland or the north of England to Glasgow, as well as from Glasgow to Edinburgh, London or Belfast and other places in Northern Ireland. Young people were also thought to be moved from Northern Ireland to Scotland by boat.

Child sexual exploitation in Scotland: The same, but different?

The social disadvantage and vulnerabilities identified as significant in relation to CSE elsewhere in the UK are, therefore, equally visible in Scotland. To this extent, and entirely unsurprisingly, it can be concluded that the nature of CSE in Scotland is largely similar to elsewhere. A slight proviso may be given in terms of geography – most of the evidence appears (though this is not always explicit) to relate to urban areas, and there is less information on small town and rural areas.

Whilst decisions have still to be taken regarding precise policy measures, one might predict that Scotland will follow the English and Welsh route. Traditionally, child protection policy in Scotland has been characterised by many similarities with that in England, Wales and Northern Ireland (McGhee and Waterhouse, 2011), even whilst there is interaction with specific cultural and historical features. The Children (Scotland) Act 1995 reflects the same principles as those of the Children Act 1989 in England, making the welfare of the child paramount and emphasising the need for a coordinated agency response from social care working with education and health services. Specifically, an increased emphasis on the integration of services and the importance of a coordinated response has been evident, reflected in the Getting It Right for Every Child (GIRFEC) approach (Scottish Executive, 2001), which shares many of the principles of Every Child Matters.

The development of expertise regarding CSE is also more visible in England and Wales, as new institutions have developed through which discussion, debate and new information is filtered. The establishment and development of the work of the Centre for Exploitation and Online Protection (CEOP) as an arm of the police has ensured that this area of work has high standing in the public realm. Organisations such as the National Working Group on Sexual Exploitation, public inquiries such as that being undertaken by the Office for the Children's Commissioner and a high level of media interest serve to reinforce the issue as one of public concern.

However, the evidence also challenges, arguably, the efficacy of statutory guidance in improving practice in relation to CSE in England and Wales. Jago and colleagues (2011) carried out a national study examining the extent to which LSCBs were actively implementing the provisions of the national guidance issued in England in 2009 and found that only a quarter were doing so. The extent of inter-agency working varied in terms of both quantity and quality, and less than a quarter of LSCBs were protecting children and proactively disrupting and prosecuting abusers, as envisaged in the dual approach outlined in the guidance (DCSF, 2009). Overall, the study concluded that the impact of the guidance had been 'limited' and that 'local histories and circumstances emerge as more influential than national policy or guidance' (p. 113). Similarly, a review of local protocols in Wales found that awareness and knowledge of these was limited to key strategic officers and individual practitioners with direct experience of cases of CSE (Clutton and Coles, 2009).

Such evidence challenges the view that the introduction of national guidance invariably permeates local policy and practice, especially where this is not backed by appropriate expertise and resources. This is important given the initial findings from practitioners in the expert seminar, which indicated considerable differences in knowledge and practice relating to CSE. Those present at the seminar were in agreement regarding the routes through which young people became exploited, but there were differences in the extent to which individuals felt the issue was being identified and addressed throughout Scotland. The question of how far guidance can be efficacious is still more problematic in the present policy and economic context, where the overall net of support to vulnerable young people and their families is being reduced (Featherstone, Broadhurst and Holt, 2012). To some extent, therefore, the effectiveness of new guidance on CSE in Scotland will be contingent on how Scotland's government protects welfare agencies and welfare support.

Where next?

> The highway code does not tell you how to drive, but how to survive the journey by flagging situations where danger may be lurking and extra vigilance is required.
>
> (Pawson et al., 2005: 34)

This chapter has reviewed the nature of the evidence base regarding CSE in Scotland. It has demonstrated that there are, unsurprisingly, more similarities than differences in the understanding of, and responses to, CSE in England. This can be explained by reference to the fact that the two countries share very similar histories in respect to child protection policies more generally, and share a broadly similar media environment. However, within that environment there are certain differences in terms of reference points, and the perception of difference in the history of the institutions associated with child protection. That said, as with other policy areas such as health, more careful consideration of the landscape indicates that the 'direction of travel' in terms of overall policy is in fact similar to that in other parts of the UK.

At the time of writing, many issues concerning CSE policy development in Scotland are still to be resolved. As illustrated above, these depend on the interaction of a range of factors. If there are lessons to be learnt, these perhaps relate to the importance of a knowledge base and recognition of the starting points of the Child Protection Committees and practitioners who will be responsible for safeguarding young people at risk of CSE. This should include acknowledgement of the disputed and contingent nature of CSE, which cannot be resolved through statutory guidance. To this extent, a greater focus on the structures of social disadvantage which underpin CSE, and the support afforded services working with young people more generally, may be most critical to addressing the problem.

7

Missing from Discourse: South Asian Young Women and Sexual Exploitation

Nicola Sharp

Introduction

The literature on child sexual exploitation (CSE) has been criticised for remaining implicitly centred on young white women, with research presenting these young women as a homogenous group, assuming similarities across racial and ethnic boundaries (Ward and Patel, 2006). This chapter addresses the neglect of black and minority ethnic young women in the dominant discourse of CSE in the UK. It does this by exploring 'going missing' as a recognised indicator of CSE vis-à-vis South Asian young women seeking to exit the threat or reality of forced marriage.

Current practice identifies particular types of risk for young black and minority ethnic women to the exclusion of other forms. This means that whilst 'honour based violence' is commonly recognised as a risk related to running away, the risk of CSE remains unnoticed. I argue that practitioners fail to consider how the intersections of age, gender and ethnicity lead to particular experiences for black and minority ethnic young runaways which, when mediated through wider systems of inequality, result in high levels of vulnerability to CSE.

This analysis focuses on children and young people from South Asian backgrounds because they are highly visible within reported cases of forced marriage (Kazimirski et al., 2009). This is likely to reflect the fact that there is a large and established South Asian population in the UK (FCO, HO and NHS, 2007) and a relatively high proportion of young people in the British Bangladeshi and Pakistani communities who are at marriageable age (Samad and Eade, 2002). However, it is important to acknowledge that forced marriage also affects children and young people from African, Middle Eastern and some Eastern European communities (Kazimirski et al., 2009; Sharp, 2010).

Going missing and forced marriage

Police statistics estimate that approximately 216,000 people were reported missing in 2010–11. The same data show that children and young people under 18 years of age are more likely than adults to go missing, representing 66 per cent of all missing incidents (NPIA, 2011). Yet whereas adults have the 'right' to go missing, this is not the case for children and young people, who are recognised in law as 'vulnerable' and therefore in need of additional protection from the risks posed to them by different forms of harm (Barter et al., 2009).

This is problematic when considering the policy response to forced marriage because the overwhelming approach in the UK has been to encourage individuals to exit the abusive situation (Phillips and Dustin, 2004). So, whilst 'going missing' to escape abuse is recognised and accepted as a protective response by adults, this is not the case for children and young people. For this group, the act of running away is instead framed within a deficit-focused, problem model and is not viewed as a form of resilience.

Despite this, multi-agency practice guidelines recognise that both male and female victims of forced marriage may feel that running away is their only option (HM Government, 2009; 2010a, b). This was first acknowledged in policy discussions by the Working Group on Forced Marriage when politicians heard evidence of the 'plight of many young women who had runaway to escape forced marriage' (Home Office Communications Directorate, 2000: 15). At the same time, concern was expressed by police forces that young females from some ethnic minority groups were 'running away from arranged marriages, domestic violence within such marriages or the prospect of an arranged marriage' (Newiss, 1999: 33).

There is a significant overlap in the profiles of victims of forced marriage and under-18s who go missing; overwhelmingly young women between 14 and 15 years of age (Kazimirski et al., 2009; NPIA, 2011). However, the picture in relation to ethnicity is more mixed. Jha (2004) suggests that the 'problem' of runaway boys and girls affects only a very small part of the Asian population. Because they are fearful of the loss of honour and respect for themselves and their families as a result of running away these young people may be more likely than those from other ethnic groups to continue coping with a difficult home situation and only leave as a last resort (Akhtar, 2002; Izzidien, 2008; Safe on the Streets Research Team, 1999). They may also risk a more final separation from family and community as a result of ensuing stigma and shame (Kelly et al., 1995).

Similarly Franks (2004) observes that lower lifetime running rates amongst South Asian young people may be connected to a high degree of surveillance experienced by some South Asian girls, making it more difficult for them to leave. Kazimirski and colleagues (2009) have noted that victims of forced marriage are often severely restricted in their movements. In this scenario, girls and young women may to have to make a premeditated escape (Akhtar, 2002; Safe on the Streets Research Team, 1999) and may require more intensive support in living away from home compared to their white counterparts since they may not have been equipped with independent living skills (Franks, 2004; Jha, 2004).

In contrast, research undertaken by Safe on the Streets Research Team (1999) suggests a different picture, with professionals identifying broadly similar rates of running away across ethnic groups, but suggesting that this behaviour might be less visible amongst Asian groups. For example, young runaways from Asian communities may not hang around on the streets for fear of the risk of being seen by somebody who knows their family (Akhtar, 2002).

Furthermore a study by Biehal and colleagues (2003) suggests that minority ethnic groups are more likely to go missing as teenagers after finding that 26 per cent of Asian young people who had gone missing did so between 13 and 17 years of age, compared to just 14 per cent of white teenagers in the same age group. The study goes on to note a significant relationship between gender and ethnic origin amongst those going missing. Women of Asian origin aged 18–25 were more likely to go missing following conflict with their parents regarding entering or remaining in a marriage than women from other ethnic age groups.

In addition to age, gender and ethnicity, risks associated with forced marriage and running away highlight other factors such as sexuality and disability. For instance, higher than average running away rates exist for young people who identify themselves as gay or lesbian

(Rees and Lee, 2005). Similarly an individual may be at greater risk of forced marriage if they are lesbian, gay, bisexual or transgender, as their parents may feel that, by forcing them to marry, their sexuality or gender identity will not be questioned and/or that marriage will 'cure' them of what are perceived to be 'abnormal' sexual practices (HM Government, 2009).

Research also suggests higher than average running away rates for young people who define themselves as being disabled or as having difficulties with learning (Rees and Lee, 2005). In cases of forced marriage disability is believed to be vastly under-reported (HM Government, 2010b), but one of the motives for forced marriage has been identified as ensuring ongoing care for a child or vulnerable adult with special needs. In some cases this may involve what Khanum (2008) terms 'false marriage' – circumstances in which a young person may consent to an arranged marriage but is not given critical information about the other party such as details of disability.

The risk of honour based violence

It is widely accepted that policy initiatives facilitating escape from abusive situations are crucial for adults and young people alike. But the 'exit' approach has been criticised for a number of reasons, not least because it imposes the burden of resolving the conflict on the individual without addressing the power relations that generate individual cases (Shachar, 2001). This is believed to result in an ongoing risk of harm to the individual and an overwhelming focus on protection (Philips and Dustin, 2004).

Evidence certainly suggests that some families will go to considerable lengths to find and bring back young women who have fled a forced marriage (Izzidien, 2008; HM Government, 2009; Home Office Communications Directorate, 2000). In many cases this will involve reporting the young person as 'missing' believing that the police will disclose the whereabouts of the victim or return them to the abuser (Bokhari, 2009; NPIA, 2009). Other methods used by families seeking to locate missing young women may include: falsely accusing them of theft; utilising extended family networks; contacting community leaders; paying 'bounty hunters' and private investigators; tracing individuals through medical and dental records, national insurance numbers, benefit records or school/college records; circulating details of the missing person to local taxi drivers, members of the community and shopkeepers; and contacting people within the Asian community who hold positions of power, such as social services and Members of Parliament (Akhtar, 2002; HM Government, 2009; 2010a; Home Office Communications Directorate, 2000; NPIA, 2010).

Once located, a young runaway may be abducted or kidnapped. Professionals working to support young runaways highlight particular concerns for Asian young people who may suffer harsh punishment and other repercussions on returning home from a perceived runaway incident (Social Exclusion Unit, 2002; Stein et al., 1994). Jha (2004) notes that runaway girls from Asian communities may be viewed as having defied the Asian code of behaviour and thereby have brought disgrace on their families. In extreme cases the young person may then be killed as a means of restoring the family 'honour' (Akhtar, 2002; Brandon and Hafez, 2008; Phillips, 2007).

This is in line with research that identifies a strong link between homicides in a domestic violence context and 'attempts to leave' (CAADA, 2012). Yet whilst the 'typical' pattern of domestic homicide within the UK is of a man killing his ex-partner or wife, minority ethnic women are also at risk of violence from their fathers, brothers and cousins, who may kill them in the name of 'honour' (Phillips, 2007). Indeed forced marriage cases reported in the press illustrate how the discovery of plans to run away have resulted in some young South Asian women being murdered by family members and, in many cases, reported as 'missing' in an attempt to cover up the crime (ACPO/ NPIA, 2008; NPIA, 2010).

Other repercussions may include the young person being held prisoner until they 'agree' to the marriage. If community gossip suggests that a girl was 'sleeping around' when she was missing then it may only be possible to secure a spouse by sending her abroad where her reputation is less likely to be damaged (Bokhari, 2009; Brandon and Hafez, 2008; Khanum, 2008). In this way, forced marriage is used as a mechanism to protect against the social rejection associated with being labelled a 'prostitute' (Richardson et al., 2009).

It is, of course, useful to assert a certain degree of commonality amongst the experiences of South Asian women when this translates into a good understanding of the risks facing them and the commissioning of effective support services. However, the danger is that asserting this commonality leads to an overemphasis of the 'difference' between their experiences and those of white women. These 'differences' are then assumed to be culturally-based and result in an essentialist and absolutist construction of South Asian young women that overlooks their agency and which constructs a sense of 'collective victimhood' (Thiara and Gill, 2010)

Meetoo and Mirza (2007) observe that, as a result of this, particular 'types' of violence facing South Asian girls and women are sensationalised, thereby entrenching stereotypes of some cultures on one hand whilst ignoring risk situations on the other. Thus, whilst honour-based violence is increasingly recognised by professionals (NPIA, 2009; HM Government, 2009) as a risk for South Asian women seeking to exit forced marriage, CSE is not highlighted as a particular risk for runaways seeking to escape forced marriage in the UK context. This is despite successive studies showing that going missing is one of the primary risk indicators for involvement in sexual exploitation (Barnardo's, 2009, 2011a, b; Beckett, 2011; Jago et al., 2011; Kelly et al., 1995; OCC, 2012a; Pearce, Williams and Galvin, 2002; Rees and Lee, 2005; Safe on the Streets, 1999; Scott and Skidmore, 2006; Stein et al., 1994).

Missing as an indicator of child sexual exploitation

Whilst many young people who run away will stay with families or friends (Rees, 2011) others will find themselves in risky situations and be vulnerable to the risk of sexual exploitation (CEOP, 2011; Jago and Pearce, 2008; Pearce, 2009; Pearce, Williams and Galvin, 2002). A missing child is believed to be at risk from sexual exploitation, irrespective of the length of time they are away from home or a caring environment (CEOP, 2011; Plass, 2007). Indeed, such is the link between going missing and CSE that Scott and Skidmore (2006: 23) describe it in a two-year evaluation of support for sexually exploited children as 'the most immediate indicator of vulnerability'. The link between missing and CSE is also identified by CEOP (2011) as particularly 'striking' within its national scoping study on CSE. Victims' experiences of running away or going missing featured in just over half the cases in the dataset where this information was recorded.

Where CSE is a cause of going missing, missing incidents are likely to form part of the 'grooming process' where an abusive adult is a significant pull factor and may encourage this behaviour. As such there is growing consensus that those children and young people who are sexually exploited are likely to 'go missing' from home or care on a regular basis and for short periods of time (CEOP, 2011). Incidents where children and young people go to meet someone by whom they have been groomed online may also only come to light when the child goes missing (CEOP, 2011). Although not all children who run away will be sexually exploited, an estimated 90 per cent of children who are sexually exploited will run away or go missing (DCSF, 2009).

Alternatively, CSE can be a consequence of going missing in situations where a child is pushed from their place of residence and is identified as vulnerable by potential exploiters. For instance, a child or young person who has run away may spend an increasing amount of time on the streets and become involved with other vulnerable young people and risky adults through a need for somewhere to hang out and to achieve acceptance (Scott and Skidmore, 2006). Abusive adults may even specifically target locations that runaways are known to frequent (Kelly et al., 1995).

In a study exploring how Bangladeshi young women experience CSE, Ward and Patel (2006) note that the outcome of family-based risk factors and stressors is that young women may seek solutions to their problems outside the home and family by running away and becoming engaged in street-based socialising. In this study, young women were reportedly meeting men and forming relationships which inevitably met with disapproval and conflict within the family. The authors note that, whilst this might not be dissimilar to social groups within the white community, it was evident there were additional cultural pressures for Bangladeshi young women. These pressures led to high levels of conflict between parents and their children as a result of young people adopting different values and traditions. Relationships were therefore usually highly secretive and hidden, adding a further risk dimension to the young women's lives.

Plass (1997) and Biehal and colleagues (2003) suggest that gender plays an important role in risk related to running away, with more girls than boys reporting experiences of risk and dangers (see also Thrane, Yoder and Chen, 2011; Van Dongen and Dawson, 2009). Almost a third of young runaways in a study by Biehal and colleagues (2003) said they had stayed with a stranger. Similarly, the most recent 'Still Running' report by the Children's Society (Rees, 2011) found that one in nine young people said they had resorted to doing 'other things' in order to survive such as exchanging sex for food and accommodation (cf. CEOP, 2011; Harris and Robinson, 2007; Jago et al., 2011).

Pearce, Williams and Galvin (2002) also suggest that if a running career evolves so that a young person moves from their immediate area into an unfamiliar area, they become increasingly vulnerable to exploitation. This is because movement into an unfamiliar area means that previous coping mechanisms based on local knowledge can become undermined. Due to safety issues, young people seeking to exit a forced marriage are likely to travel long distances to other parts of the country in order to be further away from home and actively avoid contact with their families, communities and networks (Safe on the Streets, 1999; Akhtar, 2002).

Another risk factor common to both CSE and forced marriage is going missing from school. It is observed that some British Asian girls may simply disappear from school altogether after being withdrawn from education early for the purposes of marriage. Others may be absent for short but persistent periods of time, for example, just before the summer holidays when they may be taken abroad to meet a spouse (Akhtar, 2002; Home Affairs Committee, 2008; Kazimirski, 2009). In their exploration of young people not employed, in education or training (NEET), Britton and colleagues (2002) found that a number of the Pakistani and Bangladeshi girls they interviewed reported leaving school as a consequence of running away from attempted or actual 'arranged' marriages to domestic violence refuges.

Going missing, forced marriage and child sexual exploitation

An extensive review of the research literature on CSE identifies only one research study that directly links running away with forced marriage and CSE. Undertaken by Smeaton (2009) this piece of research explored the experiences of 'detached' children and young people on the streets in the UK and presented one case study featuring a 15-year-old sexually abused by a family friend and physically abused by his father. After threats to force him into marriage, the young man ran away and stayed with a number of older men, swapping sex for accommodation.

The possibility that this might also be the experience of young women is further identified within two studies. The first, an in-depth study of four South Asian young runaways aged between 15 and 17 highlights vulnerability to CSE in the account of one young woman. In an attempt to flee a forced marriage she ran away to Manchester from another city with no money or possessions and was found hanging around a risky area with nowhere to go (Franks, 2004).

The second, a piece of exploratory research into CSE within Northern Ireland by Beckett (2011), notes links between CSE and going missing as well as between CSE and Forced Marriage Protection Orders. However it is not clear whether all three issues are linked since the forced marriage element of the findings did not emerge as a significant issue of concern within the qualitative data, meaning that the issue was not explored further.

More evidence of the links between these issues can be identified when the term 'going missing' is considered in its widest form. The missing continuum developed by Biehal and colleagues (2003) illustrates that the term 'runaway' represents only a small proportion of those who go missing and does not include those who have been forcibly removed by another person for example. Parental abduction as a feature of forced marriage can therefore result in sexual exploitation where the parents of a young person seek forcibly to remove the young person from the UK and present them with a spouse/marriage abroad (Kazimirski et al., 2009).

Although parental abduction and kidnapping are recognised within the range of criminal offences relevant to cases of forced marriage, there is less recognition that this scenario is likely to be a form of trafficking for sexual exploitation under the Sexual Offences Act introduced in 2003. This is because Section 57 of the Sexual Offences Act (2003) defines trafficking for sexual exploitation as involving circumstances in which the travel of a young person into, within or out of the UK is arranged in the belief that it is likely that rape or a child sexual offence will be committed against them (Asquith and Turner, 2008; Bokhari, 2009; Mikhail, 2002).

One notable exception is a strategic threat assessment of child trafficking undertaken by the Child Exploitation and Online Protection Centre (CEOP), which identified eight cases where girls were believed to have been trafficked and forced into marriage. Three of these cases were related to British Asian girls living in the East Midlands, two of whom were to be married in Bangladesh and one who was to be taken to Leicester to get married (CEOP, 2010).

Similarly there is a strong likelihood that young people already forced into marriage may be subjected to repeated rape and ongoing domestic abuse within the marriage. In some cases, this may be perpetrated by members of the extended family (HM Government, 2009).

It is additionally recognised that, like trafficking, forced marriage and CSE are both frequently motivated by financial gain. The policy definition of CSE used by the Department for Education (2011) recognises that a third person or persons may receive a benefit from CSE and that, in all cases, those exploiting the child/young person have power over them by virtue of their age, gender, intellect, physical strength and/or economic or other resources.

A constitutive model of intersectionality

Thiara and Gill (2010) criticise theory and research related to violence against women and girls which seeks to 'add on' issues of ethnicity and culture rather than positioning different forms of violence within existing explanatory frameworks. They argue that rather than enhancing understanding of cultural differences and practices (an approach that is typical of additive intersectionality) the 'constitutive model of intersectionality' should be used instead. This means understanding the experiences of black and minority ethnic girls as they are mediated through systems of inequality (race, class, nationality) whilst at the same time recognising different levels of agency amongst women from diverse backgrounds. In particular, access to resources and the restrictions resulting from them are considered to be integral to analysing situations of black and white women alike.

This reinforces the view of Shachar (2001), who argues that when public authorities develop routes of safety that rely on the individual's right to leave, they also need to address the substantive conditions that make the right to leave a viable option. Here parallels can be drawn with women living in the UK on spousal visas who, until very recently, were unable to escape abusive partners because they did not have access to welfare benefits and refuge accommodation as a consequence of their immigration status. The result was that these women faced a stark choice: either to stay with their abuser and risk their lives or leave and risk financial and sexual exploitation (Southall Black Sisters, 2008).

It is therefore surprising that the shortage of accessible accommodation for young females aged 16–17 is not recognised within the forced marriage literature even though a recent consultation on the Government definition of domestic violence notes that:

> Currently, many refuges can only offer accommodation to victims who are 18 or over and this can act as a barrier for those who are trying to leave their current home in order to escape abuse.
>
> (HO, 2011a: 18)

Moreover young women from minority ethnic backgrounds experience particular difficulties in locating culturally specific service provision. This is further complicated in circumstances where young runways leave home with a partner of their choice since only one specialist service exists for male and female couples fleeing family violence, including cases of honour-based violence (Quilgars and Pleace, 2010). These problems are only likely to be exacerbated following the recent Government decision to lower the age within the domestic violence definition from 18 to 16 (HO, 2011a).

Research also suggests that young Asian runaways are less likely than their white counterparts to turn to wider kin or attempt to utilise support within their communities when they go missing, again due to the dangers associated with their leaving (Rees, 2011). Furthermore, victims of forced marriage are particularly unlikely to approach statutory agencies (Safe on the Streets Research Team, 1999). Evidence shows that access to mainstream services for young runaways from minority groups is hindered because such services are not publicised in an appropriate way (Izzidien, 2008). Due to their 'white nature' there is a perceived lack of cultural awareness and sensitivity amongst agency workers towards these groups (Franks, 2004; Safe on the Streets Research Team, 1999).

Akhtar (2002) and Jha (2004) observe that even when culturally specific agencies are identified, girls and young women from South Asian backgrounds face a dilemma in seeking their support. In some cases, Asian social workers fail to evoke confidence since the young people fear they may be prone to sympathising with their parents and breach confidentiality by revealing to their family where they are. This is consistent with evidence submitted to the Social Exclusion Unit (2002), which suggested that because Asian families are believed to be more likely to keep their distance from statutory agencies, young Asian runaways may be less familiar with how social services, schools, teachers and the police operate and more distrustful of them than other young runways (see also CEOP, 2011).

Research by Kazimirski and colleagues (2009) further suggests that forced marriage victims over the age of 16 may not be considered by the local authority as requiring a child protection response. In this study, children's services were unwilling to get involved in forced marriage cases involving 16–17 year olds who were able-bodied and mentally stable. Cases of threatened forced marriage without associated physical abuse also tended to be seen as lower priority. Meetoo and Mirza (2007) cite Radford and Tsutsumi (2004), who assert that whilst feminists have seen the 'risk discourse' as an opportunity for opening up a dialogue with key agencies, uncovering violence and getting it taken seriously by the police and the courts, it has also meant rationing strategies to women who are deemed 'most at risk', thus denying protection to the majority (see also Coy and Kelly, 2011).

Conclusion

The focus on protection in forced marriage cases centres on risks associated with honour-based violence. Associated difficulties experienced by forced marriage victims, including heightened risk of CSE as a consequence of being missing, appear to be going unnoticed. This article has highlighted tensions between whether young people escaping forced marriage are located within domestic violence or child protection responses. These tensions, alongside evidence which suggests that not enough attention is paid to the abuse of adolescents, appears to indicate that this group of young people has escaped professional attention altogether.

Risk assessment related to forced marriage fails to take into account the way in which going missing is experienced when ethnicity intersects with age and gender. Similarly, risk assessment frameworks related to CSE do not take into account some of the more hidden problems and complexities that underpin this form of abuse as it may be occurring within a specific cultural context (Ward and Patel, 1996). Both models can therefore be criticised for locating abuse at the individual level and not within the context of 'deeply unequal, historical power differentials ... and inequalities' (Melrose, 2012b: 14).

Like white women who are at risk of violence as a result of patri-archal systems, this risk is amplified for some South Asian women, who face the additional risk of cultural and religious belief systems of honour and shame. Thus the tendency to individualisation in the discourse of risk combined with a multi-cultural approach to deal-ing with violent gendered practices within the private sphere of the family can lead to non-interventionism or what Mirza (2009) calls a 'multicultural paralysis'.

It is of course the interplay of going missing with other risk factors associated with CSE, taken together with exposure to someone who would take advantage of these vulnerabilities and inadequate protec-tive structures, that culminate in this form of abuse (Beckett, 2011). As Berelowitz and colleagues (OCC, 2012a) warn, professionals need to assess risk using multiple indicators not just 'going missing' as an indicator on its own since, in practice, there is substantial variation in the experience of particular risk factors amongst sexually exploited children, with individual cases characterised by a complex interplay of these factors and in some cases none of them (CEOP, 2011).

Nevertheless, as this analysis of 'going missing', forced marriage and sexual exploitation has illustrated, the possibility that a young woman who has fled a forced marriage is at risk of sexual exploita-tion should be considered, especially when other factors such as previous sexual abuse, disengagement from education and low self-esteem – all of which are features of both forced marriage and CSE cases – are present.

A young woman accessing a service for victims of forced marriage may choose not to disclose the experience of sexual exploitation if the professionals concerned do not explore what happened to her between fleeing the threat or reality of a forced marriage and access-ing safety. It is clear that the stigma and shame associated with CSE may be exacerbated for young South Asian women for whom the disclosure of sexual exploitation may in itself carry great risks. Indeed a recent study on sexual exploitation found that young people from minority ethnic backgrounds reported examples of their abusers seek-ing to control them through playing on fears associated with bringing shame on their families and the possibility of being threatened with forced marriage if they were to disclose the abuse (OCC, 2012a). These young people were aware that if their parents come to learn about their experience then this may increase the urgency and pressure felt by their parents in making their marriage choices and attempting to restore honour to the family.

Being alert to the possibility that young women running away from a forced marriage may also be at risk of CSE would therefore provide a significant addition to the conceptualisation of risk and could ensure that these young people receive a holistic response rather than just a 'forced marriage' response. If professionals do not consider the complexity of young women's identities and ask the right questions then it appears unlikely that they will provide the support required.

8

Partners in Care? Sexually Exploited Young People's Inclusion and Exclusion from Decision Making about Safeguarding

Camille Warrington

Introduction

> A lot of people have pushed us into things, have forced us to do things, and made a lot of decisions for us and we don't need the people who are there to help us to do it as well.
>
> (What Works for Us Group cited in Jago et al., 2011: 63)

This chapter considers the need to develop new ways of conceptualising young people affected by sexual exploitation as 'service users'. Specifically it seeks to address questions about what young people, rather than 'professionals', bring to the process of safeguarding. It considers the relevance of developing opportunities for young people to exert power and influence within service provision and the importance of this approach when responding to existing abusive relationships defined by control and domination. Drawing on research using in-depth interviews with service users it argues that the protective potential of services may be limited or maximised by the degree to which young people are involved in decisions about their care. It suggests that within this context young people's agency should be framed as a resource rather than a problem.

The chapter starts by placing the research study in context, presenting gaps in current knowledge and acknowledging the tension between children's participation and child protection within sexual exploitation services. It then outlines the research methods used in the study and presents examples from service users' accounts of accessing professional support for sexual exploitation. I propose that these narratives evidence the significance of concepts of control, involvement and participation for young people whose lives have been framed by limited choices and abuses of power. I argue that a commitment to enabling and supporting young people's involvement in decision making may be central to promoting their emotional and physical safety. This suggests looking beyond a consideration of service user involvement solely based on entitlement and recognising it as critical to the welfare of sexually exploited children and young people. Children's participation is thus seen as integrated with, rather than supplementary to, the aims of child protection.

Gaps in current knowledge

Children and young people's perspectives on engagement with professional welfare are rarely systematically recorded, disseminated or allowed to inform policy and practice (Charnley et al., 2009). Existing literature tends to focus on broader child protection service provision, particularly looked after, health and disability services (Cossar, Brandon and Jordan, 2011; Mainey, Ellis and Lewis, 2009; Rees et al., 2010; Voice, 2004). To date, within the field of child sexual exploitation (CSE) there is currently no literature or research focusing on young people's experiences of receiving support. Whilst a limited number of studies do include children and young people's perspectives (Coy, 2008; Melrose, Barrett and Brodie, 1999; Pearce, Williams and Galvin, 2002) comments about experiences of receiving professional support in relation to CSE are rarely considered or are ancillary to testimonies focusing on young people's experiences of abuse (Taylor-Browne, 2002).

It is possible that this absence results from a number of factors. These include the limited body of specialist services and professionals focusing on CSE within the UK (Jago and Pearce, 2008; Jago et al., 2011); ethical issues regarding engaging the children concerned in research and evaluation (Melrose, 2011); and resource implications of consultative or participatory research work with young people (Tisdall, Davis and Gallagher, 2008; Percy Smith and Thomas, 2010). I would suggest that this also represents a wider failure of adults to imagine and recognise vulnerable children's own abilities to observe, reflect on and analyse the professional services they engage with. This results from normative assumptions about children's limited capacity (James and Prout, 1990; Jenks, 2005; Lansdown, 2005) and enduring prejudices towards those who are marginalised, vulnerable or labelled 'hard to reach' (Dorling, 2011; Freire, 1970; Young, 1999; Wacquant, 2009). The study on which this discussion is based seeks to address this gap and starts from a belief that children and young people have unique knowledge and expertise. Furthermore it proposes that such knowledge provides insights on the relevance, efficacy and limitations of existing approaches to protecting victims of CSE.

Child protection and children's participation

The focus on the meaning and relevance of children's participation arises in response to evidence of specific tensions between principles of participation and protection within the field of CSE (Brown, 2006; Chase and Statham, 2004; Pearce, 2009; Warrington, 2010). This tension is rooted in the two seemingly contradictory positions on young people – that they are either 'victims' or agents of change – and which makes it difficult to conceive of them simultaneously as both. As Phoenix notes, safeguarding policy and procedures addressing CSE are unlikely to be 'structured to recognise both the victimisation of young people and their desires and abilities to fashion their own lives' (2004: 282). Such comments help to explain discrepancies between a commitment to children's participation within relevant national and international policy and guidance (CoE, 2010; DCSF, 2009) and a lack of clarity about what this means in practice (Jago et al., 2011).

Historically CSE campaigns have strategically downplayed notions of young people's agency and autonomy: an understandable response to a climate where children's access to support or justice has often been contingent on developing an understanding of them as passive and helpless victims (Brown, 2006; Melrose, this volume; Phoenix, 2004). Recognising the limits of children's own power and control within exploitative relationships is vital, yet as Pearce (2009: 4) points out, 'an uncritical acceptance of the definition of the child as a victim of abuse can undermine the development of same child's sense of agency'. This draws attention to the need for services designed to protect young people to avoid replicating the limited choices and disempowerment which may already characterise such young people's lives (Brown, 2006).

From practitioners' perspectives, the tension outlined above is often rooted in discrepancies between professionals' and young people's perception of risk (Jago et al., 2011). As one interviewee noted: 'The challenges of involving young people [in decision making] is that they [service users] obviously don't always think they're at risk'. Under these circumstances, service user participation may seem to impede the promotion of their protection. The seeming conflict between practitioner and service user understanding of risk provides justification for excluding or marginalising children's influence within decision making processes. Here child protection and participation are positioned in conflict and necessitate a hierarchy of values in which children's involvement may become marginalised. Practitioners interviewed suggested that even when children's participation was supported in principle practically it was challenging due to additional resource requirements or fears about involving young people in stressful or distressing decision making processes.

Set against this context the chapter seeks to explore how such tensions are experienced by sexual exploitation service users. It provides examples of where young people's own sense of involvement in safeguarding processes has been limited or promoted by different styles of practice and explores the possible significance of different approaches.

Research approach and methods

Before considering these ideas I present a brief overview of the study on which this discussion is based. A detailed account of the methodological approach can be found in Warrington (2013, forthcoming).

The findings on which this chapter is based are drawn from a qualitative study undertaken as part of a professional doctorate. The research aimed to explore the meaning of 'children's participation' within CSE services. The term 'child participation' here refers to young people's involvement in decision making in relation to personal welfare and safeguarding support. This contrasts with the tendency to conflate the term 'participation' solely with projects seeking to formalise children's representation and influence within strategic and policy arena (Hart, 2008; Hinton, 2008; Shier, 2001). This approach aligns with existing studies that explore children's involvement at the level of everyday social care practice (Kirby et al., 2003; Shemmings, 2000; Thomas and O'Kane, 1998; Trinder, 1997).

The research employed semi-structured, in-depth interviews with 20 young people using CSE services across England in 2011. Ten additional interviews were completed with specialist practitioners and a literature review was undertaken. Interviews with young people were conducted individually and, where requested, in pairs or small groups.

The young people who took part in the study were contacted through specialist voluntary sector CSE projects. Whilst all participants shared a similar service user identity and were engaged with professional support, they represented a diverse range of experiences of CSE. Where the nature of exploitation was shared by young people, variables included both online and offline abuse, internal trafficking, abuse by peers or by older men, abuse through a 'boyfriend', abuse through groups or individuals, exploitation occurring in party houses and exploitation via images sent via mobile phones or the Internet. These types of exploitation and risk are largely in keeping with findings from recent research (Beckett, 2011; CEOP, 2011; Jago et al., 2011). No mention was made in any interview of experiences of exchanging sex for money. The sample also included a degree of diversity in terms of age (14–19), gender (16 female: 4 male), ethnicity (17 white: 3 Black or minority ethnic) and family or care history.

Young people's inclusions and exclusion from decision making processes

What was striking throughout the interviews was the polarised ways in which young people described how they were involved or excluded from decision making in services. On the one hand they spoke about experiences in which they felt informed, involved and able to influence events, and on the other they gave examples where their rights to participate were overlooked or considered inappropriate and they remained marginalised from choices about their care.

In the following section these experiences are considered alongside the significance that young people attributed to them. Young people's involvement is considered both in relation to formal decision making processes (strategy and review meetings) relating to their care and wider processes of information sharing. The chapter then considers the specific significance of participatory principles for young people affected by sexual exploitation.

'Everybody's talking 'bout me'

Perhaps the most explicit demonstrations of young people's involvement or exclusion from decision making about their care were evidenced through accounts of strategy and review meetings. Such multi-agency meetings are significant for a number of reasons. Firstly they have come to be understood as a central aspect of safeguarding best practice in relation to supporting CSE victim (DCSF, 2009; Jago et al., 2011); secondly they represent critical opportunities for decision making, information sharing, risk assessment and planning; and thirdly their very presence acts as a signifier to young people of their status as 'service users': those whose lives are subject to scrutiny and intervention by multiple professionals. Unlike child protection case conferences, however, there is no obligation or specific guidance in policy about the need for children and young people or parents and carers to be present at CSE strategy or review meetings. This means that despite DCSF guidance stating that 'the wishes and feelings of children and young people ... should be sought and taken into account in reaching decisions about the provision of services which affect them' (2009: 13) there is little detail about what this means in practice.

When asked about the attendance of young people at these meetings, practitioners noted that whilst young people's attendance was sometimes understood as an ideal there were a number of challenges which prevented it. Reasons given for the exclusion of young people from these meetings included concerns regarding sharing third party information, conflict between young people and professionals' perspectives, the reluctance of many service users to attend and the potential for meetings to be unduly distressing for young people. Only one practitioner represented an area whose local safeguarding children's board (LSCB) systematically invited young people to attend CSE strategy meetings.

> On paper young people's views have to be taken into account – but in practice that is not what we find – and we still find really poor attitudes, and a blaming culture – they [young people] are seen as a problem and not seen as part of solution.
> (Voluntary Sector Project Manager discussing CSE strategy meetings)

In keeping with these messages young people described a spectrum of levels of involvement in these meetings. Only 13 of the 20 young people who participated in interviews referred to knowledge of professional meetings taking place in which their risk or experience of CSE was discussed and decisions about their care were taken. On the whole young people were not able to differentiate between different types of multi-agency meetings. There was an overarching sense that young people remained unclear about the purpose of many meetings and the different roles of the professionals who were attending. Evidence from interviews with young people and professionals suggested that time and again young people were overlooked as active stakeholders within this central aspect of safeguarding.

Despite these findings there was some evidence of instances where young people were invited to attend meetings and supported to have a meaningful input. Where barriers to service user inclusion were overcome, several individuals described welcoming opportunities to attend meetings and saw them as a chance to become informed about decisions being taken about them and represent themselves:

> In terms of the meetings with all the professionals and that – if you want to have an input, if you want to say something that you disagree with – that's your time to say it.
>
> (Ursula, 17)

For Ursula, a young woman accessing support from a specialist CSE project, the chance to attend meetings and represent herself was a welcome opportunity. She described it as enabling her to challenge professional assumptions made about her, influence decisions and hear what information was being shared with whom. Ursula shared examples of where her attendance in meetings allowed her to correct interpretations about her behaviour, such as her absence from school, explaining her circumstances more fully. Here she was able to inform the story being told about her and communicate the risks she experienced to professionals responsible for her care.

Elsewhere Stephanie talked about the importance of statutory social care support in enabling her personally to attend multi-agency meetings. She described one occasion where her social worker offered her the opportunity to look over information about her case prior to a strategy meeting which she and her parents were due to attend. This opportunity critically enabled her to request the removal of graphic details about her sexual activity from an account due to be read to her parents. Whilst recognising the need for her parents to learn of her sexual exploitation she was also able to challenge the necessity of including certain details. Stephanie's story draws attention to the sensitivity of information shared within these meetings and the complex dynamics that arise when discussing CSE in the presence of young people and parents or carers. Stephanie's case demonstrates the vital contribution of young people to these processes, providing an example of the ability of young people to identify successfully some of their own needs and help practitioners respond appropriately to them.

The above examples illustrate how young people's attendance at meetings could provide genuine opportunities for them to represent themselves and maintain some level of control within the safeguarding process. For young people whose lives were repeatedly interpreted and examined by multiple professionals, such inclusion appeared invaluable and often supported their willingness to continue engaging within these processes.

The importance of opportunities for young people to input into care-related decision making processes were echoed throughout the interviews. They reflected a broader group of comments about young people's simultaneous desire for specialist support alongside space and flexibility to inform the nature of that support. One young person described this careful balance as such:

> They explain what sexual exploitation is and help you get through it, but they make you kind of find your own way of dealing with it and – I don't know, it kind of calms you down in yourself and you have a chance to talk about it without you feeling crappy – because you've got a chance to make some input.
>
> (Scarlett, 16)

For other young people, opportunities to input into decision making were facilitated through their representation at meetings by a trusted adult advocating on their behalf. These included young people invited to attend meetings but who chose not to do so, usually to avoid anxiety or stress, and those who were not invited but were kept informed about them.

Young people described being supported by advocates in a variety of ways: through help preparing for meetings, representing their views within meetings, asking questions on their behalf and feeding back the content and decisions when young people were absent or uninvited. Again when young people recounted these experiences the importance of self-representation arose:

> Lucia [my CSE project worker] has helped me write stuff down. Lucia asks me if I'd like anything to be said in the meeting and it's helpful because, because sometimes everything gets said in a meeting without me even being there.
>
> (Phoebe, 17)

Young people clearly demonstrated an appetite to be informed and involved in these meetings in some way, either through advocates or in person, and to receive feedback from meetings they did not attend. Other young people, however, explained that attendance alone was not an automatic means to feeling involved and could at times compound their sense of powerlessness and mistrust. For some experiences of attending meetings represented more tokenistic participation and were associated with further marginalisation.

The excerpt below demonstrates that it is not simply a matter of inviting young people to share professionals' 'space' which creates a sense of inclusion and partnership, but also the terms on which this is undertaken.

INTERVIEWER: Have you been involved in any meetings about your care – like strategy meetings?

BETH: I don't know what's that?

SALLY: Where there's a room full of very, very important people ... [sarcastic tone] [pause] and they're all picking on you! ... yeah ... all the time.

BETH: You stick out like a sore thumb

SALLY: There's me in me trackies and hoodie and there's all them in their proper suits and I'm like ... can I go now? 'No Sally you cannot go for a fag.' ... fuck this then ... [laughter]

BETH: Our opinion don't count.

SALLY: They look at you and they say 'oh no mainstream school ...
        what? They're in a project? They're not going to school
        because they're mouthy little shits ...'
BETH: [interjecting] ... so then we don't have a say.

For Beth and Sally strategy or review meetings do not appear to
represent the 'opportunity' they do for Ursula, Stephanie or Phoebe.
Their expressions of anger and resentment about these processes
suggest that such meetings are a space in which they perceive themselves as neither listened to or welcome.

Crucially, Beth and Sally identify themselves as 'othered' or labelled
within the meeting space, repeatedly drawing attention to their
perceived image in the eyes of professionals. They suggest that they
have been invited into a space in which they do not fit and where
their difference from professionals is highlighted rather than minimised. Undercutting this is their sensitivity to what they believe to
be professionals' preconceived notions about them. Applying aspects
of Goffman's work on stigma (1963) we see how particular aspects of
young people's appearance, presentation and circumstance are interpreted by professionals as 'discrediting attributes' ('they look at you
and say, "oh no mainstream school?"'). This further limits the means
of those so labelled to redefine the situation to one in their favour
(Becker, 1963). Unlike previous examples, meetings are here depicted
as occasions in which existing images, and relations of power and
powerlessness, are reinforced rather than challenged.

In this example attempts to give the young women any real influence or control have at best left little impression and at worst did
not take place. This highlights how young people's nominal inclusion in formal information sharing processes may sometimes prove
disempowering. This supports Cornwall's theory of participation
in which she highlights the limits to the transfer of power possible
within 'invited spaces' where the terms are set by those who own and
control that space (2004). Cornwall reminds us that young people's
influence and role in decision making within such settings is vulnerable to tokenism or manipulation and remains highly dependent on
how such meetings are framed and managed.

Here and elsewhere comments suggest that existing marginalisation may be compounded by the actions (or perceived actions) of
professionals, further excluding young people from opportunities to

participate meaningfully in decision making about their care. They also reflect a recurring theme from interviews about many young people's sense of objectification within processes of care – aptly described by another young woman as the sense of 'feeling like you're being serviced.'

'Someone's missing init?' Exclusion from meetings

For other young people the right to attend, or indeed not attend, meetings was not an available option. Several interviewees noted that they were often not invited or informed about meetings or only found out due to their involvement with a voluntary sector project. For these young people CSE strategy and review meetings represented a space where they were actively excluded from processes of information sharing, often despite their express wishes to attend. Their limited knowledge about, and access to the content of, these meetings served further to emphasise young people powerlessness to represent themselves,

> Every so often they have a big massive meeting – and there's like 20 odd people there and it's like they know more about me than I do and I don't even get to go ... Sometimes afterwards we get this big massive report about everything they've talked about, about 20 pages long an' I think 'where did that come from?' 'where did that come from?' ... Someone's missing init? – Its like having a meeting without that person there – there's going to be a lot missing.
>
> (Alice, 15)

Alice highlights the irony of simultaneously recognising her centrality to the meeting alongside her physical absence. The attention she draws to the length of the report and the number of professionals attending, stand in stark contrast to both her own and her family's exclusion. The lack of her own voice within the report and her inability to recognise aspects of her own 'story' suggest this as an alienating process. Importantly, Alice does not suggest that people should not be discussing her, or making decisions about her, but rather that to do so without her involvement seems misguided, ill-informed and unjust. This discussion and similar remarks by other young people reflect an important distinction highlighted by Schofield and Thorburn (1996) between children's involvement in social care decision making and them actually making a decision themselves. Alice's desire is for a place around the table rather than an opportunity to take her own decisions. Schofield and Thorburn note a tendency in professional practice to conflate these two processes, leading to confusion about appropriate levels of young people's involvement. Understanding the modesty of Alice and other young people's desires to be informed and involved is important. They highlight how such claims do not undermine the authority of professionals authority, but potentially strengthen it by enabling decision making to be better informed and supporting young people's 'buy in' to the care plans that are made.

All of the examples above suggest how CSE strategy and review meetings can exist as both inclusive and exclusive spaces that promote or limit young people's meaningful participation. They highlight how young people's participation is not just about physical inclusion in decision making processes but about cultivating and supporting a sense of service users as genuine partners in promoting their own safety and wellbeing.

Information sharing: 'They expect you to tell them everything about your lives but tell you nothing about theirs'

Throughout the research and apparent in the quotes above is a central concern relating to remaining informed about where and how personal information about young people is shared. As Alice's quote suggests, discussions about information sharing often evoked images of information being dispersed to ever wider and more indistinct audiences – 'everyone' or 'everywhere'. Other participants conveyed a similar sense of an exponential loss of control over personal and intimate stories and the related feelings of exposure that ensued once accessing professional forms of support.

Over half of the interviewees (n = 13) provided examples of times when personal information about their abuse had been shared without their knowledge or consent. For many the realisation that such information had been passed on occurred by accident or chance. They described instances of encountering personal details about themselves and their 'case', held by those to whom they had not granted its safe holding:

> My Head teacher ... I didn't know he knew and he called me up ... he said 'Fiona, you're going to get through this – you're a strong

girl' and I was just sort of looking at him and now he sort of treats me differently. I just find it really awkward and I didn't know that he was involved in it ... I just think if they're going to get people involved, they need to let the young person know – I think the young person needs to be kept in the know the entire time.

(Fiona, 15)

Moments such as this were shockingly familiar amongst those interviewed. Understandably these unanticipated revelations were associated with a range of challenging emotions. These included: shame and embarrassment; disconcertion and indignation of hearing intimate histories and stories of sexual victimisation revealed; and an overarching loss of trust. Perhaps most crucially for this discussion they provided stark signifiers to young people of their lack of power to influence the movement of information and their representation to others. As Illy (16) explained:

Why do you think people are so scared to tell the police? It gets around and it's totally shameful. 'Oh you're that girl got raped by that man' – 'nah she didn't really get raped, she did it for money; she did it for cigs; she did it for a bottle'.

The belief that police will not, or cannot, protect victim's identity within a community is revealed here, alongside an expectation that young rape victims may become objects of gossip, shame and derision. Illy anticipates the possibility that being a known victim of rape may be reinterpreted by others in terms of prostitution and promiscuity. Such fears were familiar and highlighted specific sensitivities around information sharing associated with sexual exploitation. Here the desire of young people to avoid humiliation and maintain control over their well-being and self image overruled their need to access welfare support or advice.

The salience of these issues is also clearly heightened by previous experiences of breaches of trust by those seemingly closest to them. As Alice explained: 'because of my past – I have a really, really – how can I explain it? – I find it really hard to trust people'. Here, as with other respondents, attention is drawn to the direct impact of previous, exploitative relationships on young people's confidence and faith in all adults – professionals or otherwise.

Throughout these testimonies there appeared to be a clear, though rarely stated, parallel between some young people's experience of welfare services and aspects of their exploitative relationships. In one case a young woman remarked on the incongruity of situations, where workers 'expect you to tell them everything about your lives but then they tell you nothing about theirs' and compared this to the dynamics through which perpetrators operated, stating 'that's how the men work too'. Whilst critical differences in intent divide these two sets of relationships, the loss of control and humiliation experienced within abusive relationships can, at times, arise from professional carelessness, indiscretion or poor practice.

Despite these accounts it is important to recognise that young people did acknowledge the need for information about them to be shared. Where service users were kept informed about information sharing and were involved in the process (as in the case of Stephanie) it appeared to be largely accepted, even when it was described as uncomfortable. More than this, understanding the reasons for passing information on, and having an opportunity to inform that process, built confidence in the workers and services who applied these approaches.

> This here [sexual exploitation project] is confidential. Whatever gets said in this building stays in this building. Say if it's really, really, really important they have to report it – but if they don't think it's really important it stays confidential. But they always ask you first. They always tell you [if they're going to pass information on].
>
> (Beth, 19)

In this example Beth appears to accept information sharing by her sexual exploitation project due to her identification of it as exceptional practice ('say if it's really, really, really important') and the project's acknowledgement of her as a stakeholder in the distribution of that information ('they always ask you first. They always tell you'). Here as elsewhere, the degree to which young people saw themselves invited to be partners in their own care is directly linked with their willingness to engage and trust in systems of support.

Conclusion

This group of testimonies suggests that there are a number of similar concerns that cut across a diverse group of CSE service users' experiences of practice. Although outlining numerous aspects of good practice they also suggest that young people's experience of involvement in decision making about their care and protection remains unacceptably inconsistent and their participation rights continue to be overlooked. They highlight how professional discretion continues to determine whether to include or exclude young people from decision making about their care, to prevent service users from influencing how they and their situations are represented and defined, and to share personal and intimate information without consulting them.

Sexually exploited young people's decision's to share details about risks or abuse and engage with services are thus set against real fears about the subsequent loss of control, and further marginalisation that may result from these processes. When young people are considering their own needs for support it would appear that they are involved in complex decision making processes balancing harms that result from their relationships with perpetrators, and their interactions with professionals. Where young people were not given a means to influence decision making through legitimate processes or practice they described finding ways to resist or circumvent interventions.

From a professional perspective one might consider young people's choices to disengage with support irrational, ill-informed or short sighted. Yet we need to recognise that young people's choices to exert their power by resisting offers of professional support do appear to be rational, and perhaps more importantly, in many ways protective. Though the protection they offer is also coupled with risk, it seems critical to understand that these are not simply illogical acts of rebellion or disrespect, but often attempts to avoid humiliation, stigma and shame.

I would argue that these actions emphasise the need to adopt more participatory approaches to safeguarding that position children and young people's agency as a resource rather than a problem. Exploring how such an approach would look in practice undoubtedly presents challenges but ultimately may bear fruit where there is commitment to reducing risk whilst simultaneously empowering young people. Recognising young people as partners *in* (rather than simply recipients *of*) child protection provides an opportunity to further their trust, engagement and, subsequently, safety.

9

Constructs of Safety for Children in Care Affected by Sexual Exploitation

Lucie Shuker

Introduction

Links between child sexual exploitation (CSE) and the care system have been acknowledged for many years. Media coverage of a series of cases of 'child prostitution' involving local authority care in the 1970s triggered widespread recognition of the issue for the first time (Barrett and Brown, 2002). More recently these concerns were reignited in the media by the case of a victim of the Rochdale 'grooming ring' who had been placed a long distance from her home in a very expensive single occupancy unit, from which she regularly went missing and was abused. Despite prevention and identification being key themes of government guidance on sexual exploitation (DCSF, 2009) the Rochdale case suggests there remains a clear need for early intervention, and training for carers and professionals to recognise the signs of exploitation. In the absence of such intervention risk often escalates to the point where young people in care are moved between placements for their own safety and to disrupt an exploitative relationship. Whilst the objective of physical safety is crucial, this chapter argues that it should be achieved alongside both relational and psychological security. Where such holistic approaches are not taken, chronic insecurity is more likely, which can then become a risk factor for sexual exploitation in itself. The chapter begins by exploring the known links between the care system and risk of exploitation, before presenting a model for understanding the physical, relational and psychological aspects of safety and security for young people in care and who are affected by sexual exploitation.

Before proceeding it is important to acknowledge that whilst sexual exploitation affects young men and young women, there is little research that explores the needs of sexually exploited young men in the looked after population (Lillywhite and Skidmore, 2006). By drawing on existing research, this chapter will no doubt reflect this imbalance as well as the particular ways in which young women in care are likely to be treated, compared with their male peers.

In this discussion I employ the terminology of 'young people affected by sexual exploitation' to avoid the young people being objectified in the discussion (see Melrose, 2012a; this volume) and to acknowledge that sexual exploitation is an aspect of their experience rather than a 'master identity'.

The links between being looked after and sexual exploitation

Research suggests that most young people in England who are affected by sexual exploitation live at home with their families, but that children in the care system are disproportionately affected. A national 'snapshot' of young people at risk of, or experiencing, sexual exploitation who were being supported by statutory or voluntary agencies on 6 June 2011 revealed that of the 684 cases where data was provided for living situation, 21 per cent were in local authority care at the time (Jago et al., 2011). Again, 21 per cent of young people affected by sexual exploitation identified via submissions to the 'Child Sexual Exploitation in Gangs and Groups' inquiry were in care (OCC, 2012a). A thematic assessment of 'localised grooming' from 2008–11 found that of 896 known victims, 35 per cent were in care (CEOP, 2011). As a result of poor recognition, under-reporting and a lack of strategic investment in tackling CSE (Jago et al., 2011) most research reports exploring the prevalence and patterns of sexual exploitation qualify their findings as underestimates of the scale of the problem. Yet even if these figures are skewed, or somehow *over*-estimates, the number of looked after young people remains highly disproportionate to the general population of under-18-year-olds in England and Wales, of whom less than 1 per cent are in care (DfE, 2012; ONS, 2011; Welsh Government, 2012).

This over-representation of care backgrounds amongst young people affected by sexual exploitation has also been noted in studies with smaller samples. Pearce, Williams and Galvin (2002), for example, found that of 55 young women involved in CSE, 39 had experience of being in local authority care and 18 were homeless. Of 42 in-depth case histories of young people being supported by Barnardo's sexual exploitation services, 19 had been in care (Scott and Skidmore, 2006). Clutton and Coles (2007) report that of their sample of 367 children and young people risk assessed by a Welsh local authority, those at 'significant risk' of sexual exploitation (18 per cent) were most likely to be identified as the subject of care orders rather than as 'children in need'. Finally, retrospective research with adult women who were sexually exploited before the age of 18 has consistently identified experiences of local authority care as a situational context that facilitates entry into prostitution (Coy, 2008; Melrose, Barrett and Brodie, 1999; O' Neill, 2001).

Looked after children experience poorer outcomes than peers who live with their birth parents, but research has not robustly identified any independent effect of the care system on such outcomes, including the risk of sexual exploitation. Instead care is recognised to be a mediating experience that in some cases has an indirect influence on the risk of exploitation (Shaw and Butler, 1998) and which exacerbates the vulnerabilities that were created by the original abuse or neglect. Poor experiences at home (including neglect, parental substance abuse, disrupted and changing care placement experiences, physical or sexual abuse, or a general deficit of parenting) or then in care can 'push' young people out of home/care and into environments that increase the risk of being targeted by exploitative peers or adults (CEOP, 2011). These experiences, and the poor self-esteem that they often produce, then make young people less resilient to the 'pull' of exploitative relationships, where autonomy, excitement, gifts and someone who 'loves' them appear to be on offer (Scott and Skidmore, 2006). Various aspects of the care system can then present additional risks through exposing young people to situational hazards (Shaw et al., 1996). These include: peer introduction to exploitative men and lifestyles (Coy, 2008; Cusick, 2002; Melrose, Barrett and Brodie, 1999); social stigma and marginalisation (Kirby, 1995); lack of support networks, particularly when leaving care (Melrose, Barrett and Brodie, 1999); perpetrators targeting residential homes (Munro, 2004); the expansion of private care homes that are not well connected to local statutory services; and poor recording of, and responses to, young people going missing (OCC, 2012a).

A model of safety for sexually exploited young people

In the last 15 years CSE has increasingly been recognised as a child protection issue, and, as a result, concerns for the safety and the welfare of the child have come to dominate government policy discourse. Although a welcome shift, this development is not entirely unproblematic. Whilst binary legal definitions of adult/child position adolescents as victims of sexual abuse in need of protection, they are also predicated on notions of dependence, deficit and incapacity (Shaw and Butler, 1998; Melrose, 2012a; this volume). Despite various references to different forms of safety/security in the existing research literature on CSE, 'safety' therefore remains an under-theorised concept for young people affected by exploitative relationships. Creegan, Scott and Smith (2005), for example, conclude from their study of young people affected by sexual exploitation who were in secure accommodation in Scotland that accommodation should be provided at the highest level of relational security possible and the lowest level of physical security necessary. However physical safety is paramount for young people who have been trafficked for sexual exploitation, given the threat of being re-trafficked and further abused (Pearce et al., 2009). From a psycho-social perspective, Coy (2008, 2009b) argues that multiple placement moves undermine young women's ontological security, thus helping to create pathways into prostitution.

Drawing on this, and other literature, I suggest that physical, relational and psychological security are all vital for safeguarding the welfare of young people affected by sexual exploitation (see Figure 9.1 below). Crucially, where physical safety is achieved at the *expense* of relational and psychological security, interventions will only ever be short-term solutions that may ultimately hinder exit from an exploitative situation. Physical, relational and psychological safety are mutually reinforcing, and a child-centred approach is needed to recognise which type of security is the first priority for services to work towards in the case of each individual child. For some young people, a stable trusting relationship will be a necessary pre-condition for attempting to achieve physical safety by disrupting a relationship with a perpetrator. For others in immediate danger, physical safety will be the foundation for work to achieve psychological and then relational security.

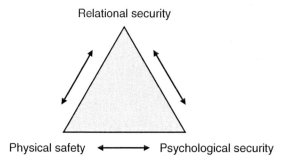

Figure 9.1 Model of safety for young people in care affected by sexual exploitation

These three kinds of safety are related to ecological assessments of risk and resilience in which risk and protective factors exist at the individual, familial and environmental levels (Rutter, 1985). Risks to physical safety may exist at both familial and environmental levels, for example. Likewise, patterns of risk at these levels may also interact to create or undermine safety. Coy (2009b), for instance, describes the way that 'cultures of care' (an environmental risk) can have a profoundly negative relational and ultimately psychological impact. The rest of this chapter will discuss each of these constructs in turn, critically considering some of the dynamics between exploitation and care, and the implications for safeguarding young people.

Physical safety

At the heart of the UK's child protection systems is the duty to protect children from physical, sexual and emotional abuse, and neglect. When a child is at risk of, or is suffering, significant harm through such abuse they may ultimately be physically removed from the source of harm. For young people affected by sexual exploitation, such short-term physical safety can be achieved through disruption tactics that include issuing civil orders and/or abduction notices to known or suspected exploiters. However, this relies on commitment to early intervention and strategic partnerships, which are not practised by the majority of Local Safeguarding Children's Boards in England (Jago et al., 2011). For children in care, a far more common approach is moving the young person to a new location where distance prevents them from seeing adults or peers who pose a risk. Farmer and Pollock (2003), for example, recommend that the most effective foster placements for children involved in prostitution are out of authority where they are forced to break links with pimps/clients (*their language*), and where negative behaviour can be modified without being reinforced in the community.

The 'disruption by distance' strategy has often been deployed alongside placing young people affected by sexual exploitation, in particular young women, in residential or secure accommodation rather than foster care (Harper and Scott, 2005; Hayes, 1996; Jesson, 1993). Although we have no robust data on placement pathways of young people who are affected by sexual exploitation Jago and colleagues (2011) found that 55 per cent of their sample of young people affected by sexual exploitation who were looked after were in residential care, whilst 12 per cent of the general population of looked after children are in residential care (DfE, 2011b). This will partially be explained by the age at which young people enter residential care, but it also reflects a lack of early intervention, whereby physical safety becomes a sudden priority for high risk young people who need emergency placements for their own protection, or because they are 'out of control' (Roesch-Marsh, 2012). Whereas many practitioners acknowledge that secure accommodation in particular is unhelpful, and may have a damaging impact on these young people (Creegan, Scott and Smith, 2005; Harper and Scott, 2005), the most clearly accepted benefit is immediate physical safety (Roesch-Marsh, 2012). This produces gendered patterns of secure accommodation placements. Girls are more likely than boys to be admitted to secure accommodation under Section 25 of the Children Act (1989) because of absconding and concerns about sexual harm rather than because they have committed criminal offences. They are therefore being cared for in an environment that is primarily designed for young offenders, and where they are often outnumbered by young men (Coy, 2008; T. O'Neill, 2001). A clear risk of achieving short term physical safety through control is therefore that young people perceive the response as punitive.

Physical safety is of significant, but limited, value for looked after young people who are affected by sexual exploitation. Part of the rationale of secure accommodation is that physical control may offer the space and support for young people to regain self-control and that parental control may then be more viable (Roesch-Marsh, 2012).

However, a study of six secure units across England found that despite an expectation that children would receive therapeutic care, staff did not feel able to address such needs, and most felt that a secure placement could not prevent abuse continuing on the young people's release (T. O'Neill, 2001). In their study of young people affected by sexual exploitation in secure units in Scotland, Creegan, Scott and Smith (2005) found that most staff felt the setting was not appropriate for the needs of these young people, and that the physical security achieved offered little value, especially once young people had returned to their communities. Even where young people value the relationships and help they receive in secure accommodation, a lack of support on leaving the secure placement can mean these positive experiences are ultimately absorbed into a wider narrative of disruption and vulnerability (Coy, 2008).

Previous research has also highlighted that the use of residential and secure accommodation can potentially increase the risk of sexual exploitation, rather than disrupting it (Harper and Scott, 2005; Jago and Pearce, 2008). A lack of training and support for carers and residential workers can mean they fail to identify the indicators of sexual exploitation for young men and women. It may also account for staff not being comfortable discussing sexual exploitation and violence, and in some situations actively reproducing gender stereotypes about young women that blame them for their own abuse (Barter, 2006; Green, 2005). Barter and colleagues (2004) report that peer sexual violence is a serious concern for young women in residential units, who were three times more likely to experience it than boys in their study, but only reported around half of these incidents. There is also some evidence of adult perpetrators deliberately targeting young people in residential accommodation (Beckett, this volume; Creegan, Scott and Smith, 2005; Munro, 2004). This is particularly concerning given a rapid expansion in the number of private children's homes, which local authorities may not be sufficiently aware of in their area. The clustering of these private homes in areas where property is cheaper may also then make children more accessible to abusers (OCC, 2012a).

The physical safety of young people affected by sexual exploitation should be a serious concern. However, a lack of resources, poor understanding of sexual exploitation and low investment in prevention and early intervention tends to lead to disruption though distance and control, where emergency and 'crisis' placements into residential or secure accommodation are driven by a lack of alternatives. In contrast, local authorities with higher awareness of, and better responses to, sexual exploitation are able to avoid the use of secure accommodation completely (Harper and Scott, 2005).

Relational security

Whilst physical safety is often a priority in cases where young people are affected by sexual exploitation, relational security is equally significant, especially over the longer term. The importance of stable, positive relationships for looked after children is well established and usually underpinned in public discourse by references to attachment theory (Bowlby, 1969). In particular, it is recognised that a good relationship with a carer can provide the 'secure base' that children and young people need if they are confidently to explore and manage the world (Howe, 2005; Schofield and Beek, 2005). Whilst this research has tended to focus on younger children, attachment is also integrally linked to adolescent psychosocial functioning (Allen et al., 1998), and friends, teachers and other close relationships can also be used selectively by adolescents as secure base figures (Waters and Cummings, 2000).

For many young people in care, the 'pull' of what becomes an exploitative relationship is related to a very real need for positive caring relationships through which they know they are valuable and loved. Low self-esteem is a common vulnerability in the profile of young women and men who are affected by sexual exploitation, as is the exchange of sex for small objects or displays of affection (Scott and Skidmore, 2006). Young women in a residential unit, for example, found the attentions of older men offered 'friendship networks and a sense of belonging, easing the loneliness and dislocation of being away from families and home' (Coy, 2008: 1409). For those with backgrounds of sexual abuse, exploitative experiences may be embedded in networks of family, friends and community so that alternative relationships are not easily viable in that context. Furthermore, young people may not recognise their own abuse and exploitation, and so reject offers of support from professionals. Here Pearce (2009) advocates for 'therapeutic outreach', where support is offered to young people in a way that is meaningful and accessible to them. A good attachment to 'a supportive, non-abusive adult', is therefore an intervention in itself, and may, over time, provide a context for 'hooking' a young person out of abusive relationships (Pearce, 2009: 146).

Despite recognition of the significance of stable positive relationships for children in care, many children's services departments struggle to operate relationally. High case loads, pressure and 'burnout' all affect the stability of the workforce and lead to high turnover (Ward and Skuse, 2001), or at the least, insufficient time for a social worker to spend with a child. As a result statutory services are rarely in the position to be able to offer the kind of therapeutic outreach described by Pearce, whilst constrained resources mean that the voluntary sector often has to work in a time-limited way as well. It is well recognised that young people affected by sexual exploitation usually need a great deal of support before they even begin to trust specialist project workers, so there is a risk that some interventions are over at just the moment when young people are ready to open up and trust an adult (Scott and Skidmore, 2006).

One of the primary ways that relational security is undermined for looked after young people affected by sexual exploitation is placement instability. Attention has turned to this issue in recent years in recognition of the negative impact that disruption and relational change has on young people moving from place to place. This research highlights the importance of continuity of contact, community, education and health care (Jackson and Thomas, 1999; Ward and Skuse, 2001; Morgan, 2006). The stressors of disruption include separation from siblings, change of school, loss of contact with friends and relocation to a new geographical area (Munro and Hardy, 2006). Placement stability has been monitored for over a decade via National Indicator 62, whereby local authorities are required to report on the number of children who had three or more placements in the year. However Unrau (2007) argues that this somewhat arbitrary measure was generated by those at the top of the knowledge/influence continuum (such as researchers), and should be accompanied by children's perspectives of what moving means to them. Cashmore and Paxman (2006), for example, found that it was young people's sense of felt security, rather than placement stability per se, that was the best predictor of their outcomes after leaving care.

Young people affected by sexual exploitation are likely also to be at risk of greater placement instability when they experience crisis moves and/or go missing. Crisis moves and emergency placements are not uncommon for young people affected by sexual exploitation (Coy, 2009b), and this increases the risk of placement breakdown (Sinclair, Wilson and Gibbs, 2005). Likewise, going missing is a powerful risk indicator of sexual exploitation (Sharp, 2012), which can then destabilise a placement further. Coy (2009b) argues that the converse is also true, with placement instability increasing the risk of sexual exploitation. In her study of women in care who were affected by sexual exploitation, all 14 described frequent placement changes and frequent absconding, with two counting over 35 changes of foster care placement over periods of seven and four years in care.

Vulnerable young people and those affected by sexual exploitation are often described as 'hard to reach' (Melrose, 2002), and there may be a range of behavioural and emotional issues young people face that make it difficult for practitioners to support them. Pearce (2009) argues that some young people will have defence mechanisms against creating new attachments that might cause further neglect and abuse, or may want to avoid acknowledging and experiencing their own pain. Young people who have insecure attachment patterns as a result of placement instability may distance themselves from carers, for example, in order to trigger rejection and further breakdown (Leathers, 2002; Morrison-Doire and Eisner, 1993). Whilst these coping mechanisms are often described as 'maladaptive' because of their negative impact on the child, there is a sense in which they are also coherent, well judged responses to systems that cannot sustain positive relationships. Where children and young people have been abused by adults they should be able to trust, it is all the more imperative that the care system reduces, rather than compounds, the impact of the harm done. However, long waiting times for CAMHS provision, issues around accessing support for out of authority placements, poor social worker/foster carer recruitment and retention, and the need for better liaison with educational services all present systemic challenges to relational stability (Holland, Faulkner and Perez-del-Aguila, 2005). Pearce (2009: 91) writes that 'It is not the one-off incident that might damage the young person's longer term ability to cope; it is the ongoing, somewhat relentless experience of abuse, rejection, change and instability that impacts negatively on the young person's capacity to manage, to be resilient'.

Psychological security

In this section I discuss the ontological and psychological security of young people who are affected by sexual exploitation and who are looked after. I use these terms to refer to the health of young people's sense of self, in terms of coherence, stability and well-being.

Strategies to cope with relational insecurity can include running away, rejecting professional support and seeking viable relationships with those who ultimately exploit young people. One of the most significant outcomes of young people's constrained choices within situations of exploitation and instability is therefore the way they come to perceive themselves, the environments and relationships they chose, and the consequences for their long-term recovery from abuse. One of the primary tasks in the adolescent stage of psychological development is the consolidation of the self-concept, as the young person develops physically and intellectually, and experiences more autonomy from their parents (Coleman, 2011). Schofield (2001) suggests that the question 'Who am I?' is not easy to answer for children who have experienced multiple families and where complex identity issues of ethnicity, class, culture and religion may be compounded by dilemmas about the value and the meaning of self. Perhaps, then, relational and physical safety are important (pre-) conditions for psychological security in terms of a stable, coherent and positive self-identity.

Coy (2008, 2009b) reports on life-history narratives produced with young women involved in prostitution who were all sexually exploited as children whilst in care. She argues that their identity development is dominated by a failure to develop a viable relational self as a result of the instability produced by their multiple disrupted care placements. Following Laing (1961) she argues that this produces a feeling of ontological insecurity which means that attempts to develop a coherent self are consistently undermined through a 'culture of care'. This results in the young person 'knowing not to feel settled, having no-one to talk to and learning not to trust, being stigmatised and different' (2009b: 255). As Beckett (this volume) has argued, it is particularly experiences of disruption and instability within care that are associated with higher risk of sexual exploitation, rather than the experience of care per se, and Coy's sample exemplifies the worst effects of this kind of chronic disruption. Nearly all of her participants ascribed the cause of their entry into underage prostitution to this culture of care, and had, over time, shifted from seeing themselves as abused children, to sex objects, to survivors and finally to professional prostitutes. Coy argues that, for these women, the profound instability they experienced as part of a 'habitus of care' then transferred to the 'familiar' world of street prostitution, where no routine or permanency was expected.

Whilst the psychosocial journeys of Coy's participants may seem extreme, many of the markers along the way are familiar to those working with young people affected by sexual exploitation who have experienced instability in care. One of these stages – sex object – refers to the way in which an aspect of a young person's identity becomes the defining feature of the whole person. For any vulnerable young person, professional support carries the risk of more permanently labelling them in terms of a need they have for a period of time. Gilligan (2006) cautions that young people in care can develop a stigmatised 'master identity' ('at risk', 'in care' or even 'sexually exploited') in the absence of alternative social roles. Young women deprived of their liberty in secure accommodation may adopt the deviant label, even if they are there for their own protection, as a result of their sexual behaviour being more heavily monitored than their male peers (T. O'Neill, 2001).

Barter (2006: 354) describes girls in residential units being positioned as sexually manipulative by staff, and as a result of their lack of social power placing 'great weight on the one area of social privilege, heterosexuality, they can obtain'. This investment in a particular kind of heterosexual identity meant the young women were then very reluctant to reflect critically on their relationships in terms of gender roles or self-esteem. Similarly, the women in Coy's study identified the labelling, record keeping and environment of residential care as alienating them from their 'normal' peers, and they resisted such 'othering' by actively embracing the role of an outsider, or 'deviant other' (2008: 1417).

Powerlessness and stigmatisation both threaten an individual's ontological security, when their competence, worthiness and lovability is questioned (Douglas, 1984). In that moment, Douglas argues, people look to return to their roots in some way through 'home grounding', which as a form of self grounding is vital to a sense of ontological security. If this is so, young people who have experienced disruption in care, and whose sense of worth and self is threatened, need the very thing they may not have: a stable, secure base to call home. Instead they may consider what other sources of self-identity and social belonging are available to them. Young women have made explicit links in interviews between the loneliness, rejection, stigma and insecurity they experienced in care and their decision to have a baby, for example (Knight et al., 2006). It is not hard, then, to recognise such ontological insecurity as a further push factor into sexually exploitative relationships and contexts.

Conclusion

Young people in care who have experienced, or who are affected by, sexual exploitation need to be protected from harm and given support to recover from abuse. This support should recognise that safety is multi-faceted, comprising, at least, physical, relational and psychological security. Where the signs of sexual exploitation are recognised and effective multi-agency partnerships exist, it should be possible to disrupt the actions of perpetrators without having to disrupt the young person's whole environment. Early intervention is therefore crucial to physical safety and protection. Where disruption by distance is attempted, physical safety or control should be used alongside measures to protect and enhance young people's relational and psychological security or it will only ever be respite. For example, services should consider how to safeguard continuity and stability, and ensure the young person is in contact with at least one adult in their new placement whom they trust. In light of the time it takes to build new trusting relationships, it is likely that placements and support packages for young people affected by sexual exploitation need to be at least 12–18 months long to address the issues around exploitative relationships.

Investing in psychological security must involve expanding the options young people have when considering how to cope with their experiences, and the roles and identities that are available to them in that process. Where young women, in particular, see the self and body as primarily sexualised, Coy (2008: 1421), for example, advocates for the development of alternative understandings of the self (skills, interests). She recognises that young women need 'intensive emotional and practical support' to engage them in 'finding a positive and healthy sense of belonging' and to prevent them from finding a psychosocial 'home' as a 'survivor' with others in the same situation.

All these observations are, of course, contingent on resources being invested in creating systems that recognise the value of sustainable relationships: whether for social workers experiencing stress because of heavy caseloads, young people faced with another new placement or specialist project workers having to end their support for a young person who has moved across local authority boundaries. Finally, it is important to recognise that safety is subjectively experienced. Very few constructs and categorisations that apply to young people in care are generated by young people themselves (including those in this chapter). In order to avoid continually constructing young people with master identities such as 'sexually exploited' 'vulnerable' and 'at risk', researchers, practitioners and policy makers need to take advantage of every opportunity to listen to what young people themselves have to say about what makes them feel safe and secure.

10
Intersections in 'Trafficking' and 'Child Sexual Exploitation' Policy

Lorena Arocha

Introduction

Trafficking and child sexual exploitation (CSE) are two policy areas whose histories are intertwined with processes of modernity and late-modernity. They have both been recognised as global social problems of alarming proportions requiring urgent and immediate action to eradicate them. These concerns have translated into a range of preventative and protective measures to ensure the well-being of those identified as 'vulnerable' to such 'risks' and prosecuting and punishing those who commit these heinous acts. Trafficking and CSE are constructed as risks that threaten the breakdown of social order and disturb the core notions which have come to govern our world: free/unfree, adult/child, sexual/asexual, deserving/undeserving, legal/illegal, victim/perpetrator (O'Connell-Davidson, 2005). But, as this chapter shows, trafficking and CSE emerged as social problems precisely in contexts where these problems could be articulated as such (Aradau, 2008: 14). It focuses on how trafficking and CSE came to be defined as global social problems and reviews some of the incongruities present in some of the initiatives implemented to address them.

The chapter describes the re-emergence of trafficking and CSE as social problems in the 1980s, concentrating on such developments at the European level as a case study, The discussion is divided into three sections. The first analyses the contradictions in social policymaking, especially with respect to trafficking and CSE. The second focuses on the re-emergence of trafficking and CSE in the 1980s and how this related to social processes of the time. The third concentrates on the European situation and the role of the Council of Europe (CoE) and the European Union (EU) in consolidating shared values and policy responses to trafficking and CSE. I draw on my involvement in a recent research project to identify where trafficking and CSE meet and consider the tendency to blur the boundaries between them.

The paradox of social policy

Social policy has traditionally developed as a panoply of discrete policy areas, which corresponds to a classificatory regime of problems and peoples. The categorisation of problems and peoples and/or particular peoples as social problems (Wedel et al., 2005: 37) has allowed complex and chaotic social processes of modernity and late-modernity to be turned into intelligible and manageable 'objects of knowledge'. Policymaking involves two processes: problem setting and problem solving (Schön, 1993: 138). This is what Foucault called 'problematisation' (Rabinow, 2003: 18 cited in Aradau, 2008: 15); that is, 'the discursive and non-discursive practices' through which a specific social issue is considered 'true or false' and 'constituted as an object of knowledge' (ibid.). Such problematisation becomes possible under specific historical and contextual conditions only (ibid.: 14). The ways in which particular social problems are framed are however not unique. Different positions regarding the origin and most appropriate response to such problems often abound within different policy areas (Schön, 1993: 138).

Although aimed at ensuring social order and cohesion, social policy often results in discriminatory practices (Crewe and Axelby, 2013: 184). Due to the limited and shrinking availability of funds and the requirement to spend them efficiently to obtain maximum results (Mayhew et al., 2005), assessment is considered necessary to identify those 'most vulnerable' or 'most at risk' and ensure only the 'most deserving' get access to assistance and support. 'Needs assessments' are therefore fundamental tools in policy making and implementation. They are considered 'objective' tools, but some have demonstrated that these are not unproblematic, but rather biased (Brown, 2012; Olivier de Sardan, 2005: 85). These processes of identification and assessment, instead of overcoming social inequalities, often build on, and reproduce, them (Wedel et al., 2005: 36).

There has been a change in the way in which we 'do' social policy in late-modernity. This is associated with the globalisation of risks and the consequent diminished capacity of national governments to deal with the resulting collateral damage at the local level (Bauman, 2001). Fears are liquid, more diffuse (Bauman, 2006) and therefore harder to address through 'conventional' social policy. National governments and other institutions can only 'shift [these] anxieties to [attempt to offer] individual safety' (Aradau, 2008: 52–3). There has been, therefore, a change in policymaking towards individualisation; that is, to offering solutions to social problems only at the level of the individual, with less consideration to the wider structural and contextual forces that create them (Melrose, 2010: 24). Because contemporary social problems and their many interconnections are deemed too complex to untangle, contemporary policy making is primarily about 'risk management' (Pupavac, 2001: 360). This has resulted in a retreat from belief in social progress towards a position that is defensive, only managing social inequalities and conflict (ibid.). The lack of attention given to the structural basis for such inequalities and conflicts has also resulted in a complete de-politicisation in policymaking (ibid.: 369). Policy solutions offered are instead within a regime of therapeutic governance, where rights are defined as the capability of individuals to claim official identification amongst a competing array of victim statuses. 'Experts' have the upper hand in these identification processes. Under this regime, the victims' entitlements are reduced to the right to therapeutic intervention and self-esteem (ibid.).

This is no different in trafficking and CSE. Identification mechanisms in place allow access to support services and other resources only to those lucky few who are successfully identified by practitioners either as 'trafficked' or as being a 'sexually exploited child'. But what about those who might have been 'trafficked' and 'sexually exploited' but are not officially identified as such (ATMG, 2010; Jago et al., 2011)? Those who are identified as 'victims' may also suffer as a result: for example, the status of 'victim' may carry a social stigma, which can be very disabling in allowing individuals to move on with their lives (Poudel, 2011).

The identification of groups 'most at risk' is closely connected to moral principles and the desire to maintain changing cultural categories, such as those of 'woman' and 'child' (O'Connell-Davidson, 2005: 26). Identification is intimately influenced by images of victimhood often used in awareness raising and preventative campaigns, which in this context have become essential (ibid.: 7–8): essential for ensuring that trafficking and CSE are maintained as priorities in governments' and other transnational institutions' political agendas through alarmist repetition of their magnitude; essential to packaging messages and stories that do away with complexity and present these problems as realisable and singular policy goals; essential to maintaining the sense of urgency necessary to sustain the flow of resources that permit the support of a whole range of professionals with specialist knowledge capable to deploy it where and when is 'most needed' (cf. Melrose, this volume).

Identification processes are therefore highly ambiguous and can be rather undemocratic for a number of reasons: they fail to address structural factors, they are implemented at the individual level but can be extremely disempowering to the individual in question, they separate individuals into 'deserving' and 'undeserving' according to simplified imagery of victimhood, they depend on professional discretion and they are based on economic and competitive liberal models of citizenship (Brown, 2012).

In these liquid times (Bauman, 2007) to be is to be incessantly in motion, adaptable, mutable and flexible to rapid changing circumstances. Mobility is the new stratifying element differentiating those who can choose to move (white, male, adult, educated, agentic economically and from the Global North) and those who are unable to do so (Bauman, 1998). As a result of all this, it is unsurprising to see which policies and interventions are promoted to address trafficking and CSE: identifying, punishing and expelling 'perpetrators', especially when they do not respect national boundaries; effectively identifying 'victims' through the implementation of what are believed to be 'objective' referral mechanisms (OSCE/ODIHR, 2004); providing expert support services and therapeutic interventions only to those successfully identified as such; raising awareness about the risks of trafficking and CSE amongst population groups deemed 'at risk' or 'vulnerable' in the hope that this knowledge would lead individuals to make the 'right' decisions; and curbing migration, especially of those groups considered 'vulnerable', through restrictive policies and higher control of their movement, such as through the setting up of vigilante committees. It is interesting to see how many of the policies to address trafficking and CSE directed at the level of the individual victim actually impose immobility. This is paradoxical, as there are often significant risks and dangers attached to such immobility.

Calls to improve policy responses are reduced to insubstantial demands: to expand definitions, to revise identification and referral mechanisms, to improve standards of support and therapeutic services, to provide more training to professionals, to increase the number of convictions of 'perpetrators' and levels of compensation to 'victims', and to provide age, ethnic and gender-appropriate education and training to identified groups 'at risk' (Arocha, 2012; ATMG, 2010; Jago et al., 2011). This is to be accomplished only over the short life of two or three year projects, funded by an array of multilateral and bilateral governmental and independent non-governmental bodies with volatile funding strategies. This approach often leads to a fragmented and ad hoc implementation on the ground, and does not lend itself to a cohesive and integrated approach to addressing trafficking and CSE that might also consider other relevant policy areas, such as 'child protection', 'immigration', 'violence against women', 'development' and 'poverty reduction', amongst others. The impact of policies so developed is often contradictory because these policy intersections are not considered.

As policy areas, trafficking and CSE conform to 'conventional' social policy making and reflect the contradictions inherent to the field. The range of policies available to tackle these issues is short-sighted and not comprehensive, and their implementation, directed at the individual level, is often unsatisfactory. Unsurprisingly, these policies have been incapable of obtaining the long-term eradication of these practices. In the next section, I turn my attention to the social processes that allowed trafficking and CSE to be problematised as global social problems after the 1980s.

The re-emergence of trafficking and CSE as social problems

The historical development of trafficking as a social problem is irrevocably intertwined with that of CSE. Nearly a hundred years after the 'first wave' of feminist campaigns against the 'white slave trade' and children's involvement in prostitution, renovated concerns about these issues re-emerged in the late 1980s. But why did such concerns re-emerge then?

Trafficking and CSE were presented as growing problems from the 1980s (Doezema, 2010; O'Connell-Davidson, 2005). This was in part to appease general levels of anxiety and fear associated with the onset of globalisation and its associated changes in the 1980s. Processes of globalisation profoundly unsettled understandings of life as we knew it, rendering lived experience incredibly uncertain and unpredictable.

The identities of the 'victims' of trafficking and CSE changed over the course of the twentieth century, from 'white' women and children to women and children 'of colour' (Gallagher, 2010: 16). Changes in female labour participation and the consequent reorganisation of the gender division of labour within families gave rise to a global care chain (Hochschild, 2000). In order to avoid conflict in the home, (white) women from the Global North who were in employment in turn employed foreign women (poorer and often of colour) to take on the responsibilities of homemaker and carer. These women were often seen as subservient (read not liberated like her Northern counterpart) and hence were considered more docile and more 'naturally' inclined to domestic chores (Anderson, 2000). Women of the Global South were bearing the brunt of the costs of economic restructuring policies but were discriminated against in employment and migration (Kempadoo, 1998). Women were willing to migrate as autonomous agents, searching for economic opportunities (ibid.: 17–18). This resulted in an international racialised and hierarchical division of reproductive labour (ibid.; Parreñas, 2004) and the appearance of transnational families (ibid.). And, with the expansion of sex industries, some were migrating for sex work too (ibid.). This led to an upsurge of anxiety over how this changing role of women would impact on the future of the 'traditional' family and the 'nation'. It is only when taking this context into consideration that we can understand the anxieties and fears played out in the campaigns against trafficking and CSE that emerged from the late 1980s.

Preventative campaigns based on awareness raising became the main tool to persuade women and children 'vulnerable' to trafficking against migration. Campaigns (re)presented the 'child' or 'woman' as a generalised suffering individual (Aradau, 2008: 4), turning them into objects, easier then for audiences to pity (O'Connell-Davidson, 2005: 26). The subtext of these campaigns was often contradictory. Images which aimed to disgust, shock and scare encouraged a voyeuristic (male) gaze (Andrijasevic, 2007: 26; Arthurs, 2009: 309–10; 2010), as 'pious pornography' (Stockton, 2009: 123). These representations also contributed to setting ideals on victimhood. Paradoxically, campaign imagery used the very victimisation and objectification they opposed, in an attempt to recapture the shifting meanings associated with the categories 'woman' and 'child'. Presented in situations of helplessness, immobility and entrapment (Andrijasevic, 2007: 26, 30), these images conceived the 'child' as latency, as delay (Stockton, 2009: 4; 2011), innocent, asexual, naive and dependent; and the 'woman' as domestic, pure, naive, family-oriented, docile and dependent. The images were so produced that it is often difficult to see the particular child or woman in front of us as our gaze is impeded by the projection of these ideal categories (Stockton, 2011). Campaigns would portray images of a 'suffering black child' as a device to recuperate that disappearing 'child' so longed for. This was also accompanied by a re-definition of the category 'child' in the Global North towards recognition of a 'queer child', whose sexuality is no longer retrospective but present (Stockton, 2009). The black child is however not embodying the 'traditional' conception of 'innocence' (white, middle-class) (ibid.). It is through the depiction of the child's 'suffering' that the 'imagined innocence' lost and searched for is recovered (ibid.; Aradau, 2008: 34). This is what some call 'kid orientalism' (Stockton, 2011). These strategic devices are essential for non-governmental organisations (NGOs) and activists who aim to maintain interest on trafficking and CSE, to fundraise and carry on advocacy work (O'Connell-Davidson, 2005: 26; cf. Melrose, this volume).

Anxieties over the impact of social changes and shifts in our understanding of these categories were also reflected in legislation. In 1989, the United Nations adopted the Convention on the Rights of the Child (UNCRC). Being the UN treaty with nearly universal assent, it introduced a new language to refer to children in prostitution. Children would now be considered to be 'sexually exploited', as this would emphasise their victimhood (Phoenix, 2002: 354; cf. Melrose, this volume). Three World Congresses against the Commercial Sexual Exploitation of Children organised by the NGO Group for the Convention on the Rights of the Child alongside UNICEF and ECPAT International reinforced this change. The first Congress, organised in Stockholm in 1996, concentrated more strongly on the commercial aspects of the sexual exploitation of children, although the background documentation shifted between commercial and non-commercial forms of sexual exploitation in line with the broader approach adopted in Article 34 of the UNCRC. Such a distinction had disappeared by the Third World Congress. The practices included under the term 'sexual exploitation', which until very recently had not been specifically defined, have expanded over the years. This trend to broaden definitions and their interpretations was aimed at taking 'advantage of political momentum [or] to advance a particular policy agenda' (Gallagher, 2010: 50) From the very beginning, the Congresses connected the ever-broadening sexual exploitation of children to that of women, to trafficking and slavery (ECPAT International, 1996).

Examining the development of the latest international legislation, it is difficult to uncouple trafficking from CSE. In 1974, the Working Group on Slavery set up under the United Nations Commission on Human Rights, defined child prostitution and trafficking as severe forms of exploitation (Santos País, 2011: 46). It was the Working Group's thrust to develop a programme to address the sale of children, child prostitution and pornography that led to a series of further actions in the 1990s. In 1995, the UN General Assembly called for the adoption of an optional protocol to the UNCRC to specifically deal with the practice (ibid.: 47). However, developments to adopt it were very slow, and five years in, Argentina sought what transpired as a very timely course of action. Argentina pushed for the trafficking for sexual exploitation of minors to be considered during the negotiations for a Convention on Transnational Organized Crime at the UN level (Gallagher, 2010: 77). This resulted in the 2000 UN Protocol to Prevent, Suppress and Punish Trafficking in Persons, especially Women and Children (the UN Trafficking Protocol from now on). Coincidentally, in the same year, the UN also adopted the Optional Protocol to the Convention on the Rights of the Child on the sale of children, child prostitution and child pornography.

The UN Trafficking Protocol problematised trafficking as a security issue (Aradau, 2008: 3), and it was only when 'trafficking' was conceived as a security/sovereignty issue, rather than an issue of women's rights or child protection, that it gained international prominence (Gallagher, 2010: 71). The UN Trafficking Protocol was the catapult to a series of regional and national laws on trafficking (Arocha, 2012). The efforts of NGOs and activists worldwide were rewarded and 'trafficking' finally became a global priority, with many governments adopting policies and their corresponding plans of action and allocating a substantial amount of resources to address it (Weitzer, 2007). This was possible because 'trafficking' was seen as challenging national sovereignty and allowed for restrictive migration policies as a trafficking prevention measure. Campaigners on CSE would use the success of trafficking to assist in recognising CSE as a global social problem too. I will use the situation at the European level to highlight this trend in the next section.

The policy context in Europe on trafficking and CSE

Consideration of the European regulatory system on trafficking and CSE requires an examination of legislation under the Council of Europe (CoE) and the European Union (EU): two different organisational bodies. The CoE was set up in 1949 to promote cooperation amongst European countries after the end of the Second World War and to strengthen core values, specifically the promotion of human rights. Currently, 47 countries are Member States to the CoE. The EU, first set up in 1957, consists of a smaller number of European States (27 at this moment). It was committed to establishing a single market through a gradual process of homogenisation and integration, mostly on economic, but also political and social matters.

As elsewhere, the historical development of legislation on trafficking and CSE is equally intertwined at the European level. The CoE first discussed trafficking in the late 1980s. To start with, the CoE concentrated its efforts on regulating against the trafficking of women for sexual exploitation (Gallagher, 2010: 20). The CoE organised an initial seminar on the subject as early as 1991. A few years later, they agreed on a Plan of Action against Trafficking in Women. In 1997 at the Strasbourg Summit, the CoE broadened its focus to include all forms of sexual exploitation and first defined trafficking as a security issue, as it was considered that 'trafficking pose[s] a *threat to citizens' security* and democracy' (emphasis added), although a sole focus on women was maintained. The CoE supported research on matters related to the trafficking of women for sexual exploitation and encouraged the development of region-wide responses in South-Eastern Europe and the South Caucasus. Such regional focus is unsurprising, given the series of revolutions and political upheavals which took place in the region at the time (Andrijasevic, 2010: 11; Brown and Shah, 2000), with the fall of the Berlin Wall in 1989, the dissolution of the Soviet Union in 1991 and the conflict in the former Yugoslavia in the mid-1990s. Such transformations and the economic and social reorganisation that ensued, translated in an increase in women's migration and the growing reliance on criminal and other underground activities for economic profit, activities which included prostitution (for women) and the facilitation of trafficking (for men) (ibid.; Barrett et al., 2000; Mai, 2010). The recommendation that the Committee of Ministers of the CoE issued considering trafficking and CSE in 1991 covered sexual exploitation, pornography and prostitution of, and trafficking in, children and young adults.

In contrast, the EU begun considering trafficking as involving more than the sexual exploitation of women and children much earlier (Gallagher, 2010: 21). The EU first passed a resolution on trafficking in human beings in 1996. The special vulnerability of women continued to be emphasised within the EU system. But, by the early 2000s, trafficking and CSE had started to appear as two different policy issues with their separate specialisms.

Following the adoption of the UN Trafficking Protocol and the UN Optional Protocol to the UNCRC in 2000 a re-energised period of legislating recommenced in both the CoE and the EU. Under the CoE, recommendation No. R (2000) 11 was concerned specifically with trafficking in human beings, though still seen only for the purpose of sexual exploitation. Recommendation Rec (2001) identified the protection of children against sexual exploitation as a case apart. Similarly, the EU passed two Council Framework Decisions, one dealing with 'trafficking in human beings' (2002) and another to combat the 'sexual exploitation of children' (2004). The CoE then abandoned its stance against considering trafficking in all its forms (ibid., 2010: 46).

In 2005, the CoE adopted the Convention on Action against Trafficking in Human Beings (CoE Trafficking Convention). This was followed by a campaign across the region to secure the minimum number of ratifications. The campaign was accompanied by a limited but efficient flow of resources, as the Convention came into force in 2008. The CoE Trafficking Convention improved the UN Trafficking Protocol through the expansion of the definition, which incorporated all forms of 'trafficking', including those which did not involve an organised crime group; and the strengthening of the identification and protection provisions for victims of trafficking. In 2007, the CoE opened another Convention for signature, this time on CSE: the Convention on the Protection of Children against Sexual Exploitation and Sexual Abuse in Lanzarote (the Lanzarote Convention). This improved international legislation by specifically defining both sexual abuse and sexual exploitation of children. The CoE did not want to 'confine solely to offences committed for commercial purposes and did not want to introduce a distinction between "child sexual abuse" and "child sexual exploitation"' (Ruelle, 2011: 60), even if this would be much harder to achieve in practice. The Lanzarote Convention came into force in 2010.

The legislation under the EU and the CoE 'feed into each other in a dynamic process of revision and improvement' (ibid.: 72). Following these two CoE Conventions, the EU adopted two Directives on trafficking and child sexual exploitation in 2011. The EU Trafficking Directive, for example, not only incorporated the merits of the CoE Trafficking Convention, but also expanded its definition to include other forms of exploitation, that is, the exploitation for begging or for other criminal activities (ibid.: 71).

This clearly demonstrates the blurring boundaries between CSE and trafficking at the European level. However, in practice, each Convention at the CoE has a Secretariat responsible for it, which often means that activities are developed in silos. Furthermore, the structure of the CoE often makes the coordination across working streams difficult, especially when such Secretariats might be competing for internal resources and external recognition. This has a number of implications in practice.

As an example, I will consider how shifting political priorities at the CoE level has had an impact on the activities of governmental and non-governmental agencies delivering work on the ground. The Lanzarote Convention has not as yet proved a favourite amongst Member States. Given the slow pace at which ratifications were taking place, a campaign was launched in 2010. A limited flow of resources was allocated for the purpose and it has succeeded in securing the ratification of 14 Member States thus far.

In 2011, whilst conducting some research on the effects of campaigns to raise awareness on child trafficking (Arocha, 2012), I contacted a number of governmental and non-governmental organisations in

South-Eastern Europe working directly with children and adults who were 'at risk'. Two of these NGOs, members of the same network, had been involved in anti-trafficking work since the late 1990s or early 2000s. During their first five to ten years of work, they had implemented a series of one- or two-year programmes to address trafficking in their respective countries. From the information shared with me then (Arocha, 2012), it is clear that a marked shift took place in the focus of their work in 2009–10. Whilst before 2009 their work was on trafficking, since then it was on CSE or 'commercial sexual exploitation of children'. The way in which their work was framed changed. Why?

As mentioned earlier, funding regimes are highly volatile and responsive to political priorities set by governments and other international bodies (Crewe and Harrison, 1998; Mayhew et al., 2005; Olivier de Sardan, 2005; Wedel, 1998). This is not dissimilar in trafficking and CSE and the organisations above are examples of that. It was in 2009–10, that the CoE shifted priorities towards the Lanzarote Convention, allocating resources to organisations in Member States to secure ratification. Coincidentally, in 2009, ECPAT International and the Body Shop launched a global campaign to 'Stop sex trafficking of children and young people', which the CoE also recognised in its own preparatory campaign material (Sakulpitakphon, 2011: 313). ECPAT International is known for exerting a powerful influence on public and political discourse on CSE in all its forms (Black, 1995 and Montgomery, 2001, both cited in O'Connell-Davidson, 2005: 31). And on this occasion, it was no different. Given changing funding streams and shifts in priorities, organisations which once had exclusively worked on trafficking were now diversifying to develop work under the new framework. This has a number of implications.

It could be argued that those who have already worked with the same populations (or similar) and on similar issues (trafficking for sexual exploitation) are best placed and have the most appropriate knowledge to implement these programmes. This could be questioned if we believe that trafficking and CSE are separate policy areas, with their corresponding specialisms, target populations and codes of practice. At the same time, changes in priorities and allocation of funds are known for preventing continuity and follow-up of previously implemented programmes. These hinder reflection and learning from old programmes to be incorporated into new programme development, which results in very poor outcomes in terms of eradicating such practices. This reveals how trafficking and CSE become interchangeable at times and used towards political ends.

This is also reflected in the work of the Dutch Rapporteur on Trafficking in Human Beings. Considered as an example of 'good practice' in 'trafficking' in Europe (ATMG, 2010: 66), the Rapporteur was established in the year 2000 (BNRM, 2002: 34). It reports on the progress that the Dutch government, in collaboration with civil society, is making to address 'trafficking in human beings'. The first report was published in 2002. In 2012, the Dutch Rapporteur published its first report on 'child pornography'. In this report, the Rapporteur acknowledges the Lanzarote Convention and confirms a change in name will reflect her new responsibilities. From 2012, the Dutch Rapporteur will report not only on the Trafficking in Human Beings, but also on Sexual Violence against Children. The Rapporteur explains how she will review progress on all forms of sexual violence against children – that is, sexual abuse, sexual exploitation and child pornography – because the Dutch government recognised that although the 2012 report only looked at child pornography, this is 'but one of the forms of sexual violence against children and [therefore] it needs to be tackled as such' (BNRM, 2002: 19).

Using Europe as a case study, I have here shown changes in policy making in trafficking and CSE – the device which allowed them to be recognised as 'global' social problems – and how legislation developed and fed into each other to maintain 'trafficking' and CSE as priorities in the European political agenda. I have also shown how such developments could affect programme development on the ground and the likely implications of this.

Conclusion

The tendency to blur the boundaries between trafficking and CSE and the impetus continuously to stretch and review definitions is best understood when examining policy making in its context. The UN Trafficking Protocol problematised 'trafficking' as a security issue, which allowed it to be recognised as a priority global social problem. General trends in policy making towards an individualised risk management approach were also the rule in trafficking and CSE. As in other policy areas, this has resulted in a complete de-politicisation of trafficking and CSE

Campaigns are used as devices to do away with the related complexity of addressing global social problems and present them instead as realisable and singular policy goals. The kind of policies and interventions developed however do not tend to produce the intended results. Changes in political priorities and funding streams affect the work that is developed on the ground and explain the lack of consistent and significant results. This approach often leads to fragmented and ad hoc programme development on the ground, as we have seen in the case of Europe. Moreover, it does not lend itself to a cohesive and integrated approach across other policy areas relevant to trafficking and CSE. This ultimately fails to provide the fundamental understanding of the complex social processes that contribute to creating the conditions for trafficking and CSE.

11
Trafficking of Children and Young People: 'Community' Knowledge and Understandings

Patricia Hynes

Introduction

Trafficking of children and young people into, within, and out of the UK has, in the past decade, been increasingly acknowledged by Governments, statutory and non-statutory agencies. Little is known, however, about how non-statutory organisations working within minority ethnic populations understand this issue. This chapter seeks to address this gap, by exploring knowledge and understandings of trafficking of children and young people within migrant and refugee community organisations.

The chapter argues that to identify proactively trafficked children or young people the role of migrant and refugee community organisations should be elevated. It suggests that the contexts in which children and young people from minority ethnic populations become vulnerable to trafficking are best understood by representatives working within these communities and community based organisations. These representatives might potentially identify a broader range of forms of trafficking above and beyond the contemporary UK focus on CSE. Evidence shows that children and young people are trafficked for a variety of purposes but practitioners are currently more likely to identify trafficking for CSE than for other purposes (Arocha, this volume).

Contemporary understandings of trafficking within community organisations are variable, thus organisations that may be able to identify and safeguard children and young people from trafficking may need resources to improve awareness and ability to identify those at risk. Furthermore, non-statutory organisations may need to work closely within minority ethnic populations to enable a more rounded picture to emerge. It is also possible that through existing social networks the global reach of community organisations might allow the formulation of preventative strategies.

The chapter will highlight issues of trust within and between statutory and non-statutory organisations alongside the contradictions of UK government policies that promote initiatives to combat trafficking whilst preventing the establishment of social, political and institutional trust with refugee and asylum seeking communities (P. Hynes, 2009; T. Hynes, 2003).

Methodology

This chapter draws on empirical evidence generated through two different studies. Firstly, qualitative research was undertaken into practitioners' responses to trafficking of children and young people (Pearce, Hynes and Bovarnick, 2009). This involved nine focus groups and semi-structured interviews with 72 practitioners as well as the collation of 37 individual case studies from three anonymised locations within the UK.

Secondly, the chapter draws on emerging findings from an ongoing study involving in-depth qualitative interviews with members of the non-statutory sector across London. This study aims to explore knowledge and understandings of trafficking within that sector and to generate knowledge relating to global points of vulnerability for children and young people trafficked into, within and out of the UK, focusing mainly on those trafficked for CSE, The study seeks to broaden current understandings of trafficking of children by exploring knowledge held within migrant and refugee community organisations across London.

The section below discusses how trafficking might be conceptualised as a sociological process before proceeding to explore understandings of trafficking from the point of view of practitioners in community organisations.

Inter-disciplinary knowledge and trafficking of children

Understanding the ways that CSE may intersect with other forms of exploitation and the ways in which it may be linked to or hidden by other forms of exploitation is complex. It may therefore be helpful to look at inter-disciplinary studies such as forced migration for suitable contextual frameworks. In studies of forced migration globally, mono-causal explanations for migration have, for many years, been rejected (see, for example, Kunz, 1973; Richmond, 1994). These have been replaced by multi-faceted understandings that draw not only on country of arrival contexts but also circumstances in countries of origin and the global dynamics that generate migration. Migration is thus often explained as a result of structural forces beyond the control of individuals (Zolberg, 1989). Also relevant is the argument by Castles and Loughna (2004) that globalisation is a process of differential inclusion and exclusion of the world's population with different levels of income and human rights being obvious causes for migration.

Historical legacies of empire, technologies that connect the global 'South' to the 'North' and social networks that connect people across the globe all present the challenge of thinking across borders when investigating unexpected and unplanned reconnections. As such there is a theoretical emphasis on people being 'forced' to migrate under conditions wherein individual agency is severely compromised. Sociological accounts have illustrated conditions in countries of origin outlining the lived experiences of refugees, asylum seekers and/or other forced migrants. In contrast literature on 'trafficking' often describes this form of forced migration in terms of the elements of the Palermo Protocol: that is in terms of the 'act', the 'means' and for the 'purpose' of exploitation. The ways in which deception, coercion, force and being misled render people 'vulnerable' to trafficking is also often a primary focus.

Trafficking, like migration and forced migration, is inextricably linked to processes of globalisation. Ongoing conflicts across the world, famine, political upheaval, poverty and associated problems create situations whereby children may be separated from their families. It is within this global context that trafficking of children and young people can be contextualised. There are global points of 'vulnerability' for children and young people and understanding trafficking as a broader, global sociological *process* rather than a nationally-bounded *event* might lead to an enhanced ability to identify children who are at risk (Hynes, 2010) and enable pre- and post-arrival 'vulnerabilities' and contexts to be better understood (see also Bokhari and Kelly, 2010).

Children, young people, trafficking and child sexual exploitation

According to statistics compiled by the UK Human Trafficking Centre (UKHTC) in conjunction with the Serious Organised Crime Agency (SOCA) (2011), between April 2009 and June 2011, some 1,664 referrals (f = 1,192; m = 472) were made to UKHTC. Of these, 438 cases related to 'minors', (that is, under 18 years of age), mainly from countries such as Vietnam, Nigeria, China and including cases of children and young people trafficked within the UK. The forms of 'exploitation' encountered by these 438 children and young people were labour exploitation (n = 154), sexual exploitation (n = 132), domestic servitude (n = 57) and other, unknown, forms of exploitation (n = 95). Thus what is known officially about trafficking in the UK indicates a range of exploitative practices.

In subsequent UKHTC (2012) statistics children and young people made up 489 of the 2,077 potential victims of trafficking identified in the UK. Again, forms of exploitation were identified as sexual exploitation (30 per cent), criminal exploitation (26 per cent), labour exploitation (13 per cent) and domestic servitude (7 per cent). In 2011 the main sending countries were Romania, Vietnam and Nigeria. Internal trafficking within the UK featured as the fourth highest total involving children originally from China.

Figure 11.1 shows that for the top ten 'sending' countries 'criminal exploitation' is predominantly an issue for Romanian and Slovakian young people, whereas 'sexual exploitation' relates mainly to 'internal' trafficking (30 per cent of cases) and, to a lesser extent, Nigerian children (14 per cent of cases). Nevertheless, the danger of stereotyping children or young people from particular ethnic communities should not be overlooked in the presentation of such statistics.

Government guidance on safeguarding children who may have been trafficked highlights the potential role of 'community groups, faith groups and voluntary organisations' in the identification process (DCSF, 2008: 22). However, there are few organisations from minority ethnic populations who are involved in safeguarding children and young people that are involved in the National Referral Mechanism (NRM) in a formal way. CSE is one form of exploitation identified in official statistics, but without the involvement of minority ethnic populations its prevalence remains unknown.

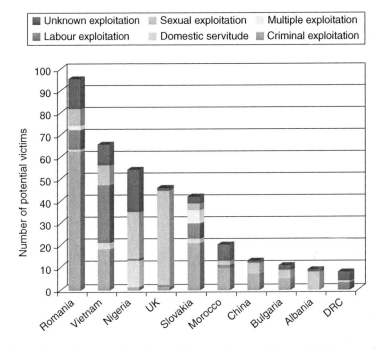

Figure 11.1 Country of origin and forms of exploitation of children and young people in 2011
Source: UKHTC statistics (2012).

Emerging findings in relation to what is known about trafficking for CSE and other purposes within minority ethnic, migrant and refugee community organisations is outlined in the next section.

What is known within minority ethnic, migrant and refugee community organisations

Within the UK organisations such as the Victoria Climbié Foundation (VCF) and Africans Unite Against Child Abuse (AFRUCA) are actively working within communities to raise awareness of issues such as trafficking – including sexual exploitation; female genital mutilation (FGM); child abuse linked to faith and belief systems, witchcraft and spirit possession; and so-called honour crimes or 'honour-based' violence. They also work on safeguarding within private, or informal, fostering arrangements, an issue of course highlighted in 2000 within minority ethnic populations as a result of the death of Victoria Climbié.

The establishment of VCF by the parents of Victoria Climbié has resulted in work on issues around child protection, policies and practices through 'education and dialogue' in 'diverse communities' (see http://vcf-uk.org/). Another organisation already working closely on this issue is AFRUCA, a charity that promotes the rights and welfare of African children in the UK. AFRUCA works with policy makers and service providers with the aim of developing better understandings of the needs of African children. Topics tackled to date include the over-representation of African children within the child protection system and issues around faith and belief systems. In terms of trafficking of children, they work across continents to highlight and understand the reason African children might be trafficked in the first instance (for further information see http://www.afruca.org/). AFRUCA have supported over 250 young people suspected of being trafficked since they began in 2001 (AFRUCA, 2012). Their literature suggests that children are often trafficked by someone they know, rather than criminal networks, for exploitation through domestic servitude, CSE and other forms of exploitation (AFRUCA, 2007).

These are two examples of established organisations that have articulated their understandings of trafficking of children and young people. There are many other non-statutory organisations with such aims, although understandings of 'trafficking' within them appear at this early stage of research to be as diverse as those found amongst practitioners in the statutory sector (Pearce, Hynes and Bovarnick, 2009).

Referring back to data from UKHTC, the statistics suggest that domestic servitude made up 7 per cent of identified trafficking cases whereas sexual exploitation made up 30 per cent. However, until much more is known about different forms of trafficking and the plethora of coercive contexts within which children may find themselves it is not possible to say categorically that sexual exploitation is de facto the dominant form. For organisations such as AFRUCA, the suggestion is that other forms may be equally present.

A spectrum of understanding

Within statutory agencies it was found that there was a spectrum of understanding about trafficking (Pearce, Hynes and Bovarnick,

2009). This same spectrum appears to currently exist within refugee and community organisations in the UK:

> In our community ... we don't see that type of child trafficking issues. You can see rape, you can see domestic violence, you see problems with gangs, but you don't see much child trafficking.
> (Interview with community representative, June 2012)

This quote suggests a conceptualisation of trafficking that entailed a narrow understanding of it being about moving a child from one country to another as a 'slave or sex object' (Interview, June 2012). In a subsequent interview there were suggestions that migrants within the community arrived in married units, gained legal status to remain, and subsequently brought only their own children into the country. However, as the discussion continued areas of exploitation within this particular community were discussed without reference to trafficking but framed within a labour exploitation lens:

> Exploitation through the textile industry in this community is well known in earlier years.
> (Interview with community representative, June 2012)

Documented cases of children and young people being trafficked were not outlined and it was clear that the interviewee did not consider that labour exploitation within the textile industry was related to trafficking.

The renunciation of trafficking as an issue within this community is similar to earlier discourses on trafficking. A decade on, it is recognised that not only does trafficking occur but also that it can lead to multiple and overlapping forms of exploitation. This resonates with understandings of trafficking expressed by practitioners in statutory organisations such as the police, local authorities, youth offending teams and legal services. These earlier interviews demonstrated understandings of trafficking for CSE being more complex than one form of abuse:

> We realised it wasn't always about sex trafficking ... there were kids being used as domestics ... people were bringing kids in

under the wire, so smuggling them in but going on to exploit them here.

> (Pearce, Hynes and Bovarnick, 2009: 71)

In stark comparison, a quotation from a representative of another community organisation currently engaging with community groups provides an alternative view. This organisation aimed to incorporate the experience and views of the community into broader processes of safeguarding and protecting children from trafficking, as noted below:

> Well, we have taken a proactive approach really... I think the headline is engaging communities in the process of identification and referral into statutory services. It is a difficult balance because we don't want to say this is a particular issue in your community, a bit like the FGM scenario. But, we take the view that communities, and people living in the community, are in a position to understand slightly better what is going on on the ground. They see individuals and ... have a sense of, like everybody does, children at risk.
>
> (Interview with community representative, July 2012)

The approach of this organisation is very much about raising awareness, exploring issues around exploitation and abuse as well as the trafficking of children and young people. In this interview, the representative was mindful of the dangers of 'profiling' communities, being conscious not to label the community as one that might be involved in the trafficking of children. This representative went on to suggest:

> We feel the community groups are best placed to be at the forefront of this. Statutory agencies tend to be reactive as opposed to proactive around prevention. So this is part of our vision, strategy and approach in Europe, African and the UK.
>
> (Interview with community representative, July 2012)

Another organisation working beyond the borders of the UK suggested that contextualising the vulnerabilities and journeys that children and young people make is essential when considering trafficking.

For example, in relation to movement within countries of origin prior to movement beyond the national borders, one participant said:

> We work with children who are vulnerable to a trafficking situation. Children who live on the streets, they may not be completely separated from their parents all of the time, but they may be. Most of the time they will have come from a rural place and have moved to a city, with their parents who may or may not be homeless. ... They need to support their families quite often. They may work ... to support their families.
>
> (Interview with community representative, August 2012)

The partial absence of parents appeared central to understanding those vulnerable to trafficking. This partial absence plus previous migration within countries of origin prior to any potential further migration is of note. Such nuanced and detailed understandings of the context from which children and young people can be made vulnerable to 'trafficking situations' are helpful:

> It does not seem to be uncommon. Quite young children can migrate to the cities to find work. They go for periods of time to raise money, sometimes for their education. Sometimes they go and they get trapped – they go thinking I will make some money and I'll come back, so they are quite ill-informed about what it is really like once they get there. In the process of being there they end up getting trapped. I'm away from home and they are not going to want me back, or they get in with crowds. They get trapped into this very day-to-day existence and there are very few success stories.
>
> (Interview with community representative, August 2012)

The getting 'trapped' element in this quote relates to a position of vulnerability through socio-economic circumstances. That children are 'ill-informed' about their destinations would relate to the 'means' of being trafficked, should this not already be ruled out by the Palermo Protocol's consideration of those under 18.

As outlined in the introduction, the argument that these organisations have a greater global reach in terms of rich understandings of the constellations of 'vulnerabilities' that might lead to trafficking in the first instance was relevant here. Greater links between such domestic and international work was seen by another representative as being essential:

> That is the UK dimension. But it also stretches across. I'll use the word global, every country in the world. It stretches across globally in that these community groups have connections back in their original countries of origin. *Use* [original emphasis] those connections to link up with organisations and people who can prevent trafficking. There would already be a prevention strategy embedded in that approach.
>
> (Interview with community representative, July 2012)

In these terms, knowledge stretching across borders and the potential for prevention of trafficking using social networks and comprehensive understandings of country of origin conditions appears a potentially fruitful route for future safeguarding. Research and empirical data collection paralleling this would also enable an evidence-base to emerge. Such transnational social networks and linkages are well recognised in forced migration literature (Baker, 1990; Boswell and Crisp, 2004; Castles, 2005; Marx, 1990) and the 'strength of weak ties' (Granovetter, 1973) well-rehearsed in discussions around social capital.

Issues of trust and mistrust

In some theories of social capital, relationships of trust and reciprocity are paramount (Coleman, 1988; Granovetter, 1973; Newton, 2006; Putnam, 1993). In child protection circles it is well documented that disclosure of any form of abuse requires a trusting environment to be present, with trust taking time to build up between practitioners and children (Allnock, 2010). As Kohli (2007) suggests, disclosing 'thin stories' to practitioners to access essential services leave out the 'thick stories' that contextualise their migration. Ishola (2010) suggests children being asked what makes them 'feel safe' needs to be incorporated into protection plans and 'incorporated back into enhancing the risk profiles and identification tools' currently available to practitioners (Warrington, this volume). Pearce, Hynes and Bovarnick (2009) found that disclosure was difficult for children if they were within the asylum system:

> The way the screening unit at the Home Office interviews children mean they do not disclose the information professionals need to identify a child as trafficked.
>
> (Pearce, Hynes and Bovarnick, 2009: 127)

Improvement of interviewing environments and techniques aside, an understanding of coercive contexts that generate vulnerability is essential. Children and young people may be told not to say anything by their traffickers or may be under threat by traffickers or members of their 'community'. Children may simply be afraid to speak out as they do not know their rights and entitlements within the UK.

> Understanding that it can take a while gaining her trust, understanding where she has come from, where she is, where she needs to be and what she needs to do to get there.
>
> (Pearce, Hynes and Bovarnick, 2009: 89)

Previous research has demonstrated that young people may feel stigmatised by the experience of abuse or exploitation and they may consequently keep them secret. 'Victimhood' is not a desirable space to inhabit and children and young people may not therefore see themselves as 'victims':

> Some girls that we had disappeared and had a 'boyfriend'. These girls did not see themselves as sexually exploited. They thought this guy loved them.
>
> (Pearce, Hynes and Bovarnick, 2009: 69)

Trust, or mistrust, has been a central consideration in studies around forced migration for the past two decades (Daniel and Knudsen, 1995; P. Hynes, 2009; T. Hynes, 2003; Muecke, 1995; Peteet, 1999; Robinson, 2002; Robinson and Segrott, 2002). A theme already emerging from the study discussed in this chapter is the issue of trust. This is considered one of the main barriers to working with communities to improve the safeguarding of children who had been, or were vulnerable to trafficking. As one representative from a community-based organisation suggested:

> Well I think, trust. If I am brutally honest in the first instance. When we talk about culture, we talk about migrants in the UK from different countries and there are a number of factors that impinge on that. One being asylum. People can be involved in the asylum process which is quite difficult, quite stressful, and also it can put a barrier up where people feel, we don't want to get involved because it draws attention. They don't quite understand the UK Borders Agency approach or motives, so they worry about that, so there is a disconnect – people just keep their heads down and get on with their lives, you know, family lives in that context, there is a real reluctance to engage.
>
> (Interview with community representative, July 2012)

Broader community relations were also commented upon:

> Again with the police, and I'm talking in broad terms now, because it is more applicable to certain areas than others ... where the relationship with authority shall we say can be difficult sometimes and, again, that is not just something that is relevant to migrant communities that live as part of our community.
>
> (Interview with community representative, July 2012)

The notion of 'communities', which may simultaneously offer protective and risk factors to children, needs to be problematised. Private fostering is an example wherein these risk and protective factors are evident for children who may be practically invisible in safeguarding terms. Whilst fostering of children is widespread as a form of childcare across the globe, trafficked children may be kept hidden within informal or private fostering arrangements. As Shaw and de Sousa (2012: 85) outline:

> There have been longstanding concerns about the welfare and potential vulnerability of children living in informal private arrangements ... [that] dates back to the baby-farming scandals of the 19th century and continued through the mass evacuation of children during the Second World War.

It is pertinent to return here to consideration of Victoria Climbie and the work that has developed since her death, as the Laming Report detailed how there had been several occasions when practitioners might have intervened to protect her. In a critique of this report, Garrett (2005) argued that issues relating to asylum and immigration could be interpreted as the 'absent presence' within its pages, linking issues of New Labour's deterrence of new arrivals and hostility towards asylum seekers and the creation of an atmosphere of indifference towards migrant children. This overarching mistrust of asylum seekers continues to undermine UK government policies that require engagement with refugee and migrant communities to address issues around trafficking, forced marriage, issues of 'honour' crimes as well as broader debates around social cohesion and social exclusion (Hynes, 2009). Trust is a key aspect of such policies. To manage any balance between statutory and non-statutory agencies, trust is also a key component.

In the UK, debates about trafficking of children for CSE and other forms of exploitation are particularly framed within debates on immigration and asylum. The systems that are set up to control migration on the one hand, and child protection concerns on the other are often at odds with each other (Bovarnick, 2010). Since the mid-1990s, the portrayal of asylum seekers as 'bogus' versus 'genuine', or 'deserving' versus 'undeserving' has entered public consciousness within the UK (Sales, 2005). These socially constructed labels have had consequences for trafficked children. In the UK, migration for those fleeing persecution is also linked to separate policy agendas surrounding the deterrence of non-EU international migration whilst simultaneously promoting the freedom of movement of UK and EU skilled nationals (Craig, 2010). Understanding the vulnerabilities of a child's history is thus tied up in broader political agendas of immigration control and practitioners' responses to children and young people thus inevitably occur within a complex policy and legislative environment.

For children who are trafficked disbelief encountered whilst moving through the administratives processes of these systems is damaging, and for children trafficked for CSE issues of shame and betrayal may be compounded by these experiences. That children and young people might be disbelieved, mistrusted, betrayed and shamed during such vulnerable moments of their lives cannot continue.

Conclusion

Trafficking children and young people into, within and out of the UK occurs due to a multitude of reasons and, like other forms of child maltreatment, it is unlikely that single or mono-causal risk factors will ever be identified to explain it. This needs to be held in mind when we are looking to identify children who have been trafficked for CSE.

Many children throughout the world live within high-risk contexts but do not experience abuse, neglect or trafficking. Risks may be moderated by protective factors within 'communities' that can reduce the likelihood of abuse or vulnerabilities being exploited. Simple 'push' or 'pull' theories are also unlikely to hold the key to understanding the trafficking of children and young people in a more comprehensive way. An emphasis on multi-faceted and interacting factors may ultimately be a more useful way forward. What we already know about multiple, or overlapping, forms of child abuse dictate that understanding the trafficking of children and young people also requires a conscious effort to use multiple lenses through which we come to know the day-to-day methods of exploitation.

Throughout this paper an argument has been made that refugee and migrant community organisations, as well as other more established 'community'-based organisations, could assist in providing a more nuanced and complex understanding of the reasons why such vulnerability to trafficking occurs in the first instance. It has also been suggested that non-statutory agencies could play a more significant role in identification and safeguarding of children affected by, or vulnerable to, trafficking. At present there is a spectrum of understanding within such organisations around trafficking that, if resourced, may lead to enhanced identification of suspected cases.

Given their knowledge of contexts within countries of origin and unique linkages within communities in the UK, the potential position of refugee and migrant communities in enhancing prevention of trafficking is clear. Their rich understanding of the particular constellations of 'vulnerabilities', as well as protective and/or risk factors requires further exploration. Combining this with a broader understanding of the sociological and transnational processes holds greater potential for safeguarding more children from CSE and trafficking for other forms of exploitation and abuse.

Concluding Thoughts

Jenny Pearce and Margaret Melrose

Different authors in this book have drawn on their research, policy and practice experience to engage in a critical appraisal of a range of approaches to child sexual exploitation (CSE) and related trafficking, looking at what these terms mean, how they are interpreted, how and why the exploitation occurs, and what may be done to enhance the safety of young people. The main theme throughout the book is that a critical appraisal will help us to unravel and work with the complex issues involved with identifying, understanding and working with CSE and related trafficking. We unashamedly challenge any oversimplified portrayal of the problems involved. For example, recent media coverage of a number of prosecutions for CSE has raised public attention to the exploitation of white girls by Asian (mainly Pakistani) men. It is clear that this pattern of exploitation exists, but it is only one of many forms of CSE and we will overlook different forms of abuse, including the abuse of boys and young men, by allowing attention to focus on only one. Also, CSE has traditionally been understood as an offence committed by adults, whereas more recent work is revealing worrying numbers of young people both abusing through CSE and being abused, making the distinction between perpetrator and victim harder to assert. Young people who go missing from home or care might be thought of as a homogenous group, overlooking the complex experiences of those from different minority ethnic groups. What we mean by safe accommodation and its provision to those who are sexually exploited may rely too much on a predetermined understanding of care, failing to address the subtle ways that exploiters abuse both the cared for and the carer.

Local and national variations in policy may bring about different foci for intervention and the relationship between different policy areas aiming to support children who have been trafficked may mean that some slip through the net or are 'siloed' into different practice interventions. Important lessons from NGOs who have experience and expertise in working with migrant communities may not be incorporated into thinking about how to protect children. Critically, the role that young people themselves have in securing their own safety is beginning to be better understood. The complexity of the language that is used to understand their behaviour and the social pressures placed upon them to consent to abuse is increasingly coming to the attention of policy makers and practitioners.

It is evident that whilst great strides have been made to improve interventions to support sexually exploited young people, each step forward brings new questions to be addressed.

It is the appraisal of these lessons emerging from research and practice that this book hopes to engage. As noted in the introduction to the book, this is not a complacent exercise that assumes a definitive body of knowledge, but a critical engagement with what we know and what we still need to find out. We do not know enough about the dynamics impacting on boys and young men who are sexually exploited, despite fantastic moves forward in practice that raise attention to the issues. We do not have any research that has focused on the problems faced by the disproportionally high numbers of children with learning difficulties who are sexually exploited. We need to support and evaluate better the ongoing work with young people affected and make significant strides into improving general education about sexual exploitation to both children (particularly those making the transition into secondary schools) and their parents/carers. In summary, we need a complete conceptual shift to include adolescents within child protection. It is not until young people's strengths and vulnerabilities are addressed by child protection policy and practice and by the broader society overall that we will begin to confront and stop child sexual exploitation.

Bibliography

Aapola, S., Gonick, M. and Harris, A. (2005) *Young Femininity: Girlhood, Power and Social Change*, Basingstoke: Palgrave Macmillan.

ACPC (2005) *Regional Child Protection Policy and Procedures*, Northern Ireland: ACPC.

ACPO/NPIA (2008) *Guidance on Investigating Domestic Abuse* http://www.npia. police.uk/en/docs/Domestic_Abuse_Guidance_2008.pdf.

AFRUCA (2007) *What is Child Trafficking?* London: Africans Unite Against Child Abuse.

—— (2012) *An Evaluation of AFRUCA's Anti–Trafficking Project*, January, London: Africans Unite Against Child Abuse.

Akhtar, S. (2002) *No-One Asked Us Before!* Manchester: The Children's Society.

Aldridge, J., Medina, J. and Ralphs, R. (2008) 'Dangers and Problems of Doing Gang Research in the UK', in F. van Gemert., L. Peterson and I. Lien (eds) *Street Gangs, Migration and Ethnicity*, Cullompton: Willan.

All-Parliamentary Group for Runaway and Missing Children and Adults and the All Parliamentary Group for Looked After Children and Care Leavers (2012) *Report from the Joint Inquiry into Children Who Go Missing From Care.* London: HM Government.

Allen, J., Moore, C., Kuperminc, G. and Bell, K. (1998) 'Attachment and Adolescent Psychosocial Functioning', *Child Development*, 69, 1406–19.

Allen, L. (2003) 'Girls Want Sex, Boys Want Love: Resisting Dominant Discourses of (Hetero) Sexuality', *Sexualities*, 6, 215–36.

Allnock, D. (2010) *Children and Young People Disclosing Sexual Abuse: An Introduction to the Research,* NSPCC Research Briefing, London: NSPCC.

Alexander, C. (2008) *(Re)thinking 'Gangs'*, London: Runnymede Trust, 14.

Andell P. and Pitts J. (2010) Youth Gangs and Gang Culture in West Yorkshire, West Yorkshire Constabulary.

Anderson, B. (2000) *Doing the Dirty Work? The Global Politics of Domestic Labour*, London and New York: Zed Books.

Anderson, E. (1999) *Code of the Street: Decency, Violence, and the Moral Life of the Inner City*, New York: W.W. Norton.

Andrieu-Sanz, R. and Vasquez-Anton, K. (1998) 'Young Women Prostitutes in Bilbao', in M. Cain (ed.) *Growing Up Good: Policing the Behaviour of Girls in Europe*, London: Sage.

Andrijasevic, R. (2007) 'Beautiful Dead Bodies: Gender, Migration and Representation in Anti-Trafficking Campaigns', *Feminist Review*, 86, 24–44.

—— (2010) *Migration, Agency and Citizenship in Sex Trafficking*, Basingstoke and New York: Palgrave Macmillan.

Appleyard, C. (2011) 'Worried what your Teen's up to on Holiday? You should be, says this 18-year-old (who was astounded by what she saw on her post-exam break)', *Daily Mail* 11 August.

Aradau, C. (2008) *Rethinking Trafficking in Women: Politics out of Security*, London: Palgrave Macmillan.

Aries, P. (1962) *Centuries of Childhood*, Harmondsworth: Penguin.

Arnott, M. and Ozga, J. (2008) *Education and Nationalism: Education Policy and the SNP Government*, Paper presented at *Social Policy Association Annual Conference*, University of Edinburgh, 23–5 June, 2008.

Arocha, L. (2012) *What are the Key Components of a Successful Awareness Raising and Prevention Campaign to Combat Cross-Border Trafficking of Young People up to 25 Years Old?* Unpublished report, Comic Relief Review, London: UK.

Arthurs, J. (2009) 'Brands, Markets and Charitable Ethics: MTV's EXIT Campaign', *Journal of Audience & Reception Studies*, 6, 301–19.

—— (2010) *Deliciously Consumable: The Uses and Abuses of Irony in Counter-Trafficking Campaigns*, Paper presented at the Conference *Representations of Prostitution, Sex Work and Sex Trafficking*, 9–10 September 2010, Exeter University, Exeter: UK.

Asquith, S. and Turner, E. (2008) *Recovery and Reintegration of Children from the Effects of Sexual Exploitation and Related Trafficking*, Geneva: Oak Foundation.

ATMG (2010) *Wrong Kind of Victim – One Year on, An Analysis of UK Measures to Protect Trafficked Persons*, http://www.antislavery.org/includes/documents/cm_docs/2010/a/1_atmg_report_for_web.pdf, accessed October 2012.

Attwood, F. (2006) 'Sexed Up: Theorising the Sexualisation of Culture', *Sexualities*, 9 (1), 99–116.

Attwood, F. (2010) 'The Sexualisation of Culture', in F. Attwood (ed.) *Mainstreaming Sex*, London: I.B. Tauris & Co. Ltd.

BAAF (2012) *Regional Statistics on Children in Public Care*, http://www.baaf.org.uk/res/stats, accessed 16 January 2013.

Bailey, R. (2011) *Letting Children be Children: Report of an Independent Review of the Commercialisation and Sexualisation of Childhood*, London: Department for Education.

Baker, R. (1990) 'The Refugee Experience: Communication and Stress, Recollections of a Refugee Survivor', *The Journal of Refugee Studies*, 3, 64–71.

Balasunderam, A. (2009) 'Gang-Related Violence amongst Young People of the Tamil Refugee Diaspora in London', *Safer Communities*, 8, 34–41.

Bannister, T., Pickering, J., Batcelor, S., Burman, M., Kintra, K. and McVie, S. (2010) *Troublesome Youth Groups, Gangs and Knife Carrying in Scotland*, Edinburgh: Scottish Government.

Barnardos (1998) *Whose Daughter Next?* Essex: Barnardos.

—— (2009) *Whose Child Now? Fifteen Years of Working to Prevent the Sexual Exploitation of Children in the UK*, Barkingside: Barnardos.

—— (2011a) *Puppet on a String: The Urgent Need to Cut Children Free from Sexual Exploitation*, Barkingside: Barnardos.

—— (2011b) *Cut Them Free: Tackling Child Sexual Exploitation in Scotland*, Edinburgh: Barnardos.

Barrett, D. (1994) 'Social Work on the Streets: Responding to Juvenile Prostitution in Amsterdam, London and Paris', *Social Work in Europe*, 1, 29–32.

Barrett, D. (1997) (ed.) *Child Prostitution in Britain: Dilemmas and Practical Responses*, London, The Children's Society.

Barrett, D. with Barrett, E. and Mullenger, N. (eds) (2000) *Youth Prostitution in the New Europe: the Growth in Sex Work*, Dorset: Russell House Publishing.

Barter, C. (2006) 'Discourses of Blame: Deconstructing (Hetero) Sexuality, Peer Sexual Violence and Residential Children's Homes', *Child and Family Social Work*, 11, 347–56.

—— (2009) 'In the Name of Love: Exploitation and Violence in Teenage Dating Relationships', *British Journal of Social Work*, 39, 211–32.

—— (2011) 'A Thoroughly Gendered Affair: Teenage Partner Violence and Exploitation', in C. Barter and D. Berridge (eds) *Children Behaving Badly? Peer Violence Between Children and Young People*, West Sussex: John Wiley & Sons Ltd.

Barter, C., McCarry, M., Berridge, D. and Evans, K. (2009) *Partner Exploitation and Violence in Teenage Intimate Relationships*. London: NSPCC.

Barter, C. A., Renold, D., Berridge, D. and Cawson, P. (2004) Peer Violence in Children's Residential Care. London: Palgrave Macmillan.

Batchelor S. (2009) 'Girls, Gangs & Violence: Assessing the Evidence', *The Probation Journal*, 56 (4), 399–414.

Bauman, Z. (1998) *Globalization: The Human Consequences*, New York: Columbia University Press.

—— (2001) *Collateral Damage: Social Inequalities in a Global Age*, Cambridge: Polity Press.

—— (2006) *Liquid Fear*, Cambridge and Malden, MA: Polity Press.

—— (2007) *Liquid Times: Living in an Age of Uncertainty*, Cambridge and Malden, MA: Polity Press.

Becker, H. (1963) *Outsiders: Studies in the Sociology of Deviance*, New York: The Free Press.

Beckett, H. (2011) *Not a World Away: The Sexual Exploitation of Children and Young People in Northern Ireland*, Belfast: Barnardos NI.

Beckett, H., Brodie, I., Factor, F., Melrose, M., Pearce, J., Pitts, J., Shuker, L. and Warrington, C. (2012) *Research into Gang-Associated Sexual Exploitation and Sexual Violence: Interim Report*, Luton: University of Bedfordshire.

Bernstein, E. (1999) 'What's Wrong with Prostitution? What's Right with Sex Work? Comparing Markets in Female Sexual Labour', *Hastings Women's Law Journal*, 10, 91–117.

Biehal, N., Mitchell, F. and Wade, J. (2003) *Lost from view: Missing persons in the UK*, Bristol, The Policy Press.

Bokhari, F. (2009) *Stolen Futures: Trafficking for Forced Marriage in the UK*, London: ECPAT.

Bokhari, F. and Kelly, E. (2010) 'Child Rights, Culture and Exploitation: UK Experiences of Child Trafficking', in G. Craig (ed.) *Child Slavery Now: A Contemporary Reader*, Bristol: Policy Press.

Boswell, C. and Crisp, J. (2004) *Poverty, International Migration and Asylum,* Policy Brief No. 8, United Nations University, World Institute for Development Economics Research: Finland.

Bourdieu, P. (1993) *The Field of Cultural Production,* Cambridge: Polity Press.

Bovarnick, S. (2010) 'How do You Define a Trafficked Child? A Discursive Analysis of Practitioners' Understandings of Trafficking', *Youth & Policy,* 104, 80–96.

Bowlby, J. (1969) *Attachment and Loss,* Vol. I., London: Hogarth.

Bragg, S. (2012) 'Dockside Tarts and Modesty Boards: A Review of Recent Policy on Sexualisation', *Children and Society,* 26 (5) 406–14.

Bragg, S. and Buckingham, D. (2010) 'Too Much Too Young? Young People, Sexual Media and Learning', in F. Attwood (ed.) *Mainstreaming Sex: The Sexualisation of Western Culture,* London: I.B. Tauris & Co. Ltd.

Brandon, J. and Hafez, S. (2008) *Crimes of the Community: Honour-based Violence in the UK,* London: Centre for Social Cohesion.

Britton, B., Chatrik, B., Coles, B., Craig, G., Hylton, C. and Mumtaz, S. with Bivand, P., Burrows, R. and Convery, P. (2002) *Missing ConneXions: The Career Dynamics and Welfare Needs of Black and Minority Ethnic Young People at the Margins,* Bristol, The Policy Press.

Brodie, I. with Melrose, M., Pearce, J. and Warrington, C. (2011) *Providing Safe and Supported Accommodation for Young People who are in the Care System and who are at Risk of, or Experiencing, Sexual Exploitation or Trafficking for Sexual Exploitation,* Luton: University of Bedfordshire, http://www.beds.ac.uk/iasr/ publications, accessed 8 January 2012.

Brodie, I. and Pearce, J. (2012) *Review of Child Sexual Exploitation in Scotland,* Edinburgh: Scottish Government, www.scotland.gov.uk, accessed 15 December 2012.

Brown, K. (2006) 'Participation and Young People Involved in Prostitution', *Child Abuse Review,* 15, 294–312.

—— (2012) 'Re-moralising 'vulnerability'', *People, Place & Policy,* 6(1), 41–53.

Brown, A. and Barrett, D. (2002) Knowledge of evil: child prostitution and child sexual abuse in twentieth century England. Devon: Willan Publishing.

Brown, A. and Shah, A. (2000) 'Reflections on a Changing Europe', in D. Barrett with E. Barrett and N. Mullenger (eds) *Youth Prostitution in the New Europe,* Lyme Regis: Russell House Publishing.

Buckley, R. and Brodie, S. (2000) 'Child Prostitution: A Scottish Perspective' in Barrett, D. With E. Barrett and N. Mullenger (eds) *Youth Prostitution in the New Europe.* Lyme Regis: Russell House Publishing.

Bullock, K. and Tilley, N. (2003) *Shooting, Gangs and Violent Incidents in Manchester: Developing a Crime Reduction Strategy,* London: Home Office.

Bureau Nationaal Rapporteur Mensenhandel (National Rapporteur on Trafficking in Human Beings) (BNRM) (2002) *Trafficking in Human Beings – First report of the Dutch National Rapporteur,* BNRM, The Hague, The Netherlands, Available at http://english.bnrm.nl/reports/1st-report-CP/ Last accessed January 2013.

Burman, M. and Cartmel, F. (2006) *Young People's Attitudes towards Gendered Violence,* Scotland: Edinburgh, NHS Health.

Burton, L. (1990) 'Teenage Childbearing as an Alternative Life Course Strategy in Multigenerational Black Families', *Human Nature*, 1, 123–43.

Butler, J. (1999) *Excitable Speech: A Politics of the Performative*, New York: Routledge.

CAADA (2012) *Domestic Abuse, Stalking and 'Honour'-based Violence (DASH) Risk Identification Checklist*, http://www.caada.org.uk/dvservices/RIC_and_severity_of_abuse_grid_and_IDVA_practice_guidance.pdf, accessed 20 January 2013.

Cabezas, L. (1998) 'Discourses of Prostitution: The Case of Cuba', in K. Kempadoo and J. Doezema (eds) *Global Sex Workers: Rights, Resistance and Redefinition*, London: Routledge.

Calder, M. (2001) 'Child Prostitution: Developing Effective Protocols', *Child Care in Practice*, 7, 98–115.

Cashmore, J. and Paxman, M. (2006) 'Predicting After-Care Outcomes: The Importance of "Felt" Security', *Child and Family Social Work*, 11, 232–41.

Castles, S. (2005) Policy-driven research or research-driven policy? Challenges to, and dilemmas for, forced migration studies, paper presented at the conference 'Seeking Refuge, Seeking Rights, Seeking a Future', Oxford Brookes University, Oxford, 13–14 May.

Castles, S. and Loughna, S. (2004) Globalization and Asylum, in George, V. and R. M. Page (eds.) *Global Social problems and Global Social Policy*, Cambridge: Polity Press.

Centre for Social Justice (2009) *Dying to Belong: An In-depth Review of Street Gangs in Britain*, London: Centre for Social Justice.

CEOP (2011) *Out of Mind, Out of Sight: Breaking Down the Barriers to Understanding Child Sexual Exploitation*, London, Child Exploitation and Online Protection Centre.

—— (2012) Personal communication.

Cepeda, A. and Valdez, A. (2003) 'Risk Behaviours among Young Mexican-American Gang-Associated Females: Sexual Relations, Partying, Substance Use, and Crime', *Journal of Adolescent Research*, 8, 185–99.

Charnley, H., Roddam, G. and Wistow, J. (2009) 'Working with service users and carers', in Adams, R. and Dominelli, L.P.M. (eds) *Social work: themes, issues and critical debates*, 3rd edition, Basingstoke: Palgrave Macmillan.

Chase, E. and Statham, J. (2004) *The Commercial Sexual Exploitation of Children and Young People: An Overview of Key Literature and Data*, London: Thomas Coram Research Unit, Institute of Education.

—— (2005) Commercial and Sexual Exploitation of Children and Young People in the UK: A Review. *Child Abuse Review*, 14, 4–25.

Clutton, S., and Coles, J. (2007) *Sexual Exploitation Risk Assessment Framework: A Pilot Study*, Cardiff: Barnardos.

—— (2009) *Child Sexual Exploitation in Wales: 3 Years On*, Cardiff: Barnardos.

Cohen, K. (2011) *Dirty Little Secrets: Breaking the Silence on Teenage Girls and Promiscuity*, Naperville, IL: Sourcebooks Inc.

Coleman, J. (1988) 'Social Capital and the Creation of Human Capital', *American Journal of Sociology*, 94, 95–121.

—— (2011) *The Nature of Adolescence*, 4th Edition (Adolescence and Society Series), Howe, East Sussex: Routledge.

—— (2012) *The Nature of Adolescence*, 4th edition, London: Routledge.

Corby, D., Shemmings, D. and Wilkins, D. (2012) *Child Abuse: An Evidence Base for Confident Practice*, 4th edition, Maidenhead: McGraw Hill, Open University Press.

Connell, R. and Messerschmidt, J.W. (2005) 'Hegemonic Masculinity: Rethinking the Concept', *Gender and Society*, 19, 829–59.

Cornwall, A. (2004) 'Spaces for Transformation: Reflections on Issues of Power and Difference in Participation in Development', S. Hickey and G. Mohan (eds) *Participation: From Tyranny to Transformation. Exploring New Approaches to Participation in Development*, London: Zed Books.

Cossar, J., Brandon, M. and Jordan, P. (2011) *Office of the Children's Commissioner: 'Don't Make Assumptions': Children's and Young People's Views of the Child Protection System and Messages for Change*, London: OCC.

Council of Europe (2010) *Campaign to stop sexual violence against children/ One in Five* [Online]. Available at: www.coe.int/oneinfive, accessed 14 June 2012.

Cousineau, M. (2002) 'Girls and Street Gangs: When the Dream Becomes a Nightmare', *Preventing Violence against Girls: Should Programmes be Gender-Specific?* Conference Proceedings, Montreal, October 25, 2002.

Coy, M. (2008) 'Young Women, Local Authority Care and Selling Sex', *British Journal of Social Work*, 38, 1408–24.

—— (2009a) 'Milkshakes, Lady Lumps and Growing Up to Want Boobies: How the Sexualisation of Popular Culture Limits Girls' Horizons', *Child Abuse Review*, 18, 372–83.

—— (2009b) 'Moved around like Bags of Rubbish Nobody Wants: How Multiple Placement Moves can Make Young Women Vulnerable to Sexual Exploitation', *Child Abuse Review*, 18, 254–66.

Coy, M. and Kelly, L. (2011) *Islands in the Stream: An Evaluation of Four London Independent Domestic Violence Advocacy Schemes*, London: CWASU, London Metropolitan University.

Craig, G. (2010) (ed.) *Child Slavery Now: A Contemporary Reader*, Bristol: Policy Press.

Creegan, C., Scott, S. and Smith, R. (2005) *The Use of Secure Accommodation and Alternative Provisions for Sexually Exploited Young People in Scotland*, Barkingside: Barnardos.

Crewe, E. and Axelby, R. (2013) *Anthropology and Development: Culture, Morality and Politics in a Globalised World*, Cambridge: Cambridge University Press.

Crewe, E. and Harrison, E. (1998) *Whose Development? An Ethnography of Aid*, London and New York: Zed Books.

Crosby, S. and Barrett, D. (1999) 'Poverty, Drugs and Youth Prostitution: A Case Study of Service Providers' Practical Responses', in A. Marlow and J. Pitts (eds) *Managing Drugs and Young People*, Lyme Regis: Russell House Publishing.

Crown Prosecution Service (CPS) (2012) 'Fact Sheet: Sexual Offences', http://www.cps.gov.uk/news/fact_sheets/sexual_offences/, accessed 9 October 2012.

Cusick, L. (2003) 'Youth Prostitution: A Literature Review', *Child Abuse Review*, 11, 230–51.

Daniel, E. and Knudsen, J. (eds) (1995) *Mistrusting Refugees*, Los Angeles and London: University of California Press.

DCSF (2008) *Young Runaways Action Plan*, London: DCSF.

—— (2009) *Safeguarding Children and Young People from Sexual Exploitation: Supplementary Guidance to Working Together to Safeguard Children*, London: DCSF.

Dennis, J. (2008) 'Women are Victims, Men make Choices: The Invisibility of Men and Boys in the Global Sex Trade', *Gender Issues*, 25, 11–25.

DfE (2011a) *Tackling Child Sexual Exploitation Action Plan*, http://media. education.gov.uk/assets/files/pdf/c/tackling%20child%20sexual%20exploit ation%20action%20plan.pdf, accessed 29 November 2012.

—— (2011b) *Children Looked After by Local Authorities in England* (including adoption and care leavers) – year ending 31 March 2011, http://www. education.gov.uk/rsgateway/DB/SFR/s0001026/sfr21–2011.pdf, accessed 12 January 2012.

—— (2012) *Difference between Child Protection and Safeguarding*, http:// www.education.gov.uk/popularquestions/a0064461/what-is-the-difference- between-safeguarding-and-child-protection, accessed 3 August 2012.

DHSSPSNI (2003) *Co-operating to Safeguard Children*, Belfast: DHSSPSNI.

—— (2006) *Our Children and Young People, Our Shared Responsibility: Inspection of Child Protection Services in Northern Ireland*, Belfast: DHSSPSNI.

—— (2008) Tackling Sexual Violence and Abuse: A Regional Strategy 2008–2013 Belfast: DHSSPSNI.

—— (2011) *Children in Care in Northern Ireland 2010/11: Statistical Bulletin*, Belfast: DHSSPSNI.

—— (2012) *Children's Social Care Statistics for Northern Ireland 2011/2012*, Belfast: DHSSPSNI.

Dillane, J., Hill, M. and Munro, C. (2005) *A Study of Sexual Exploitation of Looked After and Accommodated Young People*, Glasgow: Centre for the Child and Society and Barnardos Street Team.

Doezema, J. (1998) 'Forced to Choose: Beyond the Voluntary v. Forced Prostitution Dichotomy', in K. Kempadoo and J. Doezema (eds) *Global Sex Workers: Rights, Resistance and Redefinition*, London: Routledge.

—— (2010) *Sex Slaves and Discourse Masters: The Constructions of Trafficking*, London and New York: Zed Books.

DoH/HO (2000) *Safeguarding Children Involved in Prostitution: Supplementary Guidance to Working Together to Safeguard Children*, London: Department of Health, National Assembly for Wales, Home Office, Department for Education and Employment.

DoJ (2011) *Research Paper Investigation the Issues for Women in Northern Ireland Involved in Prostitution and Exploring Best Practice Elsewhere*, Belfast: DoJ.

Dorling, D. (2011) *Injustice: Why Social Inequality Persists*, Bristol: The Policy Press.

Douglas, J. (1984) 'The Emergence, Security, and Growth of the Sense of Self', in J. Kotarba and A. Fontana (eds) *The Existential Self in Society*, Chicago: University of Chicago Press.

Dudley, R. (2006) *Crossing Borders: Preliminary Research on Human Trafficking in Northern Ireland*, Belfast: Women's Aid Federation NI.

Eagleton, T. (1991) *Ideology*, London: Verso.

ECPAT International (1996) *The International Legal Framework and Current National Legislative and Enforcement Responses*, http://www.csecworld congress.org/PDF/en/Stockholm/Background_reading/Theme_papers/ Theme%20paper%20legal%201998_EN.pdf, accessed October 2012.

Education Select Committee (2012) *Children First: the child protection system in England*, London.

Edwards, S. (1992) 'Prostitutes: Victims of Law, Social Policy and Organised Crime', in P. Carlen and A. Worrall (eds) *Gender, Crime and Justice*, Buckingham: Open University Press.

Elias, N. (2000) *The Civilizing Process: Sociogenetic and Psychogenetic Investigations*, Oxford: Basil Blackwell.

EVAW (2010) *Almost a third of girls experience unwanted sexual touching in UK schools – new YouGov poll*, www.endviolenceagainstwomen.org.uk.

Family Lives (2012) *All of Our Concern: Commercialisation, Sexualisation and Hypermasculinity*, London: Family Lives.

Farmer, E. and Pollock, S. (2003) 'Managing Sexually Abused and/or Abusing Children in Substitute Care', *Child and Family Social Work*, 8, 101–12.

FCO, HO and NHS (2007) *Dealing with Cases of Forced Marriage*, http://www. forcedmarriage.net/media/images/FMU-FMGuidanceHealthProfessionals_ 74.pdf, accessed 3 February 2008.

Featherstone, B., Broadhurst, K. and Holt, K. (2012) 'Thinking Systemically – Thinking Politically: Building Strong Partnerships with Children and Families in the Context of Rising Inequality', *British Journal of Social Work*, 42, 618–33.

Firmin, C. (2008) *Building Bridges Project, Final Report*, London: Race on the Agenda.

—— (2009) 'Girls around Gangs', *Safer Communities*, 8, 14–16.

—— (2010) *Female Voice in Violence Project: A Study into the Impact of Serious Youth and Gang Violence on Women and Girls*, London: Race on the Agenda.

—— (2011) *This Is It, This Is My Life: Female Voice in Violence Final Report*, London, Race on the Agenda (ROTA).

—— (2013) 'Busting the 'Gang Rape' Myth: Girls' Victimisation and Agency in Gang-Associated Sexual Violence', Woodhams, J. and Horvath, M. (eds) *Handbook on the Study of Multiple Perpetrator Rape: A Multidisciplinary Response to an International Problem* (eds), London, Routledge.

Flood, M. (2009) 'The Harms of Pornography Exposure among Children and Young People', *Child Abuse Review*, 18, 384–400.

FPA (2011) *The Law on Sex Factsheet*, http://www.fpa.org.uk/professionals/ factsheets, accessed 28 May 2013.

Franklin, D. (1988) 'Race, Class and Adolescent Pregnancy: An Ecological Analysis', *American Journal of Orthopsychiatry*, 58, 339–54.

Franklin, K. (2004) 'Enacting Masculinity: Antigay Violence and Group Rape as Participatory Theatre', *Sexuality Research and Social Policy*, 1, 25–40.

Franks, M. (2004) *The Work of Safe on Our Streets with Minority Ethnic Runaways: An Analysis of Work Carried out with Four Young Women from South Asian, Muslim Backgrounds*, http://www.childrenssociety.org.uk/sites/default/files/tcs/work_with_four_south_asian_young_women.pdf, accessed 6 September 2004.

Freire, P. (1970) *Pedagogy of the Oppressed*, London and New York: Penguin.

Fusco, C. (1998) 'Hustling for Dollars: Jineterismo in Cuba', in K. Kempadoo and J. Doezema (eds) *Global Sex Workers: Rights, Resistance and Redefinitions*, London: Routledge.

Gallagher, A. (2010) *The International Law of Human Trafficking*, Cambridge and New York: Cambridge University Press.

Garrett, P. M. (2005) 'Protecting Children in a Globalized World: "Race" and "Place" in the Laming Report on the Death of Victoria Climbie', *Journal of Social Work*, 6 (3), 315–36.

Gibson, B. (1995) *Male Order: Life Stories from Boys who Sell Sex*, London: Cassell.

Gill, R. (2003) *Participation and Access of Women to the Media and Information Technologies and Their Impact on and Use as an Instrument for the Advancement and Empowerment of Women*, 47th Commission on the Status of Women, United Nations, New York, 3 March.

—— (2007) *Post-Feminist Media Culture: Elements of Sensibility*, LSE Research Online at http://eprints.lse.ac.uk, accessed March 2011.

—— (2010) 'Supersexualise Me! Advertising and the Midriffs', in F. Attwood (ed.) *Mainstreaming Sex*, London: I.B. Tauris and Co. Ltd.

Gilligan, R. (2006) 'Creating a warm place where children can blossom', *Social Policy Journal of New Zealand*, 28 (July), 36–45.

GMC (2012) *Protecting Children and Young People: The Responsibility of All Doctors*, http://www.gmc-uk.org/static/documents/content/Child_protection_-_English_0712.pdf, accessed 3 November 2012.

Goffman, E. (1963) *Stigma: Notes on the Management of Spoiled Identity*, New York: Simon and Schuster.

Granovetter, M. (1973) 'The Strength of Weak Ties', *American Journal of Sociology*, 78, 1360–80.

Green, J. (1992) *It's No Game: Responding to the Needs of Young Women at Risk or Involved in Prostitution*, Leicester: National Youth Agency.

Green, L. (2005) 'Theorizing Sexuality, Sexual Abuse and Residential Children's Homes: Adding Gender to the Equation', *British Journal of Social Work*, 35, 453–81.

Hagedorn, J. (2008) *A World of Gangs: Armed Young Men and Gangsta Culture*, Minneapolis: University of Minnesota.

Hallsworth, S. (2011) 'Gangland Britain? Realities, Fantasies and Industry', in B. Goldson (ed.) *Youth in Crisis: Gangs Territoriality and Violence*, London: Routledge.

Hallsworth, S. and Young, T. (2008) 'Gang Talk and Gang Talkers: A Critique', *Crime, Media and Culture*, 4, 175–95.

—— (2011) 'Young People, Gangs and Street-based Violence', in C. Barter and D. Berridge (eds) *Children Behaving Badly? Peer Violence between Children and Young People*, West Sussex: John Wiley & Sons Ltd.

Hardman, K. (1997) 'A Social Work Group for Prostituted Women with Children', *Social Work with Groups*, 20, 19–31.

Harding, S. (2012) *The Role and Significance of Social Capital and Street Capital in the Social Field of the Violent Youth Gang in Central Lambeth*, Doctoral Thesis, University of Bedfordshire.

Harper, Z. and Scott, S. (2005) *Meeting the Needs of Sexually Exploited Young People in London*, Ilford, Essex: Barnardo's.

—— (2006) *Meeting the Needs of Sexually Exploited Young People in London*, Barkingside: Barnardos.

Harris, J. and Robinson, B. (2007) *Tipping the Iceberg: A Pan Sussex Study of Young People at Risk of Sexual Exploitation and Trafficking, Final Report*, Barkingside: Barnardos.

Hart, R. (2008) 'Stepping Back from "The Ladder": Reflections on a Model of Participatory Work with Children', in A. Reid, B. Jenson, J. Nikel and V. Simovska (eds) *Participation and Learning*, Amsterdam: Springer.

Hatfield, E. (2010) '"What it Means to Be a Man": Examining Hegemonic Masculinity in *Two and Half Men'*, *Communication, Culture and Critique*, 3, 526–48.

Haydon, D. and Scraton, P. (2002) 'Sex Education as Regulation', in B. Goldson., M. Lavalette and J. McKechnie (eds) *Children, Welfare and the State*, London: Sage.

Hayes, C. (1996) *Young People and Prostitution: A Report for the Law Society Working Group*, Manchester: The Law Society.

Hebdige, D. (1979) *Subculture: The Meaning of Style*, London: Routledge.

Hinton, R. (2008) 'Children's Participation and Good Governance: Limits of Theoretical Literature', *International Journal of Children's Rights*, 16, 285–300.

Hird, M. and Jackson, S. (2001) 'Where "Angels" and "Wusses" Fear to Tread: Sexual Coercion in Adolescent Dating Relationships', *Journal of Sociology*, 37, 27–43.

Home Affairs Committee (2008) *Domestic Violence, Forced Marriage and 'Honour'-based Violence*, Sixth Report of Session 2007–08, London: UK Parliament.

HM Government (2009) *Multi-Agency Practice Guidelines: Handling Cases of Forced Marriage*, London: Stationary Office.

—— (2010a) *Call to End Violence against Women and Girls*, London: Stationary Office.

—— (2010b) *The Right to Choose: Multi-Agency Statutory Guidance for Dealing with Forced Marriage*, London: Stationary Office.

—— (2011) *Ending Gang and Youth Violence: A Cross-Government Report including Further Evidence and Good Practice Case Studies*, London: Stationary Office.

HO (2000) *Setting the Boundaries: Reforming the Law on Sex Offences*, Vol. 1, London: Home Office.

—— (2008) *Tackling Gangs Action Programme – Tackling Gangs: A Practical Guide for Local Authorities, CDRPS and Other Local Partners*, London: Home Office.

—— (2011a) *Cross-Government Definition of Domestic Violence: A Consultation*, London: Home Office.

—— (2011b) *Call to End Violence against Women and Girls: Action Plan*, London: Home Office.

—— (2011c) *Teenage Relationship Abuse Campaign*, London: Home Office.

Hochschild, A. (2000) 'Global Care Chains and Emotional Surplus Value', in W. Hutton and A. Giddens (eds) *On The Edge: Living with Global Capitalism*, London: Jonathan Cape.

Hoggart, L. and Phillips, J. (2009) *London Teenage Abortion and Repeat Abortion Research Report*, London: Policy Studies Institute.

Holland, S., Faulkner, A. and Perez-del-Aguila, R. (2005) 'Promoting Stability and Continuity of Care for Looked After Children: A Survey and Critical Review', *Child and Family Social Work*, 10, 29–41.

Home Office Communications Directorate (2000) *A Choice by Right: The Report of the Working Group on Forced Marriage*, http://www.fco.gov.uk/resources/en/pdf/a-choice-by-right, accessed 6 June 2000.

Home Office (2008) *Tackling Gangs Action Programme – Tackling Gangs: A Practical Guide for Local Authorities, CDRPS and Other Local Partners*, London, Home Office.

—— (2010) *Statutory Guidance: Injunctions to Prevent Gang-Related Violence*, London, Home Office.

Horvath, M. and Kelly, L. (2009) 'Multiple Perpetrator Rape: Naming an Offence and Initial Research Findings', *Journal of Sexual Aggression*, 15, 83–96.

Howe, D. (2005) *Child Abuse and Neglect*, Basingstoke: Palgrave Macmillan.

—— (2011) *Attachment across the Life Course*, Basingstoke: Palgrave Macmillan.

HSC Board (2010) *Strategic Action Plan on Children Missing from Home or Care*, Belfast: HSC Board.

HSSB, PSNI and SBNI (2004) Protocol for joint investigation by social workers and police officers of alleged and suspected cases of child abuse Belfast: DHSSPSNI.

Hynes, P. (2009) 'Contemporary Compulsory Dispersal and the Absence of Space for the Restoration of Trust', *Journal of Refugee Studies*, 22, 97–121.

—— (2010) 'Global Points of "Vulnerability": Understanding Processes of the Trafficking of Children and Young People into, within and out of the UK', *The International Journal of Human Rights*, 14, 952–70.

Hynes, T. (2003) *The Issue of 'Trust' or 'Mistrust' in Research with Refugees: Choices, Caveats and Considerations for Researchers*, United Nations High Commissioner for Refugees (UNHCR), Evaluation and Policy Analysis Unit, Working Paper No.98.

Ishola, P. (2010) 'Identification of Separated Children in the UK', in E. Kelly and F. Bokhari (eds) *Safeguarding Children from Abroad: Refugee, Asylum Seeking and Trafficked Children in the UK*, London and Philadelphia: Jessica Kingsley Publishers.

Izzidien, S. (2008) *'I Can't Tell People What is Happening at Home': Domestic Abuse within South Asian Communities: The Specific Needs of Women, Children and Young People*, London: NSPCC.

Jackson, S. and Thomas, N. (1999) *On the Move Again? What Works in Creating Stability for Looked After Children*, Ilford: Barnardos. Jago, S., Arocha, L., Brodie, I., Melrose, M., Pearce, J. and Warrington, C. (2011) *What's Going On to Safeguard Children and Young People from Sexual Exploitation? How*

Local Partnerships Respond to Child Sexual Exploitation, Luton: University of Bedfordshire.

Jago, S. and Pearce, J. (2008) *Gathering Evidence of the Sexual Exploitation of Children and Young People: A Scoping Exercise*, Luton: University of Bedfordshire.

James, A., Jenks, C. and Prout, A. (1998) *Theorising Childhood*, Cambridge: Polity Press.

James, A. and Prout, A. (1990) *Constructing and Reconstructing Childhood: Contemporary Issues in the Sociological Study of Childhood*, Basingstoke: Falmer Press.

Jeffner, S. (2000) *Different Space for Action: The Everyday Meaning of Young People's Perception of Rape*, Paper at ESS Faculty Seminar, University of North London, May.

Jenks, C. (2005) *Childhood*, 2nd edition, Oxon: Routledge.

Jesson, J. (1993) 'Understanding Adolescent Female Prostitution: A Literature Review', *British Journal of Social Work*, 23, 517–30.

Jha, K. (2004) 'Runaway Asian Girls in Glasgow: The Role and Response of the Community', *Scottis Affairs*, No. 48, http://www.scottishaffairs.org/backiss/2004.html#summer, accessed 1 October 2004.

Joseph Rowntree Foundation (2011) *Monitoring Poverty and Social Exclusion*, York: Joseph Rowntree Foundation.

Kazimirski, A., Keogh, P., Kumari, V., Smith, R., Gowland, S., Purdon, S. and Khanum, N. (2009) *Forced Marriage: Prevalence and Service Response, National Centre for Social Research*, London, Department for Children, Schools and Families.

Keeling, J. and Mason, T. (2008) Domestic Violence. Maidenhead: Open University Press.

Kelly, L. (1988) *Surviving Sexual Violence*, Minneapolis: University of Minesota Press.

Kelly, L. and Gill, A. (2012) 'Reading the Riots through Gender: A Feminist Reflection on England's 2011 Riots', in D. Briggs (ed.) *The English Riots of 2011: A Summer of Discontent*, Hampshire: Waterside Press.

Kelly, L., Lovett, J. and Regan, L. (2005) *A Gap or a Chasm? Attrition in Reported Rape Cases*, Home Office Research Study 293, London: Home Office.

Kelly, L., Wingfield, R., Burton, S. and Regan, L. (1995) *Splintered Lives: Sexual Exploitation in the Context of Children's Rights and Child Protection*, Essex: Barnardos.

Kempadoo, K. (1998) 'Introduction: Globalizing Sex Workers' Rights' in Kempadoo, K. and Doezema, J. (1998) *Global Sex Workers: Rights, Resistance, and Redefinition*, New York and London: Routledge, 1–28.

Khanum, N. (2008) *Forced Marriage, Family Cohesion and Community Engagement: National Learning through a Case Study of Luton*, Watford: Equality in Diversity.

Kirby, P. (1995) *A Word from the Street: Young People who Leave Care and Become Homeless*, London: Centrepoint/Community Care/Reed Business Publishing.

Kirby, P., Lanyon, C., Cronin, K. and Sinclair, R. (2003) *Building a Culture of Participation: Involving Children and Young People in Policy, Service Planning, Delivering and Evaluation*, Nottingham: DfES.

Knight, A., Chase, E. and Aggleton, P. (2006) '"Someone of Your Own to Love": Experiences of Being Looked After as Influences on Teenage Pregnancy', *Children and Society*, 20(5), 391–403.

Kohli, R. (2007) *Social Work with Unaccompanied Asylum-Seeking Children*, Basingstoke: Palgrave Macmillan.

Kunz, E. (1973) 'The Refugee in Flight: Kinetic Models and Forms of Displacement', *International Migration Review*, 7, 125–46.

Laing, R. (1960) *The Divided Self: An Existential Study in Sanity and Madness*, Harmondsworth: Penguin.

Lansdown, G. (2005) *Evolving Capacities of the Child*, Sweden: UNICEF/Save the Children.

Lea, J. and Young, J. (1984) *What is to be Done about Law and Order?* Harmondsworth: Penguin.

Leathers, S. (2002) 'Foster Children's Behavioural Disturbance and Detachment from Caregivers and Community Institutions', *Children and Youth Services Review*, 24, 239–68.

Lees, S. (1993) *Sugar and Spice: Sexuality and Adolescent Girls*, London: Penguin Books.

Levi-Strauss, C. (1966) *The Savage Mind*, translated by George Weidenfeld and Nicolson Ltd, Chicago: The University of Chicago Press.

Levy, A. (2005) *Female Chauvinist Pigs: Women and the Rise of Raunch Culture*, London: Simon and Schuster.

Lillywhite, R. and Skidmore, P. (2006) 'Boys are Not Sexually Exploited? A Challenge to Practitioners', *Child Abuse Review*, 15, 351–61.

London Safeguarding Children Board (2009) *Safeguarding Children Affected by Gang Activity and/or Serious Youth Violence*, London: LSCB.

Mac an Ghaill, M. (1994) *The Making of Men: Masculinities, Sexualities and Schooling*, Buckingham: Open University Press.

Mai, N. (2010) *The Psycho-Social Trajectories of Albanian and Romanian 'Traffickers'*, Institute for the Study of European Transformations Working Paper No. 17, http://www.londonmet.ac.uk/fms/MRSite/Research/iset/Working%20Paper%20Series/WP17%20N%20Mai.pdf, accessed June 2012.

Malloch, M. (2006) *Running: Other Choices Refuge Evaluation*, Stirling: University of Stirling.

Mainey, A., Ellis, A. and Lewis, J. (2009) *Children's Views of Services – A Rapid Review*, London: NCB.

Marie, A. and Skidmore, P. (2007) *A Summary Report Mapping the Scale of Internal Trafficking in the UK Based on a Survey of Barnardos Anti-Sexual Exploitation and Missing Services*, Barkingside: Barnardos.

Martynowicz, A., Toucas, S. and Caughey, A. (2009) *The Nature and Extent of Human Trafficking in Northern Ireland*, Belfast: NIHRC and ECNI.

Marx, E. (1990) 'The Social World of Refugees: A Conceptual Framework', *Journal of Refugee Studies*, 3, 189–203.

Matthews, R. (2008) *Prostitution, Politics and Policy*, Oxon: Routledge-Cavendish.

Matthews, R. and Pitts, J. (2007) *An Examination of the Disproportionate Number of Young Black Men Involved in Street Robbery in Lewisham*, Lewisham: Children and Young People's Directorate and Lewisham's Youth Crime Group.

Matthews, R. and Young, J. (1992) *Issues in Realist Criminology*, London: Sage.

Matza, D. (1969) *Becoming Deviant*, Englewood Cliffs, NJ: Prentice Hall Inc.

Mauss, M. (1934) 'Les Techniques du corps', *Journal de Psychologie*, 32, 3–4, Reprinted in M. Mauss, *Sociologie et anthropologie*, 1936, Paris: PUF.

Mayhew, S., Walt, G., Lush, L. and Cleland, J. (2005) 'Donor Agencies' Involvement in Reproductive Health: Saying One Thing and Doing Another?' *International Journal of Health Services*, 35, 579–601.

Maxwell, C. and Aggleton, P. (2010) 'Agency in Action – Young Women and Their Sexual Relationships in a Private School', *Gender and Education*, 22, 327–43.

McClung, M. and Gayle, V. (2010) 'Exploring the care effects of multiple factors on the educational achievements of children looked after at home and away from home', *Child and Family Social Work*, 15, 409–431.

McGhee, J. and Waterhouse, L. (2011) 'Locked Out of Prevention? The Identity of Child and Family Oriented Social Work in Scottish Post-Devolution Policy', *British Journal of Social Work*, 41, 1088–104.

McNay, L. (2000) *Gender and Agency: Reconfiguring the Subject in Feminist and Social Theory*, Cambridge: Polity Press.

McMullen, R. (1987) Youth Prostitution: A Balance of Power, *Journal of Adolescence*, 10 (1), 35–43.

McRobbie, A. (1991) *Feminism and Youth Culture: From 'Jackie' to 'Just Seventeen'*, Basingstoke: Macmillan.

—— (2004) 'Notes on Post-Feminist and Popular Culture: Bridget Jones and the New Gender Regime, in A. Harris (ed.) *All About the Girl: Culture, Power and Identity*, London: Routledge.

Meetoo, V. and Mirza, H. S. (2007) 'Lives at Risk: Multiculturalism, Young Women and 'Honour' Killings' in Thom, B., Sales, R. and Pearce, J. (2007) *Growing Up With Risk*, Bristol, The Policy Press.

Melrose, M. (2002) 'Labour Pains: Some Considerations of the Difficulties in Researching Juvenile Prostitution', *International Journal of Social Research Theory, Methodology and Practice*, 5, 333–52.

—— (2004) 'Young People Abused through Prostitution: Some Observations for Practice', *Practice*, 16, 17–29.

—— (2010) 'What's Love Got to Do With It? Theorising Young People's Involvement in Prostitution', *Youth and Policy*, 104, 12–30.

—— (2011) 'Regulating Social Research: Exploring the Implications of Extending Ethical Review Procedures in Social Research', *Sociological Research Online*, 16, http://www.socresonline.org.uk/16/2/14.html, accessed 23 January 2012.

—— (2012a) 'Twenty-First Century Party People: Young People and Sexual Exploitation in the New Millennium', *Child Abuse Review*, [Early View] doi: 10:1002/car.2238.

—— (2012b) 'Enlightenment or Mystification? Shifting Paradigms in Child Sexual Exploitation', *Professorial Inaugural Lecture*, Luton: University of Bedfordshire, 19 March.

—— (2012c) 'Young People, Welfare Reform and Social Insecurity', *Youth and Policy*, 108, 1–21.

Melrose, M. with Barrett, D. (2004) *Anchors in Floating Lives: Interventions with Young People Abused through Prostitution*, Lyme Regis: Russell House Publishing.

Melrose, M., Barrett, D. and Brodie, I. (1999) *One Way Street: Retrospectives on Childhood Prostitution*, London: The Children's Society.

Messerschmidt, J. (1993) *Masculinities and Crime: Critique and Reconceptualisation of Theory*, Lanham, MD: Rowman and Littlefield.

—— (2012) 'Engendering Gendered Knowledge: Assessing the Academic Appropriation of Hegemonic Masculinity', *Men and Masculinities*, 15, 56–76.

Mikhail, S. (2002) 'Child Marriage and Child Prostitution: Two Forms of Sexual Exploitation', *Gender and Development*, 10, 43–9.

Miller W. B. (1958) Lower Class Culture as a Generating Milieu for Gang Delinquency, *Journal of Social Issues*, 15, 5–19.

Miller, J. (1998) 'Gender and Victimization Risk among Young Women in Gangs', *Journal of Research in Crime and Delinquency*, 35, 429–53.

—— (2001) *One of the Guys*, New York: Oxford University Press.

—— (2009) 'Young Women and Street Gangs', in M. Zahn (ed.) *The Delinquent Girl, Girls, Gangs and Sexual Exploitation in British Columbia*, Philadelphia: Temple University Press.

Mirza, H. S. (2009) *Race, Gender and Education Desire: Why Black Women Succeed and Fail*, London, Routledge.

Montgomery, H. (1998) 'Children, Prostitution and Identity: A Case Study from a Tourist Resort in Thailand', in K. Kempadoo and J. Doezema (eds) *Global Sex Workers: Rights, Resistance and Redefinition*, London: Routledge.

Montgomery-Devlin, J. (2008) 'The Sexual Exploitation of Children and Young People in Northern Ireland: Overview from the Barnardos Beyond the Shadows Service', *Child Care in Practice*, 14, 381–400.

Morgan, R. (2006) *Placements, Reviews, Decisions: A Children's Views Report*, Newcastle upon Tyne: Commission for Social Care Inspection.

Morrison-Doire, M. and Eisner, E. (1993) 'Child-Related Dimensions of Placement Stability in Treatment Foster Care', *Child and Adolescent Social Work Journal*, 10, 301–17.

MPS (2012) *The Trident Gang Strategy*, London: Metropolitan Police Service.

Muecke, M. (1995) 'Trust, Abuse of Trust, and Mistrust among Cambodian Refugee Women: A Cultural Interpretation', in E. Daniel and J. Knudsen (eds) *Mistrusting Refugees*, Los Angeles and London: University of California Press.

Mullins, C. (2007) *Holding Your Square: Masculinities, Streetlife and Violence*, Cullompton: Willan Publishing.

Munro, C. (2004) *Scratching the Surface … What We Know about the Abuse and Sexual Exploitation of Young People by Adults Targeting Residential and Supported Accommodation Units*, Unpublished Paper, Glasgow: Barnardos Street Team.

Munro, E. and Hardy, A. (2006) *Placement Stability – A Review of the Literature. Report to the DCSF*, Loughborough: CCFR.

National Policing Improvement Agency (2012) *Missing Persons Data and Analysis 2010–11*. London: NPIA.

Newburn, T. and Stanko, E. (1994) *Just Boys Doing Business? Men, Masculinities, and Crime*, New York: Routledge.

Newiss, G. (1999) *Missing Presumed...? The Police Response to Missing Persons*, London: Home Office.

Newton, K. (2006) *Social Trust and Politics*, Conference Presentation, ESRC Research Methods Festival, Oxford, 17–20 July 2006.

NICCY (2009) *Children's Rights: Rhetoric or Reality? A Review of Children's Rights in Northern Ireland 2007/2008*, Belfast: NICCY.

Noonan, R. and Charles, D. (2009) 'Developing Teen Dating Violence Prevention Strategies: Formative Research in Middle School Youth', *Violence Against Women*, 15, 1087–105.

NPIA (2009) *Guidance on Investigating Child Abuse and Safeguarding Children*, http://www.npia.police.uk/en/14532.htm, accessed 24 March 2010.

—— (2010) *Guidance on the Management, Recording and Investigation of Missing Persons*, http://www.acpo.police.uk/documents/crime/2011/20110301%20Management_Recording%20and%20Investigation%20of%20Missing%20Persons%202010_2nd%20Edition.pdf, accessed 3 February 2011.

—— (2011) *Missing Persons: Data and Analysis*, London: National Policing Improvement Agency.

OCC (2012a) *'I Thought I was the Only One, the Only One in the World'*, London: Office of the Children's Commissioner.

—— (2012b) *Briefing for the Rt Hon Michael Gove MP, Secretary of State for Education, on the Emerging Findings of the Office of the Children's Commissioner's Inquiry into Child Sexual Exploitation in Gangs and Groups, with a Special Focus on Children in Care*, http://www.childrenscommissioner.gov.uk/, accessed 9 September 2012.

O'Connell-Davidson, J. (1995) 'The Anatomy of Free Choice Prostitution', *Gender, Work and Organisation*, 2, 1–10.

—— (1998) *Prostitution, Power and Freedom*, Cambridge: Polity Press.

—— (2005) *Children in the Global Sex Trade*, Cambridge: Polity Press.

Oliver, M. (1996) *Understanding Disability: From Theory to Practice*, London: Macmillan.

Olivier de Sardan, J. (2005) *Anthropology and Development: Understanding Contemporary Social Change*, translated by Antoinette Tidjani Alou, London and New York: Zed Books.

O'Neill, M. (1994) 'Prostitution and the State: Towards a Feminist Practice', in C. Lupton and T. Gillespie (eds) *Working with Violence*, Basingstoke: Macmillan.

—— (1997) 'Prostitute Women Now', in G. Scambler and A. Scambler (eds) *Rethinking Prostitution: Purchasing Sex in the 1990s*, London: Routledge.

—— (2001) *Prostitution and Feminism*, Cambridge: Polity Press.

O'Neill, M., Goode, N. and Hopkins, K. (1995) 'Juvenile Prostitution: The Experience of Young Women in Residential Care', *Childright*, 113, 14–16.

O'Neill, T. (2001) *Children in Secure Accommodation: A Gendered Exploration of Young People in Trouble*, London: Jessica Kingsley.

ONS (2011) *Annual Mid-Year Population Estimates for England and Wales, Mid 2011*, http://www.ons.gov.uk/ons/dcp171778_277794.pdf, accessed 6 November 2011.

Organization for Security and Co-operation in Europe (OSCE) and the Office for Democratic Institutions and Human Rights (ODIHR) (2004) *National Referral Mechanisms: Joining Efforts to Protect the Rights of Trafficked Persons. A Practical Handbook*, Warsaw: Poland, Available at http://www. osce.org/documents/odihr/2004/05/2903_en.pdf Last accessed December 2012.

Palmer, S. (2009) 'The Origins and Emergence of Youth Gangs in a British Inner City Neighbourhood', *Safer Communities*, 8, 14–21.

Palmer, S. and Pitts, J. (2006) 'Othering the Brothers: Black Youth, Racial Solidarity and Gun Crime', *Youth & Policy*, 91, 5–22.

Papadopoulos, L. (2010) *Sexualisation of Young People Review*, London: Crown Copyright.

Parreñas, R. S. (2004) *Servants of Globalization: Women, Migration and Domestic Work*, Stanford: Stanford University Press.

Paterson, L. and Iannelli, C. (2007) 'Social class and educational attainment: a comparative study of England, Wales and England', *Sociology of Education*, 80(4), 330–58.

Pawson, R., Greenhalgh, T., Harvey, G. and Walshe, K. (2005) 'Realist Review – A New Method of Systematic Review Designed for Complex Policy Interventions', *Journal of Health Services Research and Policy*, 10, 21–34.

Pearce, J. (2009) *Young People and Sexual Exploitation: It's Not Hidden, You Just Aren't Looking*, London: Routledge.

—— (2010) 'Safeguarding Young People from Sexual Exploitation and from being Trafficked: Tensions within Contemporary Policy and Practice', *Youth and Policy*, 104, 1–11.

Pearce, J., Hynes, P. and Bovarnick, S. (2009) *Breaking the Wall of Silence: Practitioners' Responses to Trafficked Children and Young People*, London: NSPCC and University of Bedfordshire.

—— (2013) *Trafficked Young People: Breaking the Wall of Silence*, London: Routledge.

Pearce, J., Williams, M. and Galvin, C. (2002) *It's Someone Taking a Part of You: A Study of Young Women and Sexual Exploitation*, London: National Children's Bureau.

Pearson, G. (1983) *Hooligan: A History of Respectable Fears*, Basingstoke: MacMillan.

Percy-Smith, B. and Thomas, N. (eds) (2010) *Handbook of Children and Young People's Participation: Perspectives from theory and practice*, Oxon: Routledge.

Peter, J. and Valkenburg, P. (2007) 'Adolescents' Exposure to a Sexualised Media Environment and Their Notions of Women as Sex Objects', *Sex Roles*, 56, 381–95.

Peteet, J. M. (1995) Transforming trust: dispossession and empowerment among Palestinian refugees, in Daniel, E. V. and J. C. Knudsen (eds) *Mistrusting Refugees*, Berkeley, CA: University of California Press.

Phillips, A. (2007) *Multiculturalism without Culture*, Oxford: Princeton.

Phillips, A. and Dustin, M. (2004) *UK Initiatives on Forced Marriage: Regulation, Dialogue and Exit*, London: London School of Economics.

Phillips, R. (2003) 'Education Policy, Comprehensive Schooling and Devolution in the Disunited Kingdom: An Historical "Home International" Analysis', *Journal of Education Policy*, 18, 1–17.

Phoenix, J. (2001) *Making Sense of Prostitution*, Basingstoke: Palgrave Macmillan.

—— (2002) 'In the Name of Protection: Youth Prostitution Reforms in England and Wales', *Critical Social Policy*, 71, 353–75.

—— (2004) 'Regulating Sex: Young People, Prostitution and Policy Reform', in B. Brooks-Gordon, L. Gelsthorpe, A. Baimham and M. Johnson (eds) *Sexuality Repositioned: Diversity and the Law*, Oxford: Hart Publishing.

Pilcher, J. (1996) 'Gillick and After: Children and Sex in the 1980s and 1990s', in J. Pilcher and S. Wagg (eds) *Thatcher's Children? Politics, Childhood and Society in the 1980s and 1990s*, London: Falmer Press.

Pitts, J. (1997) 'Causes of Youth Prostitution: New Forms of Practice and Political Responses', in D. Barrett (ed.) *Child Prostitution in Britain: Dilemmas and Practical Responses*, London: The Children's Society.

—— (2008) *Reluctant Gangsters: The Changing Shape of Youth Crime*, Exeter: Willan Publishing.

Plass, P. S. (2007) 'Secondary Victimizations in Missing Children Events', *American Journal of Criminal Justice*, 32, 30–44.

Poudel, M. (2011) *Dealing with Hidden Issues: Social Rejection Experienced by Trafficked Women in Nepal*, LAP Lambert Academic Publishing.

Powell, A. (2008) 'Amor Fati? Gender Habitus and Young People's Negotiation of (Hetero)Sexual Consent', *Sociology*, 44, 167–84.

—— (2010) *Sex, Power and Consent: Youth Culture and the Unwritten Rules*, Cambridge: Cambridge University Press.

Pupavac, V. (2001) 'Therapeutic Governance: Psycho-Social Intervention and Trauma Risk Management', *Disasters*, 25, 358–72.

Putnam, R. (1993) *Making Democracy Work: Civic Traditions in Modern Italy*, Princeton: Princeton University Press.

Quilgars, D., Johnsen, S. and Pleace, N. (2008) *Youth Homelessness in the UK – A Decade of Progress?* York: Joseph Rowntree Foundation.

Quilgars, D. and Pleace, N. (2010) *Meeting the Needs of Households at Risk of Domestic Violence in England*, York: University of York.

Radford, L., Corral, S., Bradley, C., Fisher, H., Bassett, C., Howat, N. and Collishaw, S. (2011) *Child Abuse and Neglect in the UK Today*, London: NSPCC.

Raws, P. (2001) *Lost Youth: Young Runaways in Northern Ireland*, London: The Children's Society.

Rees, G. (2011) *Still Running 3: Early Findings from Our Third National Survey of Young Runaways*, London: The Children's Society.

Rees, G. and Lee, J. (2005) *Still Running 2: Findings from the Second National Survey of Young Runaways*, London: The Children's Society.

Rees, G., Gorin, S., Jobe, A., Stein, M. and Goswami, H. (2010) *Safeguarding Young People: Responding to Young People Aged 11 to 17 who are Maltreated*, London: The Children's Society.

Rees, G., Stein, M., Hicks, L. and Gorin, S. (2011) Adolescent neglect: research, policy and practice. London: Jessica Kingsley.

Richardson, D., Poudel, M. and Laurie, N. (2009) 'Sexual Trafficking in Nepal: Constructing Citizenship and Livelihoods in Gender, Place and Culture', *A Journal of Feminist Geography*, 16 (3), 259–78.

Richmond, A. (1994) *Global Apartheid: Refugees, Racism and New World Order*, Oxford: Oxford University Press.

Ringrose, J. and Renold, E. (2011) 'Boys, Girls and Performing Normative Violence in Schools: A Gendered Critique of Bully Discourses', in C. Barter and D. Berridge (eds) *Children Behaving Badly? Peer Violence Between Children and Young People*, West Sussex: John Wiley & Sons Ltd.

Ringrose, J., Gill, R., Livingstone, S. and Harvey, L. (2011) *A Qualitative Study of Children, Young People and 'Sexting'*, London: NSPCC.

Robinson, V. (2002) '"Doing Research" with Refugees and Asylum Seekers', *Swansea Geographer*, 37, 61–7.

Robinson, V. and Segrott, J. (2002) *Understanding the Decision-Making of Asylum Seekers*, Home Office Research Study 243, London: Home Office.

Rodger, J. (2008) *Criminalising Social Policy: Anti-social Behaviour and Welfare in a De-civilised Society*, Cullompton: Willan Publishing.

Roesch-Marsh, A. (2012) '"Out of Control": Making Sense of the Behaviour of Young People Referred to Secure Accommodation', *British Journal of Social Work*, 42, 1–17.

Royal College of General Practitioners (RCGP) (2011) *Confidentiality and Young People Toolkit*, RCGP Adolescent Health Group, London: Royal College of General Practitioners.

RQIA (2011) *A Report on the Inspection of the Care Pathways of a Select Group of Young People who Met the Criteria for Secure Accommodation in Northern Ireland*, Belfast: RQIA.

Ruelle, E. (2011) 'Sexual Violence against Children – The European Legislative Framework and Outline of Council of Europe Conventions and European Union policy', in Council of Europe, 2011, *Protecting Children from Sexual Violence – A Comprehensive Approach*, 55–72, http://www.coe.int/t/dg3/children/1in5/whatweknow/publication_EN.asp, accessed October 2012.

Rutter, M. (1985) 'Resilience in the Face of Adversity: Protective Factors and Resistance to Psychiatric Disorder', *British Journal of Psychiatry*, 147, 598–611.

Safe on the Streets Research Team (1999) *Still Running: Children on the Streets in the UK*, London: The Children's Society.

Sakulpitakphon, P. (2011) 'Stop Sex Trafficking of Children and Young People – A Unique ECPAT and Body Shop Campaign', in Council of Europe, 2011, *Protecting Children from Sexual Violence – A Comprehensive Approach*, 313–20, http://www.coe.int/t/dg3/children/1in5/whatweknow/publication_EN.asp, accessed January 2013.

Sales, R. (2005) 'The Deserving and the Undeserving? Refugees, Asylum Seekers and Welfare in Britain', *Critical Social Policy*, 22, 456–78.

Samad, Y. and Eade, J. (2002) *Community Perceptions of Forced Marriage*, London: Foreign and Commonwealth Office.

Santos País, M. (2011) 'The United Nations legislative framework for the protection of children from sexual exploitation, including sexual abuse and exploitation' in Council of Europe, 2011, *Protecting children from sexual violence – A comprehensive approach*, 45–54, Available at http://www.coe.int/t/dg3/children/1in5/whatweknow/publication_EN.asp. Last accessed December 2012.

Schofield, J. and Thorburn, J. (1996) *Child Protection: The Voice of the Child in Decision Making*, London: Institute for Public Policy Research.

Schofield, G. (2001) 'Resilience and Family Placement: A Lifespan Perspective', *Adoption and Fostering*, 25, 6–19.

Schofield, G. and Beek, M. (2005) 'Risk and Resilience in Long-Term Foster-Care', *British Journal of Social Work*, 35, 1283–301.

Schutt, N. (2006) *Domestic Violence in Adolescent Relationships: Young People in Southwark and Their Experiences with Unhealthy Relationships*, London: Safer Southwark Partnership.

Scottish Commissioner for Children and Young People (2011) *Scotland: A Safe Place for Child Traffickers? A Scoping Study into the Nature and Extent of Child Trafficking in Scotland*. Edinburgh: SCCYP.

Scottish Executive (2001) *For Scotland's Children*, Edinburgh: Scottish Executive.

—— (2003) *Vulnerable Children and Young People: Sexual Exploitation through Prostitution*, Edinburgh: Scottish Executive.

—— (2009) *Safeguarding Children in Scotland Who May Have Been Trafficked*, Edinburgh: Scottish Executive.

Schön, D. (1993) *Generative metaphor: A perspective on problem-setting in social policy*, Cambridge: Cambridge University Press.

Scott, G. and Wright, S. (2012) 'Devolution, Social Democratic Visions and Policy Reality in Scotland', *Critical Social Policy*, 32, 440–53.

Scott, J. (2010) 'The Concept of Consent under the Sexual Offences Act 2003', *Plymouth Law Review*, 1, 22–41.

Scott, S. and Skidmore, P. (2006) *Reducing the Risk: Barnardos Support for Sexually Exploited Young People: A Two-Year Evaluation*, Barkingside: Barnardos.

SECOS (2012) *Sexual Exploitation of Children on the Street Annual Report*, Middlesbrough: Barnardos.

Shachar, S. (2001) *Multicultural Jurisdictions: Cultural Differences and Women's Rights*, Cambridge: Cambridge University Press.

Sharp, N. (2010) *Forced Marriage in the UK: A Scoping Study on the Experience of Women from Middle Eastern and North East African Communities*, London: Refuge.

—— (2012) *Still Hidden? Going Missing as an Indicator of Child Sexual Exploitation*, London: Missing People.

Shaw, I. and Butler, I. (1998) Understanding young people and prostitution. A foundation for practice? *British Journal of Social Work*, 28, 177–96.

Shaw, C. and de Sousa, S. (2012) 'Living with Unrelated Adults: Private Fostering', in E. Kelly and F. Bokhari (eds) *Safeguarding Children from Abroad: Refugee, Asylum Seeking and Trafficked Children in the UK*, London and Philadelphia: Jessica Kingsley Publishers.

Shaw, I., Butler, I., Crowley, A. and Patel, G. (1996) Paying the Price: young people and prostitution. Cardiff University School of Social and Administrative Studies.

Shemmings, D. (2000) 'Professional Attitudes to Children's Participation in Decision-Making: Dichotomous Accounts and Doctrinal Contests', *Child and Family Social Work*, 5, 235–43.

Shier, H. (2001) 'Pathways to Participation: Openings, Opportunities, Obligations', *Children and Society*, 15, 107–17.

Sinclair, I., Wilson, K. and Gibbs, I. (2005) *Foster Placements: Why They Succeed and Why They Fail*, London: Jessica Kingsley Publishers.

Sinclair, R. and Geraghty, T. (2008) *A Review of the Use of Secure Accommodation in Northern Ireland*, London: National Children's Bureau.

Smeaton, E. (2009) *Off the Radar: Children and Young People on the Streets in the UK*, Sandbach, Railway Children.

Smith, K. and colleagues (2009) 'Divergence or convergence? Health inequalities and policy in a devolved Britain', *Critical Social Policy*, 29, 216–42.

Social Exclusion Unit (2002) *Young Runaways*, London: Office of the Deputy Prime Minister.

Southall Black Sisters (2008) *Campaign to Abolish No Recourse to Public Funds: How Can I Help Her?* London.

Statham, J. (1984) *Non Traditional Sex Role Socialisation: Parents' Perceptions of Non-Sexist Childrearing*, Ph.D. Thesis, The Open University.

Stein, M., Rees, G. and Frost, N. (1994) *Running – The Risk: Young People on the Streets of Britain Today*, London: The Children's Society.

Stockton, K. B. (2009) *The Queer Child or Growing Sideways in the Twentieth Century*, Durham and London: Duke University Press.

Stockton, K. (2011) 'Kid Orientalism' video available from Cornell University web channel, *CornellCast*, http://www.cornell.edu/video/?videoid=1740, accessed January 2013.

Stonewall Scotland (2009) *Understanding the Housing Needs and Homelessness Experiences of Lesbian, Gay, Bisexual and Transgender (LGBT) People in Scotland*.

Talbot, K. and Quayle, M. (2010) 'The Perils of Being a Nice Guy: Contextual Variation in Five Young Women's Constructions of Acceptable Hegemonic and Alternative Masculinities', *Men and Masculinities*, 13, 255–7.

Tan, L. and Quinlivan, J. (2006) 'Domestic Violence, Single Parenthood, and Fathers in the Setting of Teenage Pregnancy', *Journal of Adolescent Health*, 38, 201–7.

Taylor-Browne, J. (2002) *More than one chance! Young people involved in prostitution speak out*, London: ECPAT.

Thiara, R. and Gill, A. (2010) *Violence against Women in South Asian Communities: Issues for Policy and Practice*, London: Jessica Kingsley Publishers.

Thomas, N. and O'Kane, C. (1998) *Children and Decision Making*, Wales: University of Wales.

Thornberry, T., Krohn, M., Lizotte, A. and Chard-Wierschem, D. (1995) 'The Role of Juvenile Gangs in Facilitating Delinquent Behaviour', in M. Klein, C. Maxson and J. Miller (eds) *The Modern Gang Reader*, Los Angeles: Roxbury.

Thorne, B. (1993) *Gender Play*, New Brunswick, NJ: Rutgers University Press.

Thrane, L., Yoder, K. and Chen, X. (2011) 'The Influence of Running Away on the Risk of Female Sexual Assault in the Subsequent Year', *Violence and Victims*, 26, 816–29.

Thrasher, F. (1927) *The Gang: A Study of 1,313 Gangs in Chicago*, Chicago: University of Chicago Press.

Tisdall, K., Davis, J. and Gallagher, M. (2008) *Researching with Children and Young People: Research Design, Methods and Analysis*, London: Sage Publications Ltd.

Totten, M. (2000) *Guys, Gangs and Girlfriend Abuse*, Peterborough: Broadview Press.

Trinder, L. (1997) 'Competing Constructions of Childhood: Children's Rights and Children's Wishes in Divorce', *Journal of Social Welfare and Family Law*, 19, 25–37.

UKHTC (2012) *NRM Statistics*, http://www.soca.gov.uk/about–soca/about–the–ukhtc/national–referral–mechanism/statistics, accessed February 2013.

UKHTC/SOCA (2011) *UKHTC: A Baseline Assessment on the Nature and Scale of Human Trafficking in 2011*.

UNCRC (1989) United National Convention on the Rights of the Child UNICEF, London.

University of Stirling and Ipsos MORI Scotland (2010) *Grampian Police Return Homes Welfare Interview Pilot for Young Runaways: Pilot Evaluation Final Report*, Stirling: University of Stirling.

Unrau, Y. (2007) 'Research on placement moves: Seeking the perspective of foster children', *Children and Youth Services Review*, 29 (1), 122–37.

Valkenburg, P. and Peter, J. (2007) 'Online Communication and Adolescent Well-Being: Test the Stimulation Versus the Displacement Hypothesis', *Journal of Computer-Mediated Communication*, 12, 123–33.

Van Dongen, L. and Dawson, M. (2009) *Going Missing and Gender: The Risks and Perils of Going Missing for Women and Girls*, http://citation.allacademic.com/meta/p_mla_apa_research_citation/3/7/3/1/3/p373132_index.html?phpsessid=10f7cf3d077242ce238d8de7be71960c, accessed 6 December 2009.

Voice (2004) *Blueprint Project: Start with the Child: Stay with the Child*, London: National Children's Bureau.

Wacquant, L. (1998) 'Negative Social Capital: State Breakdown and Social Destitution in America's Urban Core', *Journal of Housing and the Built Environment*, 13, 25–40.

—— (2008) Urban Outcasts: A Comparative Sociology of Advanced Marginality, Cambridge, Polity Press.

—— (2009) *Punishing the Poor: The Neoliberal Government of Social Insecurity*, Durham and London: Duke University Press.

Wade, J. (2002) *Missing Out: Young Runaways in Scotland*, Glasgow: Aberlour Trust.

Walter, N. (2010) *Living Dolls: The Return of Sexism*, London: Virago.

Ward, J. and Patel, N. (2006) 'Broadening the Discussion on "Sexual Exploitation": Ethnicity, Sexual Exploitation and Young People', *Child Abuse Review*, 15, 341–50.

Ward, H. and Skuse, T. (2001) 'Performance Targets and Stability of Placements for Children Long Looked After Away from Home', *Children and Society*, 15, 333–46.

Warrington, C. (2010) 'From Less Harm to More Good: The Role of Children and Young People's Participation in Relation to Sexual Exploitation', *Youth and Policy*, 104, 62–79.

—— (2013, forthcoming) *How We See It: Sexually Exploited Young People's Involvement in Decision-Making about their Care*, Unpublished Thesis, Luton, University of Bedfordshire.

Waters, E. and Cummings, E. (2000) 'A secure base from which to explore close relationships', *Child Development*, 71, 164–72.

Wedel, J. (1998) *Collision and Collusion: The Strange Case of Western Aid to Eastern Europe 1989–1998*, New York: St. Martin's Press.

Wedel, J., Shore, C., Feldman, G. and Lathrop, S. (2005) 'Toward an Anthropology of Public Policy', *The Annals of the American Academy of Political and Social Science*, 600(300), 30–51.

Weitzer, R. (2007) 'The Social Construction of Sex Trafficking: Ideology and Institutionalisation of a Moral Crusade', *Politics & Society*, 35, 447–75.

Weitzer, R. and Kubrin, C. (2009) 'Misogyny in Rap Music: A Content Analysis of Prevalence and Meanings', *Men and Masculinities*, 12, 3–29.

Welsh Assembly (2010) Safeguarding children and young people from sexual exploitation: supplementary guidance to Safeguarding Children Wales Wales: Welsh Assembly Government.

Welsh Government (2012) *Adoptions, Outcomes and Placements for Children Looked After by Local Authorities, Year ending 31 March 2012*, http://wales.gov.uk/docs/statistics/2012/120927sdr/1622012en.pdf, accessed 26 September 2012.

'What Works For Us' (2011) Annual Report, available from The University of Bedfordshire www.beds.ac.uk/iasr, accessed 14 October 2011.

Wheeler, R. (2006) 'Gillick or Fraser? A Plea for Consistency Over Competence in Children', *British Medical Journal*, 332(7545), 807.

Wood, M., Barter, C. and Berridge, D. (2011) *'Standing on My Own Two Feet': Disadvantaged Teenagers, Intimate Partner Violence and Coercive Control*, London: NSPCC.

Woolf, H. (1985) quoted in NSPCC Inform 'What do "Gillick Competency" and "Fraser Guidelines" Refer to?' http://www.nspcc.org.uk/inform/research/questions/gillick_wda61289.html, accessed 11 June 2012.

Young, J. (1999) *The Exclusive Society*, London and Thousand Oaks: Sage.

Young, J. and Matthews, R. (1992) *Rethinking Criminology: The Realist Debate*, London: Sage.

Young T. (2009) *Girls and Gangs: 'Shemale' Gangsters in the UK?* Youth Justice December, 9 (3), 224–238.

Youth Justice Board (2007) *Groups, Gangs and Weapons*, London: Youth Justice Board.

Zolberg, A. (1989) *Escape from Violence*, Oxford: Oxford University Press.

Zuckerman, D. and Abraham, A. (2008) 'Teenagers and Cosmetic Surgery: Focus on Breast Augmentation and Liposuction', *Journal of Adolescent Health*, 43, 318–24.

Index

Printed and bound by CPI Group (UK) Ltd, Croydon, CR0 4YY